Teaching Interculturality 'Otherwise'

This edited volume focuses on the thorny and somewhat controversial issue of teaching (and learning) interculturality in a way that considers the notion from critical and reflexive perspectives when introduced to students.

Comprised of three parts, the book discusses the nuts and bolts of teaching interculturally, considers changes in the teaching of interculturality, and provides pedagogical insights into interculturalising the notion. It studies both teaching im-/explicitly about interculturality and how to incorporate interculturality into teaching practices or into an institution. By sharing varied cases and theoretical reflections on the topic, the editors and contributors from different parts of the world aim to stimulate more initiatives to enrich the field instead of delimiting it, especially in complement to and beyond the 'West' or 'Global North', and also to build up further reflexivity in the way readers engage with interculturality in education.

This will be a must-read for teachers and researchers of intercultural communication education at different educational levels, as well as anyone interested in scholarship on education for interculturality.

Fred Dervin is Professor of Multicultural Education at the University of Helsinki (Finland). He specialises in intercultural communication education, the sociology of multiculturalism, and international mobilities in education, and has widely published in different languages on identity, interculturality, and mobility/migration. Exploring the politics of interculturality within and beyond the 'canon' of intercultural communication education research has been one of his *idées fixes* in his works over the past 20 years.

Mei Yuan is Associate Professor at the School of Education, Minzu University of China. Yuan has led many research projects on Minzu and intercultural education and internationalisation, and has been recognised and awarded several times for her contributions to 'minority' education.

Sude is Professor at the School of Education, Minzu University of China, and is considered one of the most influential scholars in the field of Chinese Minzu education. His research interests include multicultural education, diversity in teacher education, and intercultural competence in superdiverse institutions.

New Perspectives on Teaching Interculturality

About the Series

This book series publishes original and innovative single-authored and edited volumes contributing robust, new and genuinely global studies to the exciting field of research and practice of interculturality in education. The series aims to enrich the current objectives of 'doing' and teaching interculturality in the 21st century by problematizing Euro- and Western-centric perspectives and giving a voice to other original and under-explored approaches. The series promotes the search for different epistemologies, cutting-edge interdisciplinarity and the importance of reflexive and critical translation in teaching about this important notion. Finally, *New Perspectives on Teaching Interculturality* serves as a platform for dialogue amongst the global community of educators, researchers, and students.

Series Editors:

Fred Dervin is Professor of multicultural education at the University of Helsinki.

Mei Yuan is Associate Professor at the School of Education, Minzu University of China.

Interculturality in Schools
Practice and Research
Robyn Moloney, Maria Lobytsyna and John De Nobile

Interculturality in Higher Education
Putting Critical Approaches into Practice
Edited by Mélodine Sommier, Anssi Roiha and Malgorzata Lahti

Teaching Interculturality 'Otherwise'
Edited by Fred Dervin, Mei Yuan and Sude

The Paradoxes of Interculturality
A Toolbox of Out-of-the-Box Ideas for Intercultural Communication Education
Fred Dervin

For a full list of titles in this series, visit https://www.routledge.com/New-Perspectives-on-Teaching-Interculturality/book-series/NPTI

Teaching Interculturality 'Otherwise'

Edited by Fred Dervin, Mei Yuan, and Sude

LONDON AND NEW YORK

This book is an outcome of the *Enhancing Intercultural Dialogue in Education* Project sponsored by the 2021 National Foreign Experts Program (G202184002L).

First published 2023
by Routledge
4 Park Square, Milton Park, Abingdon, Oxon OX14 4RN

and by Routledge
605 Third Avenue, New York, NY 10158

Routledge is an imprint of the Taylor & Francis Group, an informa business

© 2023 selection and editorial matter, Fred Dervin, Mei Yuan and Sude; individual chapters, the contributors

The right of Fred Dervin, Mei Yuan and Sude to be identified as the authors of the editorial material, and of the authors for their individual chapters, has been asserted in accordance with sections 77 and 78 of the Copyright, Designs and Patents Act 1988.

With the exception of Chapter 3, no part of this book may be reprinted or reproduced or utilised in any form or by any electronic, mechanical, or other means, now known or hereafter invented, including photocopying and recording, or in any information storage or retrieval system, without permission in writing from the publishers.

Chapter 3 of this book is available for free in PDF format as Open Access from the individual product page at www.routledge.com. It has been made available under a Creative Commons Attribution-Non Commercial-No Derivatives 4.0 license.

Trademark notice: Product or corporate names may be trademarks or registered trademarks, and are used only for identification and explanation without intent to infringe.

British Library Cataloguing-in-Publication Data
A catalogue record for this book is available from the British Library

ISBN: 978-1-032-38479-5 (hbk)
ISBN: 978-1-032-43352-3 (pbk)
ISBN: 978-1-003-34527-5 (ebk)

DOI: 10.4324/9781003345275

Typeset in Times New Roman
by Deanta Global Publishing Services, Chennai, India

Contents

List of figures	viii
List of tables	ix
List of contributors	x

1 Introduction   1
   FRED DERVIN

PART I
The nuts and bolts of teaching interculturally   13

2 Teaching and learning about interculturality in communication
   and management   15
   ALEXANDER FRAME

3 Unity in diversity: Exploring intercultural teaching and
   learning practices in secondary education and teacher training
   in Austria   34
   JASMIN PESKOLLER

4 Teaching in intercultural classrooms: An Italian perspective   55
   AGOSTINO PORTERA

5 Teaching through learning about intercultural difference(s):
   Autoethnographic experiences of a teacher aide in an
   Australian regional secondary school   71
   P. A. DANAHER

vi *Contents*

6 Interculturality and the university: The case of Jagdish Gundara and the Institute of Education Centre for Intercultural Education (UK) 88
GARY MCCULLOCH

PART II
Change in the teaching of interculturality 99

7 Teaching interculturality: Changes in perspective (A story of change) 101
ROBYN MOLONEY

8 Is there any communication that isn't intercultural? 111
ETTA KRALOVEC

9 Interculturality-as-altering: Observality as a method for 'silent' reflexivity and criticality 116
NING CHEN AND FRED DERVIN

10 Interculturality holding hands with education for emergencies 128
HEIDI LAYNE AND ABITHA CHAKRAPANI

PART III
Insights into interculturalising interculturality 141

11 Teaching interculturality 'beyond' culture: Challenges and future possibilities 143
GIULIANA FERRI

12 Interculturalising the teaching of interculturality in Swedish higher education 157
ANDREAS JACOBSSON

13 Mediated communication as an entryway into interculturality 173
MARKO SIITONEN AND MARGARETHE OLBERTZ-SIITONEN

14 Teaching interculturality: The ecology of self-reflection as a priority 187
NATHALIE AUGER

15 A Finnish approach to promoting intercultural encountering in
   primary schools   200
   OONA PIIPPONEN

16 Remarks and conclusion: Towards an endless and centreless
   glissando of interculturality   215
   FRED DERVIN

17 Afterword: Theorising and teaching interculturality otherwise:
   What 'otherwise'?   222
   HAMZA R'BOUL

   Index   227

Figures

3.1 Addressing stereotypes in the EFL classroom – example 1   44
3.2 Addressing stereotypes in the EFL classroom – example 2   45

Tables

1.1	Keys to reflecting on the chapters	10
2.1	Three phases of learning about interculturality	20
2.2	The three phases of learning about interculturality in the ICM MA course	24
3.1	Criteria catalogue for intercultural learning activities	42
13.1	A sample task for analysing social media	178
13.2	A sample task for analysing global virtual teamwork	180
15.1	Seven dimensions of the learning space influence whether a space of reciprocal encountering can be created in a children's story exchange	210

Contributors

Nathalie Auger is a full professor at the University of Montpellier-Paul-Valéry, France. She teaches students from all over the world intercultural dimensions in a teaching French as a foreign/second language master's programme. She has run many projects in Europe and Canada regarding the use of cultural and language resources to teach/learn French as a second language. She has also worked with newly arrived pupils, e.g. Roma and Gypsy students and their families, in a holistic and maximalist way to include the students with their multifaceted identities. She has published a dozen books and created films and websites on these topics in various languages.

Abitha Chakrapani is currently pursuing a master's in education at the University of Jyväskylä as part of the EDUMA program. She is interested in curriculum development and language education.

Ning Chen is Lecturer at Tianjin Academy of Fine Arts (China) and Visiting Scholar at the Faculty of Educational Sciences of the University of Helsinki (Finland). Chen specialises in the interplay between internationalisation of universities and interculturality. His latest books include *Interculturality Between East and West. Unthink, Dialogue, and Rethink* (with Dervin et al.; Springer, 2022) and *Change and Exchange in Global Education. Learning with Chinese Stories of Interculturality* (with Yuan, Dervin, and Sude; Palgrave Macmillan, 2022).

P. A. Danaher is Professor (Educational Research) in the School of Education at the Toowoomba campus of the University of Southern Queensland, Australia. He is also Adjunct Professor in the School of Education and the Arts at Central Queensland University, and in the College of Arts, Society and Education at James Cook University, both in Australia, and also Docent in Social Justice and Education at the University of Helsinki, Finland.

Fred Dervin is Professor of Multicultural Education at the University of Helsinki, Finland. Dervin specialises in intercultural communication education, the sociology of multiculturalism, and international mobilities in education. He has widely published in different languages on identity, interculturality, and mobility/migration (over 150 articles and 70 books). His latest book is *Interculturality* *in Fragments: A Reflexive Perspective* (Springer, 2022). Exploring the politics of interculturality within and beyond the 'canon' of intercultural communication education research has been one of Dervin's *idées fixes* in his work over the past 20 years.

Giuliana Ferri is Senior Lecturer in the Department of Education at Brunel University London. Before working in higher education, Ferri taught for over ten years in multicultural and multilingual primary schools in inner London, where she developed an interest in interculturalism and critical pedagogies. Ferri has a range of research interests broadly focused on language and intercultural communication, gender, ethnicity, and race.

Alexander Frame is Associate Professor in Communication Science at the Languages and Communication Faculty of the University of Burgundy (Dijon, France), where he runs the MA course in Intercultural Management. He is a member of the TIL research group (EA 4182), specialising in intercultural, interpersonal, organisational, and digital communication.

Andreas Jacobsson is Senior Lecturer in child and youth studies at the University of Gothenburg, Sweden. His latest book (co-written with F. Dervin) is *Intercultural Communication Education: Broken Realities and Rebellious Dreams* (Springer, 2022).

Etta Kralovec is Professor Emerita of Teacher Education at the University of Arizona (US). She holds a doctorate in philosophy from Teachers' College, Columbia University, from which she received a Distinguished Alumni Award in 2018. She was awarded a Fulbright Fellowship in 1996 to establish a teacher education program at Africa University in Zimbabwe. Her 2001 ground-breaking book, *The End of Homework*, ignited a national conversation about homework. In 2018, Kralovec became the founding director and principal investigator for the Bisbee Science Exploration and Research Center (BSERC). Kralovec's current work explores the importance of context in the preparation of teachers for schools in border communities.

Heidi Layne is Senior Lecturer in Sustainable and Global Education at the University of Jyväskylä, Finland. She received her PhD in education from the University of Helsinki and worked as a research scientist at the National Institute of Education, Nanyang Technological University, Singapore. Her research focuses on sustainable, critical, and global education; early childhood education; and qualitative research methods. Currently, she is engaged in research projects on the welfare and learning of children from low-income family backgrounds and on everyday multiculturalism and racism in Finland and Singapore.

Gary McCulloch is Brian Simon Professor of History of Education at University College London Institute of Education (UK). He is also the director of the International Centre for Historical Research in Education. Past president of the

British Educational Research Association (BERA), McCulloch is the editor of the *British Journal of Educational Studies*.

Robyn Moloney is a writer and educator in teacher intercultural education. Formerly a school language teacher, her many publications document research in intercultural learning and teacher development. Moloney now works with schools to develop understanding of the intercultural capability in the curriculum and in the broader school environment.

Margarethe Olbertz-Siitonen (PhD) is Senior Lecturer in Intercultural Communication and teaches in the MA programme in Language, Globalization and Intercultural Communication at the Department of Language and Communication Studies, University of Jyväskylä, Finland. Her research interests include technology in workplace interaction as well as different facets of interculturality.

Jasmin Peskoller is a researcher and lecturer in language education at the University of Innsbruck, Austria. Her research interests include intercultural learning, global (citizenship) education, and diversity-sensitive approaches to teaching and learning. She received an honorary state prize for her research on Indigenous perspectives in contemporary Australian education. Jasmin Peskoller also works as an English and Mathematics teacher at a secondary school in Austria.

Oona Piipponen completed her doctoral research at the University of Eastern Finland on the topic of children's intercultural encountering. She is also a primary teacher with an MA (Hons) in primary education from the University of Glasgow. She has many years of experience learning and now teaching in international schools.

Agostino Portera is Professor of Intercultural Education, Director of the Master in 'Intercultural Competences and Management', and Head of the Centre for Intercultural Studies, University of Verona (Italy). He specialises in education, psychology and psychotherapy in Italy and Germany and has widely published in different languages on identity, intercultural education, counselling and competences. Portera's recent work includes Education and Intercultural Identity (2021), co-written with Z. Bauman. His mission is to develop intercultural education, mediation and counseling for confronting neoliberalism by promoting justice, equity and a more robust democratic civilisation worldwide.

Hamza R'boul is a Research Assistant Professor in the Department of International Education at the Education University of Hong Kong. His works examine interculturality, power relations and the skewed geopolitics of knowledge as they shape education and society at large. They also address inequalities and discuss the demands for more epistemic justice in intercultural communication education and research, sociology of education, internationalization of higher education and English language teaching.

Marko Siitonen, PhD, is Associate Professor working in the MA programme in Language, Globalization and Intercultural Communication at the Department of Language and Communication Studies, University of Jyväskylä, Finland. His research focuses especially on technology-mediated communication across contexts ranging from virtual teams to online communities.

1 Introduction

Fred Dervin

Interculturality as a multiform *imaginary being*

In his 1979 *Book of Imaginary Beings*, Jorge Luis Borges (2002) presents fantastic and phantasmagorical creatures from around the world. The writer includes amongst others: Antelopes with six legs, the Eastern Dragon, the Gnomes, the Jinn, and the Uroboros. In the preface to the book Borges explains that he has selected 116 such beings, adding (2002: 5):

> The title of this book would justify the inclusion of Prince Hamlet, of the point, of the line, of the surface, of n-dimensional hyperplanes and hypervolumes, of all generic terms, and perhaps of each one of us and of the godhead. In brief, the sum of all things – the universe.

Teaching Imaginary Beings 'Otherwise' could have also been the title of this book, instead of *Teaching Interculturality 'Otherwise'*.

As an omnipresent phenomenon, which no one can avoid ("a universe" in itself, "the sum of all things" to refer back to Borges), interculturality is a highly complex, multiform, and changeable notion, of which global scholars, educators, and decision-makers speak in many different ways, often giving the impression that they 'own' it and shouting at others that their version of interculturality is 'fake', 'invalid', 'unacceptable', 'undemocratic', 'too philosophical'. They (we) also manipulate it – interculturality being an easily mouldable notion.

As an object of research and education – our focus in this book – interculturality *exists* under different 'theoretical' and 'ideological' guises (and, at times, it is just chosen as a random word); it is *influenced* by reported and personal experiences of itself, *subjected to* economic–political pressure in different corners of the world (with capitalism dominating; see Fraser, 2022), *spoken* in different languages, with preferred and specifically connoted words; it also *follows* trends (e.g. translanguaging, decolonial, 'European' democracy, criticality, citizenship), and *transforms* through global and local shifts and mixings (one day *intercultural*, the other *transcultural* and back). This all leads to interculturality (and companion terms, which are often opposed to it but can share resemblances in their own instabilities, such as *multicultural, global, transcultural*) being pulled in all directions, torn apart, and mistreated. And yet, as will be discussed throughout this volume,

DOI: 10.4324/9781003345275-1

interculturality is dominated by some privileged scholars from one corner of the world (the 'West') who speak about it, over others, as if it were 'theirs' only, often leading to *parasitism* whereby they gain benefits at the expense of others. Many of us in this volume (myself included), from a 'province' called Europe, have had their voices heard globally, influencing, at times, thousands of students, scholars, and educators in other parts of the world.

Considering all these, when one uses the word *interculturality* one cannot but have the impression of facing a multifaceted imaginary being like Borges's antelopes with six legs. The word *imaginary* is not meant to be negative since there is a need to reinvent and reimagine the notion ad infinitum. As such, its Latin etymology, *imaginari* reminds us that an imaginary is *picture to oneself*. I have argued that interculturality as an object of research and education can only be such a picture (Dervin, 2022). This is why the notion is not one but an uncountable number of imaginary beings.

This edited volume looks into this multiform imaginary focusing on the thorny issue of teaching interculturality. We could have used another notion in the book (*trans-, poly-, multi-, cross-, hyper-cultural*, or even *global*), but we decided to stick to interculturality, a notion that I have used for at least a decade (Dervin, 2012, 2016) and that my co-editors and I have problematised in our joint research (e.g. Dervin & Yuan, 2021; Dervin et al., 2022). We are well aware that the notion is not used everywhere and that some languages struggle in trying to offer a clear equivalent to it (e.g. Chinese and Finnish). In a sense, it does not matter what label we choose as long as we know why we pick a specific one, its *global* archaeology (beyond the 'West') and how we understand the notion at moment X (because its definition *might* and *will* probably change). Although some of us see specific economic–political and ideological meanings and connotations attached to these different labels (e.g. Meer et al., 2016), as soon as one starts looking outside one's small corner of the world, one notices that these labels are used in very unstable ways in different economic–political, educational, and multilingual contexts. For us, interculturality is preferred for its apparent flexibility (*-ality* refers to never-ending processes) and for reminding us that meeting a person, a thing, an idea, a product from another part of the world, always involves at least two persons who are made to *think beyond themselves*, even if they might resist the presence of another, disagree with and/or insult each other (*inter-*, in-betweenness). Finally, we are blind and deaf to the concept of *culture* squeezed in-between *inter-* and *-ality* in the notion, but we are tolerant of it today, considering culture as another imaginary being which deserves to live and to be imaged at will (see Dervin, 2022). We also agree that it could be replaced with other concepts such as *subject* (as in *intersubjectivity*).

Our goal in publishing this book is not to set interculturality in stone but to both showcase different perspectives and approaches in teaching and (more importantly) to continue to open it up *ad infinitum*. As Nabokov reminds us (2019: 67): "You can know more and more about one thing but you can never know everything about one thing: it's hopeless."

A first takeaway for engaging with the chapters to follow: every time the imaginary being appears, remember to look for and observe its different shapes. The end of this introduction provides you with helpful questions to read the book.

Teaching and (obviously) learning interculturality

Every week, teachers, teacher educators, and researchers engage with and/or lecture about interculturality in different languages in classrooms around the world. *Every week*, thousands of students of all ages are made to reflect im-/explicitly on the imaginary being through different lenses. *Every week*, billions of people 'do' interculturality (in)directly, face-to-face and/or online, watching a film or looking at a piece of art, and also ponder over the notion, learning new things and questioning others.

Let's clarify one thing before we move on: The book says 'teaching' since it is primarily targeted at scholars and educators. However, this does not mean that my co-editors, the authors, and I separate teaching from learning or say 'Let's focus on teaching only!.' This would make no sense since teaching and learning cannot be detached from each other – like those involved in 'doing' *inter*-culturality, they are together, what they do and say influences the other, and vice versa. The dichotomy of teaching-learning would deserve to be renamed by means of a portmanteau word like *tearning*, to remind us that *they can only be one*. The book can thus be used by students who also want to know more about our imaginary being, digging further into its complexities, contradictions, and 'magical powers'.

Although many scholars have presented their own take on the imaginary being under review in English (often labelling themselves 'critical'; see, e.g., Dervin & Jacobsson, 2022; Ferri, 2018; Halualani, 2017; Holliday & Amasi, 2020; Piller, 2017), very few have focused more specifically on teaching the notion. Some recent books relate more or less directly to teaching interculturality in different and, at times, overlapping ways: interculturality in learning Mandarin Chinese in British universities (Jin, 2020); interculturality in Australian schools (Moloney et al., 2022); unthinking, dialoguing, and rethinking the teaching of interculturality in China and Finland (Dervin et al., 2022); introducing an intercultural approach to English-language teaching (Corbett, 2022; see also Victoria & Sangiamchit, 2021); and promoting critical intercultural pedagogy for difficult times (Holmes & Corbett, 2022). Some of these books relate to teaching im-/explicitly *about* interculturality (in, e.g., a classroom), while others discuss how to 'infuse' interculturality in one's teaching practices or in an institution. In this volume, both approaches are covered, with a majority of the chapters focusing on teaching the notion.

Now let's discuss the inclusion of the adverb *otherwise* in the title of the book (*Teaching Interculturality Otherwise*).[1] Etymologically the adverb is based on the contraction of an Old English phrase *on oðre wisan*, meaning 'in the other manner'. It is based on the combination of *other* and *wise*. The word *wise* in Old English meant 'experienced', 'having the power of discerning', and 'judging rightly', and it seems to derive from the Proto-Indo European root for 'to see/know'. *Otherwise* here is not to be understood as offering an alternative that can be copied successfully to 'do' interculturality 'properly' (or something like that). Teaching interculturality otherwise has more to do with learning to consider different ways of engaging with the notion in education, to see and discern different aspects of its teaching. The book will not teach you how to 'do' it properly. No book could ever synthesise the complexities and multiformity of this

4 *Fred Dervin*

imaginary being and decide for readers from around the world how they should do it. Besides, teaching interculturality might not even be possible in itself. The book thus urges you to reflect critically with us on how we understand and teach interculturality and to get some potential inspiration for your own work – while keeping a critical eye constantly opened. The book also helps us put our finger on what influences us in speaking and delivering content about interculturality (e.g. economic–political forces, beliefs in our (subconscious) superiority–inferiority, our own experiences, biases, and imaginaries). Finally, based on the idea of *interculturalising interculturality* that I have proposed (Dervin, 2021), developed with Andreas Jacobsson (Dervin & Jacobsson, 2021, 2022) and continued exploring (Dervin, 2022), the book suggests ways of unthinking and rethinking the notion without any end in sight. Actively engaging with current discussions of the epistemological divide between the 'Global South'/'North' is also highly recommended, especially beyond mere litany and/or self-congratulating oneself.

The book is aimed at teachers and researchers of intercultural communication education at different educational levels, as well as anyone interested in scholarship on education for interculturality.

Origins of the book

> Splendid to think that we are steeped in secrets. The nicest thing about learning is that it multiplies the secrets.
>
> (Canetti, 2021: 56)

The book derives from a two-year international project led by myself (University of Helsinki) and the other editors, Mei Yuan and Sude (both from Minzu University of China). The project aimed to support Chinese and Finnish students to teach interculturality in higher education, looking into multiple perspectives, which for them were, to refer to Canetti's quote, 'secrets' in the sense that, like most students around the world, the way the notion had been introduced to them before the project was limited (see Tan et al., 2022; Dervin & Tan, 2023). During the project, the students had the opportunity to listen to and interact with the chapter authors, and to interact with students based at a Finnish university and students from another Chinese university around the project topic. For a semester, Mei Yuan and I also met the students online to discuss with them and to empower them to reflect on what they were learning and discussing with these different groups.

When we put the project together, we decided to include a range of scholars from the 'West' who had different – with some overlapping – perspectives on teaching interculturality. The chapter authors, who cooperated with our students, work in the following countries: Australia, Austria, Finland, France, Greece, Italy, Sweden, UK, USA. Only two of them are originally from outside the 'West' (China and India), and two other authors were 'navigating' intellectually between a European country, China, and Singapore at the time of writing. They also represent different generations of researchers (some are more 'senior' than others), different first languages (but they all wrote their chapters in English), different (sub-)fields of research (adult education, business, early childhood education, language education, media studies, teacher education) as well as different theoretical and ideological positions.

The Chinese students we were working with come from Minzu University of China, a very special institution in Beijing with a focus on China's 56 Minzu 'ethnic' groups (see Dervin & Yuan, 2021, for more information). They specialise in educational sciences (fourth-year bachelor's) and have been introduced to two specific perspectives on interculturality during their studies: *Minzu education* (e.g. Sude et al., 2020) and *American scholar James Banks's multicultural education* (Banks, 2006). Influenced by local professors who have studied abroad, some of the students might have come across the work of *Michael Byram* (e.g. 1997, UK), who is often referred to in Mainland China, especially in reference to his model of intercultural competence, and *J. W. Berry's model of acculturation* (e.g. 1992, Canada). Apart from these dominant ideological entries into issues of interculturality, the students were unaware of the tens of other perspectives from the 'West'. We wanted the students to get acquainted with some of them, including and beyond English-speaking countries, so that they could become more aware of the complexities of the imaginary being they were working on and enrich their takes on teaching interculturality. At the same time, we helped the students develop their sense of criticality towards the knowledge that they were introduced to by the chapter authors.[2] Schoenberg's (2003: 17) views on seeing the teacher beyond the figure of the 'demigod' describe well our intentions:

> The teacher must have the courage to admit his own mistakes. He does not have to pose as infallible, as one who knows all and never errs; he must rather be tireless, constantly searching, perhaps sometimes finding. Why pose as a demigod? Why not be, rather, fully human?

Let me share what some of the students said in their learning diaries (written in English) that seem to hint at criticality having taken place during the project. I refrain from commenting on what the students say here, preferring to let readers see for themselves:

- About the imaginary being of interculturality

> This week's teaching allowed us to share our intercultural experiences. At first, my thinking was limited. I felt that I didn't have much direct contact with foreigners, so I didn't know what to say. Later, my team members [the students cooperated with their classmates in breakout rooms in Zoom during interactions with the chapter authors] shared their feelings about watching British dramas, which reminded me of the foreign movies that I had watched. Most of the foreign films I have seen are American films, and most of these films have individual heroism, which could be related to the democratic system of the United States. In Chinese films, more emphasis is placed on win-win cooperation, which is also in line

with China's socialist system. From this, I also feel that direct contact is not the only way of intercultural communication.

At the beginning, I thought that interculturality was communication between countries. At that time, my understanding of interculturality was very limited, and I also thought that interculturality was far away from me. But I gradually discovered that interculturality is a very broad concept and that it can refer to *inter-generational exchanges, inter-ethnic exchanges, inter-gender exchanges*, etc. I also realized that interculturality is in fact always around us all the time.

In my opinion, intercultural education and communication are sometimes just like Schrodinger's cat. We never know what characteristics and needs we will have before we officially start. When we conduct interculturality activities, we are not only practitioners of *known knowledge*, but also *explorers of the unknown*.

- About some of the chapter authors' lectures

The title of Robyn Moloney's lecture was *A story of change (变化) or a story about change*. I think that Robyn was emphasizing that interculturality is a dynamic process, that we can't look at it in a static way and that we have to look at it with a developmental insight. Because the content of intercultural research is constantly changing and always full of surprises, the research process is like opening a drawer, you never know what's in the next drawer. So, we should treat it with humility and prudence. The process of our intercultural communication is also a process of constantly changing our original ideas. In this process, we not only reflect on ourselves, but also on others. And language is a tool to speed up the process of cross-cultural, because it can use specific symbols to present the culture behind a nation and country.

In class, several intercultural scholars were introduced. It is very interesting that the research fields of these professors are different, which also allows me to look at interculturality from different perspectives, and to find that the meaning of interculturality is really rich, complex and interesting.

- About interculturalising interculturality

I think that the Tang Dynasty's 兼容并蓄 (inclusiveness) is of great significance to intercultural development. The Tang Dynasty of China did not control thoughts and limit one mainstream thought like the previous dynasties, but adopted an open attitude towards the thoughts of the three schools of Confucianism, Buddhism and Taoism, reflecting strong cultural tolerance and confidence. So, it's the same across cultures. We can't just listen to the voice of one family, we must pursue 百花齐放 (letting a hundred flowers blossom). I think that an intercultural researcher who only uses books and articles produced in the US or UK, can only understand one interpretation of interculturality, and only hear a 'Western' voice. Interculturality should not be limited to the 'West'.

14 chapters, 14 ways of engaging with the imaginary being

The book contains 14 chapters, an introduction, a conclusion, and an afterword. The 14 chapters were written by colleagues who took part in the aforementioned project. I have asked my colleague and friend Hamza R'boul, with whom I published a book where we discuss and contrast our views and experiences of working on interculturality as scholars located in different parts of the world (Dervin & R'boul, 2022), to write an afterword. R'boul was based in Morocco at the time. His afterword helps us further 'unwrap' the 'otherwise' of the book title.

In writing their chapters the authors were asked to consider the following questions – which they could also question:

- How do you see interculturality? What does it mean to you? How similar and different is it compared to other educators/scholars? How have you changed in the way you conceptualise it?
- What do you make of the idea of *interculturalising interculturality* (Dervin, 2021; Dervin & Jacobsson, 2022)?
- How do you/could you teach about interculturality (give a couple of examples)? What would you consider changing about your teaching?
- When you teach about interculturality, what would you want your students to learn? What problems do they face when they try to 'learn' about it?
- What problems related to teaching interculturality would you like to see solved (if possible)?

The book is divided into three parts: Part I, 'The nuts and bolts of teaching interculturally'; Part II, 'Change in the teaching of interculturality'; and Part III, 'Insights into interculturalising interculturality'.

Part I, 'The nuts and bolts of teaching interculturally'

Alexander Frame starts with a chapter based on his experience of designing, setting up, and leading a master of arts (MA) programme in intercultural management in France. Training the students to adopt critical, interpretivist, and non-essentialising views of interculturality in organisational settings, the author highlights three key phases in learning about the notion. In Chapter 3, Jasmin Peskoller sees interculturality as an open and dynamic understanding of culture that is strongly focused on the individual and the multitude of dimensions that differentiate and connect human beings. Set in Austrian secondary and teacher education, the chapter recommends a form of intercultural pedagogy that includes activities integrating self-reflection, perspective-changing, and critical analysis. From Austria, we travel to Italy where, in Chapter 4, Agostino Portera describes how teaching in intercultural classrooms takes place in Italy. Reviewing the meanings and characteristics of intercultural education from an Italian/European perspective, and referring to his extensive research, Portera focuses on intercultural teaching competences both in theory and in practice. Based on an

8 *Fred Dervin*

autoethnography of being a teacher aide in an Australian secondary school, working with, e.g., migrant and refugee children who did not speak English, the next chapter by Patrick A. Danaher problematises a conceptual relationship between specific differences and particular ways of engaging with interculturality in education in Australia. Implications for teacher educators are discussed. Finally, Chapter 6 was written by Gary McCulloch. This original contribution interrogates the connections between university structures and the creation of a former research centre on interculturality at the Institute of Education University College London (UK). The case of Jagdish Gundara serves as a case study to understand the way the centre was created and the distinctive ideals of interculturality that it represented.

Part II, 'Change in the teaching of interculturality'

In 'Teaching interculturality: Changes in perspective (A story of change)', Robyn Moloney discusses a number of changes which have brought about shifts in her thinking and conceptualisation of interculturality as both a language teacher and teacher educator. For the author, interculturality is a fluid developmental relational process constructed from the 'inside out', which should aim at better practice and social justice. Set in the context of Australian teacher education, the chapter emphasises the importance of the growth of personal interculturality. Etta Kralovec, another teacher educator, asks the provocative but important question: Is there any communication that isn't intercultural? Reminding us that the notion of interculturality is not used in her field in the US, Kralovec presents her educational and intellectual autobiography, showing that the notion was always 'underground' in her academic and professional career. As takeaways she suggests that teachers should reflect systematically on their identities and that teaching interculturality comes down to the basic question of what education is all about. In Chapter 9, Ning Chen and Fred Dervin propose a new method called *observality*, which symbolises the complex continuum of the observer and the observed in interculturality. Chen and Dervin argue that those involved in teaching-learning ('tearning' as suggested earlier) interculturality have a need and responsibility to look at themselves in 'the' mirror of what others say and 'do' to reflect on and be critical of both their own take and criticality of interculturality. Examples of observality from the authors' engagement with China are shared for the reader to get a clear sense of what the method is about. In the final chapter of this part, Heidi Layne and Abitha Chakrapani facilitate a 'meeting' between interculturality and the fairly recent field of education for emergencies. In the midst of the multifaceted emergencies and crises that the world has experienced since 2020, the authors argue that teaching interculturality cannot do without (1) taking into account such issues and (2) listening to what students have to say about their experiences and perceptions of these emergencies. Using a short survey with students registered at Finnish universities, Layne and Chakrapani describe what interculturality joining hands with education for emergencies could entail.

Part III, 'Insights into interculturalising interculturality'

In Chapter 11, Giuliana Ferri tackles a question that has occupied interculturalists for some years now: Is it possible to teach interculturality 'beyond' culture? Starting from the argument that interculturality is never neutral but an ideological and political term, the author contextualises the notion within current perspectives of decolonising knowledge. Introducing us to the context of teacher education in the UK, Ferri suggests moving away from, e.g., an overemphasis on cultural difference to teach interculturality within the framework of social justice. In 'Interculturalising the teaching of interculturality in Swedish higher education', Andreas Jacobsson proposes a similar perspective, promoting a polycentric approach that integrates approaches to interculturality from different cultural contexts. The specific context of early childhood teacher education in Sweden serves as an illustration. The next chapter was written by Marko Siitonen and Margarethe Olbertz-Siitonen. The authors problematise utilising mediated communication in a more systematic way in teaching interculturality, using the context of Finnish higher education as an example. They argue that media- and technology-mediated communication can enhance making sense of oneself and of the other. Several concrete examples are used to illustrate how the integration of mediated communication could take place in the teaching of interculturality. For Nathalie Auger (France), the author of Chapter 14, teaching interculturality is first and foremost about cultivating self-reflection. In her work with future teachers of French as a second language, Auger focuses on stereotypes and emotions. She trains her students to recognise emotions that can lead to the 'rehearsal' of stereotypes, to identify them and to deconstruct them using specific theoretical tools from the human and social sciences. The final chapter is based on Oona Piipponen's work in Finnish primary schools, where she aims to promote children's intercultural encountering. Providing examples from an intercultural story exchange in Europe, during which children told stories to exchange partners, Piipponen insists on adopting methods that urge us to listen to children's voices – rather than imposing a specific view of interculturality on them.

Advice on how to reflect on the chapters

> We know that there is nothing higher than knowledge. But it is absurd to shout at someone: 'Know!' Knowledge is the summit, but what are the paths leading to it?
> Hohl (2021: 22)

You are about to enter the fascinating world of teaching (imaginary beings) (interculturality). Some of you will already have extensive knowledge about the complex field of interculturality, while others might be pure novices. Everyone will find something new for themselves in what follows. *I promise*. As Hohl (2021) puts it, there are different paths on the way to the unattainable summit that knowledge represents.

Over the past years I have come to realise that working on interculturality includes two interrelated and vital processes, which are well summarised by Barthes (1977: 170) in what follows:

What he listened to, what he could not keep from listening to, wherever he was, was the deafness of others to their own language: he heard them not hearing each other.

We must hear ourselves (not) hear each other. Reading this book requires listening carefully to what the chapter authors say while listening to our own thoughts, to how we absorb/reject and reformulate what they say, to our emotions, our potential biases, our (dis)comfort, our contradictory reactions to what they propose, our dialogues with ourselves and others about what we read. In order to do so, I suggest that you keep an eye on these questions while engaging with each chapter (you may obviously remove, edit, and add questions; see Table 1.1).

Table 1.1 Keys to reflecting on the chapters

- Can I summarise the author's take on interculturality and their proposal for teaching interculturality in a couple of sentences?
- Do I find the chapter to be successful at proposing teaching interculturality 'otherwise'? Why (not)?
- Does the author reveal success and/or failure of their 'otherwising'?
- Does the author have 'pet' words/terms/concepts that they use to discuss interculturality? What do I know about them? How could I translate them into other languages?
- Is the author critical of themselves? For which aspect of their work and why?
- Is the author inclusive/tolerant of other ways of conceptualising interculturality?
- How does the author engage with the idea of *interculturalising interculturality*? Can I clearly summarise their arguments?
- What is the context of the chapter (country, region, urban, rural locations, etc.)? What do I know about it? What are my potential biases and misrepresentations concerning this context?
- How much does the context of the chapter seem to influence how the author engages with teaching interculturality?
- What are my feelings towards what the author is writing? Why do I seem to feel this or that way? What seems to trigger specific emotions?
- Do I know scholars from the context of this article? How do they speak about interculturality? Is their approach similar and/or different from the chapter author?
- Who does the chapter author refer to? Are they all scholars? From which part(s) of the world? How much do they refer to people from their own context?
- How many of the references from the chapter are in a language other than English? How many are translations from another language into English? What seems to be the influence of these references on what the author writes? What purpose(s) do they serve?
- What is the subfield of the author? How much does it seem to matter in the way they write about interculturality? What other fields of research are included in the chapter?
- Have I come across some of the ideas, concepts, or theories presented as being from a specific field in the chapter in other fields of knowledge?
- If I could interact with the chapter author, what would I want to ask them about their take on teaching interculturality?
- Finally, after reading all the chapters, can I map out what the authors seem to (dis) agree about in terms of how they understand and work with interculturality in education?

I will get back to you at the end of the book to discuss some of these important issues before leaving the floor to Hamza R'boul, who will push us to think even further about teaching interculturality 'otherwise'. My co-editors and I do hope that you will enjoy reading through the chapters, acquainting yourself further with the multiform imaginary being that interculturality is.

Notes

1 As I started writing the introduction to this book, Hamza R'boul reminded me that the International Association for Languages and Intercultural Communication (IALIC) was going to hold its 2022 conference on the topic 'Diversity and Epistemological Plurality: Thinking interculturality "otherwise"' – with this same mysterious adverb *otherwise* in its title too. Organised in Portugal, the conference was based on the increasingly popular idea of 'epistemological plurality' (which could explain 'otherwise' in the call), 'promising', amongst others, to "defy[ing] geocultural, systemic, structural and symbolic invisibilizations of diversity, to name but a few, in order to think interculturality 'otherwise'" (http://ialic.international/wp-content/uploads/2022/04/IALIC2022_CfP -VF.pdf). Concretely, for the organisers, this seems to mean (amongst others) "bringing together diverse communities (scholars, researchers, practitioners, local authorities, entities of the civic society…) from different locations or geographies" (http://ialic. international/wp-content/uploads/2022/04/IALIC2022_CfP-VF.pdf). However, the fact that the conference was only going to be *face-to-face* (although we have 'experienced' fruitful online lives for nearly two years that allowed access to events one could never have imagined attending physically and bearing in mind that many scholars were still unable to travel due to COVID-19 restrictions or 'vaccinationism' at the time of writing), requiring expensive travelling to Portugal – while continuing to be a real burden to the environment; the high registration fees and the 'Western-centrism' of the conference scientific committee, all seem to contribute to a feeling of schizophrenia *otherwise*. As we shall see in this introduction and throughout *Teaching Interculturality 'Otherwise'*, one will experience a potentially similar feeling with this book. R'boul comes back to the 'otherwise' in his thought-provoking Afterword.

2 One important aspect of the project which is not covered in this book has to do with guiding the students in contrasting these approaches and 'their' Minzu perspective for differences and similarities so that they can decide for themselves what they would like to do with the notion of interculturality. Future publications will focus on this.

References

Banks, J. A. (2006). *Race, Culture and Education*. New York: Routledge.
Barthes, R. (1977). *Roland Barthes by Roland Barthes*. Berkeley and Los Angeles, CA: University of California Press.
Berry, J. W. (1992). Acculturation and adaptation in a new society. *International Migration*, *30*(1), 69–85.
Borges, J. L. (2002). *The Books of Imaginary Beings*. London: Penguin Books.
Byram, M. (1997). *Teaching and Assessing Intercultural Communicative Competence*. Clevedon: Multilingual Matters.
Canetti, E. (2021). *Notes from Hampstead*. London: Macmillan.
Corbett, J. (2022). *An Intercultural Approach to English Language Teaching*. Clevedon: Multilingual matters.
Dervin, F. (2012). A plea for change in research on intercultural discourses: A liquid approach to the study of the acculturation of Chinese students. *Journal of Multicultural Discourses*, *6*(1), 37–52.

Dervin, F. (2016). *Intercultural Education: A Theoretical and Methodological Toolbox*. London: Palgrave Macmillan.

Dervin, F. (2021). *Critical and Reflexive Languaging in the Construction of Interculturality as an Object of Research and Practice* (19 April 2021). Digital series of talks on plurilingualism and interculturality, University of Copenhagen.

Dervin, F. (2022). *Interculturality in Fragments: A Reflexive Approach*. Singapore: Springer.

Dervin, F., & Jacobsson, A. (2021). *Interculturaliser l'interculturel*. Paris: L'harmattan.

Dervin, F., & Jacobsson, A. (2022). *Intercultural Communication Education: Broken Realities and Rebellious Dreams*. London: Springer.

Dervin, F., & R'boul, H. (2022). *Through the Looking-Glass of Interculturality: Autocritiques*. Singapore: Springer.

Dervin, F., Sude, Yuan, M., & Chen, N. (2022). *Interculturality between East and West. Unthink, Dialogue, and Rethink*. London: Springer.

Dervin, F., & Tan, H. (2023). *Supercriticality and Interculturality*. Singapore: Springer.

Dervin, F., & Yuan, M. (2021). *Revitalizing Interculturality in Education: Minzu as a Companion*. London: Routledge.

Ferri, G. (2018). *Intercultural Communication: Critical Approaches, Future Challenges*. London: Palgrave Macmillan.

Fraser, N. (2022). *Cannibal Capitalism*. London: Verso.

Halualani, R. T. (2017). *Intercultural Communication: A Critical Perspective*. New York: Cognella Academic Publishing.

Hohl, L. (2021). *The Notes or On Non-Premature Reconciliation*. New Haven, CT, and London: Yale University Press.

Holliday, A., & Amasi, S. (2020). *Making Sense of the Intercultural: Finding DeCentred Threads*. London: Routledge.

Holmes, P., & Corbett, J. (Eds.). (2022). *Critical Intercultural Pedagogy for Difficult Times: Conflict, Crisis, and Creativity*. London: Routledge.

Jin, T. (2020). *Interculturality in Learning Mandarin Chinese in British Universities*. London: Routledge.

Meer, N., Modood, T., & Zapata-Barrero, R. (2016). *Multiculturalism and Interculturalism: Debating the Dividing Lines*. Edinburgh: Edinburgh University Press.

Moloney, R., Lobytsyna, M., & De Nobile, J. (2022). *Interculturality in Schools: Practice and Research*. London: Routledge.

Nabokov, V. (2019). *Think, Write, Speak*. London: Penguin Modern Classics.

Piller, I. (2017). *Intercultural Communication: A Critical Introduction*. Edinburgh: Edinburgh University Press.

Schoenberg, A. (2003). *A Schoenberg Reader: Documents of a Life*. New Haven, CT, and London: Yale University Press.

Sude, Yuan, M., & Dervin, F. (2020). *An Introduction to Chinese Ethnic Minority Education*. Singapore: Springer.

Tan, H., Zhao, K., & Dervin, F. (2022). Experiences of and preparedness for intercultural teacherhood in higher education: Non-specialist English teachers' positioning, agency and sense of legitimacy in China. *Language and Intercultural Communication, 22*(1), 68–84.

Victoria, M., & Sangiamchit, C. (Eds.). (2021). *Interculturality and the English Language Classroom*. London: Palgrave Macmillan.

Part I
The nuts and bolts of teaching interculturally

2 Teaching and learning about interculturality in communication and management

Alexander Frame

Introduction

Although courses about interculturality all around the world ostensibly deal with similar questions, there may be considerable differences and divergencies between disciplinary perspectives, course objectives, epistemological postures, and so on. These may be related to individual differences in the way that scholars understand and position themselves relating to the concepts of culture and interculturality, in an interdisciplinary field which is multifaceted and in constant evolution, but also to the institutional factors that lead to a course on interculturality being offered by a given organisation or higher education institution (HEI). From my experience, the reasoning behind a module in intercultural communication being offered in a HEI in France is often either linked to a desire to take into account the cultural dimension in a related field of study or to fulfil more-or-less vague objectives of developing 'global competences' among students. What is taught and how it is taught can vary greatly depending on institutional requirements and expectations. In the French university system, which is traditionally built around compulsory modules with few electives, interculturality is more often linked to other questions, and relatively rarely presents as an option chosen only by interested and motivated students. For instance, within different programmes at my university, I currently teach interculturality linked to the localisation of websites and multimedia products; interculturality in the context of organising and managing international projects in the arts; interculturality from the point of view of international public relations, including the ethics of stereotyping and how to deal with diverse audiences; and intercultural negotiation skills in the light of international commerce in the food and beverages sector.

Despite the variety of courses for non-specialists, this chapter focuses in particular on a specialised programme of study for interculturalists which I set up and currently coordinate at the University of Burgundy, France. This two-year English-taught master of arts (MA) programme in intercultural management deals with interculturality from the perspective of communication sciences and applied to questions of management (diversity and inclusion, international projects/teams, change management) within organisations. As a programme for specialists, it covers multiple perspectives on interculturality and aims to encourage learners

DOI: 10.4324/9781003345275-3

to develop a complex view of this phenomenon. This chapter reviews the way in which the programme design can be seen to progressively develop this complex, multiperspective view of interculturality. It is divided into three sections, structured around the questions asked by Dervin as main editor and architect of this book, concerning the way the different chapter authors conceptualise and teach about interculturality. The initial section discusses the concept of interculturality from a communication studies perspective, as a key to understanding interpersonal communication as an intersubjective process linked to sensemaking and identities. This is important insofar as it is the vision which underpins the way interculturality is taught in the MA programme. The second section addresses the question of how we might 'interculturalise interculturality' as suggested by Dervin and Jacobsson (2022) and what that might mean in such a context. The third section focuses on how this translates into course design in the MA programme, covering contents and methods used to teach and learn about interculturality, as well as potential areas for development.

Since the chapter constitutes a personal reflection on how my vision of interculturality shapes my teaching practices and this particular course design, I have chosen to use the first person to underline my proximity with the subject. The exercise naturally imposes its own limits since this self-reflective stance is likely to encourage subjective bias and some degree of self-justification. My understanding of what goes on in the programme is necessarily only partial, given that I teach some but not all of the classes described, and my colleagues do not necessarily all share the multiperspective view of interculturality that I outline here. I am thus describing an ideal theoretical situation which may correspond more or less closely to what actually takes place in the classroom. I have been coordinating the MA course for the past five years with a colleague, David Bousquet, who is a cultural studies scholar. The programme design described here reflects the current syllabus, shaped by joint decisions, and my particular rationalisation of its contents is necessarily idiosyncratic and partial. The text which follows should be read in the light of these limits, as a personal attempt to reflect on my current vision and practice of teaching interculturality in the classroom.

Interculturality from a communication studies perspective

My conceptualisation of culture and interculturality has evolved over the 25 years I have been in the field. In France, in the 1990s, difference-based approaches were dominant, based on comparative models imported from English-speaking management scholars such as Hofstede or Trompenaars. They existed alongside a 'French' school of cross-cultural psychology, linked to the French and German Youth Office (OFAJ), with a focus on bias and phenomena based on intergroup dynamics (Demorgon, 1989; Ladmiral & Lipiansky, 1989; Lipiansky, 1992).[1] My own perspective was influenced by my attachment to the field of communication studies, meaning that I first approached intercultural communication as one particular form of interpersonal communication (Dacheux, 1999), before moving on to think more generally about how we use cultures and identities in our everyday

Interculturality in communication and management 17

encounters. From this perspective, interculturality gives us useful insights into interpersonal communication as a process, linked to how individuals go about making sense of and with one another, in a given context.

In the early days of intercultural communication scholarship, emphasis was placed almost exclusively on national cultural differences, associated with differences in communication style and their supposed negative impact on interpersonal communication between people of different nationalities (Romani et al., 2018). However, more recent approaches, sometimes described as 'culture-interactional' (Spencer-Oatey & Franklin, 2009), rather than placing the emphasis on comparing national cultures (the 'positivist paradigm'), adopt an 'interpretivist' perspective. They are centred on sensemaking (Weick, 1995) and look at how cultural norms, linked to the different identities foregrounded by individuals in their interactions, are negotiated, 'performed', or 'emerge' in given settings (Frame, 2014). Another epistemological tradition, linked to cultural studies and social theory, also questions the essentialising nature of cultures, looking at the way national and other cultures and identities are constructed through discourse and used to maintain or challenge relationships of power and status between social groups. The emphasis of these 'postmodern' and/or 'critical' perspectives is not so much how these cultures emerge through interactions, but how they are used to maintain social imbalance, often from a post-colonial point of view. Postmodernists tend to focus on how national cultural identities are constructed through discourse and grand narratives (Romani et al., 2018), sometimes contrasting this with the ambiguity surrounding individuals in their interactions in today's hyperconnected world (Martin, 2004), where they are exposed to a variety of cultures and identities, many of which are rooted in digital media (Matthews, 2000). Critical scholars see their role as challenging power imbalance wherever it may occur, by deconstructing cultural discourse and identities (Nakayama & Halualani, 2010; Romani & Frame, 2020). The vision I have today is one that I believe I share with other academics who can be situated in the interpretivist, postmodern, and/or critical schools of thought, linked to practice theory. These views are increasingly common, but still do not represent the majority of scholars who use the concept.

From this perspective, cultures are seen not as distinct sets of rules or norms which strictly regiment the behaviour of everyone in a particular national group, but rather as 'repertoires of action' or 'tool-kits' (Swidler, 1986) based on anticipated behavioural patterns and routines associated with particular social groups, which constitute (partly) shared and meaningful expectations of how others might behave and expect us to behave. We all have multiple identities and, along with these identities, multiple repertoires and sets of expectations which we can use in our interactions. These identities are not only national, but may be professional, regional, generational, ethnic, family, religious, organisational, or related to many other types of social groupings (Frame & Boutaud, 2010). They may be transnational and mediatised (Hepp, 2015), focused on artefacts or areas of interest, such as pop cultures linked to music, television series, video games, or sports. In this way as a communications scholar, I see all situations of interpersonal communication as intercultural, because we all use cultural references from multiple sources in our interactions, including when there is no apparent international dimension.

This is a slightly different approach to that found in mainstream media, social, and even much academic discourse, in which something flagged as 'intercultural' is usually identified as encompassing difference, typically national difference, and as being a source of misunderstandings, tensions, and potential conflict. While it is important to take this popular representation of interculturality into account in our understanding of the way people relate to one another, my own perspective is a more positive one (Barmeyer & Franklin, 2016), building on the symbolic interactionist perspective (Blumer, 1969; Stryker, 1980) and more specifically on identity theory (Burke et al., 2003; Burke & Stets, 2009; Stryker & Burke, 2000). Our different identities and cultural repertoires provide us with tools for understanding one another and behaving in an understandable way, as we negotiate and perform our shared references in our interactions. They constitute the building blocks of meaning that we use to make sense of and for specific individuals, in a given situation, taking into account their identities and the interactional context (Frame, 2012). This does not have to be consensual or cooperative: I can also use my cultural knowledge to insult someone, or resist or oppose them, but it is always done by taking the other into account.

When intercultural 'problems', 'conflicts', or 'crises' are pointed to, I often find it useful to shift the focus from cultures to identities. Where cultures are the sources of potentially shared representations which facilitate communication, identities can be used to divide people into groups, 'us and them', often to try to maintain an advantage for one's own group. This can be in terms of self-esteem ('we're better than they are') or in order to stigmatise the others and try to maintain them in a position of (social, symbolic, economic, political, etc.) inferiority: they are not equal to us, and so do not deserve equal treatment, access to resources, etc. Culture often has very little to do with this, except being used as a pretext to try to justify the stigmatisation, with the underlying idea that people are prisoners of their 'culture', that they cannot evolve, that they are somehow different in the essence of who they are. As a scholar, I try to combat these 'solid', 'essentialising' conceptions of culture. While I realise and recognise that they reflect how we often tend to think about our fellow humans, by putting them into groups and considering these groups through certain typical, even stereotypical, traits, I believe that it is dangerous for humankind when scholars, the media, politicians, or whoever encourage the idea that we are fundamentally different from one another.

I believe that this is a particularly topical and important question since social media have considerably reinforced the fragmentation and polarisation of the public sphere over the last 20 years. We now tend to be exposed, through the work of algorithms, to people who express similar opinions to us. Social media rarely show us views opposing our own, since this would arguably reduce engagement and user satisfaction. This leads to fragmentation and our unopposed opinions becoming more radical, by being shared only with like-minded people in the digital public sphere. In the 20th century, people in societies were generally exposed to a much smaller range of more mainstream media influences, through a limited number of terrestrial television channels, newspapers, or radio stations. Now it is easy with social media to find groups of people sharing and encouraging extreme views, whether political, religious, racial, or whatever (Kaluža, 2021). This media landscape, or digital media logic (Altheide, 2013), appears to be creating new types of 'cultural bubbles' within societies, by promoting opposing world views, isolating connected online groups algorithmically in a way not dissimilar to the geographical isolation responsible for cultural differentiation in a previous era.[2]

In the last few years, I have found myself in situations where I have been faced with someone with whom I feel I am not able to find intellectual common ground, because our world views are markedly different on a particular question. This is not 'interculturality' in the international sense or the 'ethnic' one. These are people with whom I share many vectors of socialisation: we live nearby, have a similar income, are of a similar age, speak the same language, etc., but have such different political views, for example, that it appears impossible to find any shared intellectual starting point from which we can begin building a consensus on the topic. I would argue that this phenomenon runs more deeply than heartfelt differences of opinion, which have always existed, as have newspapers with their politically oriented readerships. 'Algorithmic isolation' leads to contrasting 'factual representations' of the world which underpin these differences of opinion, and in the 'post-truth' era (Keyes, 2004; Lewandowsky et al., 2017), 'fact' becomes the object not so much of debate as of belief. Affinity and affect have replaced the Habermassian ideal of *deliberation*, fuelled by polarised social media posts and conspiracy theories (Brachotte et al., forthcoming), where everyone and no one is recognised as an 'expert'. In reference to the earlier discussion of cultures, the building blocks upon which we might construct a common vision do not, in such cases, seem to fit together. I believe that this is a new form of interculturality, where the word takes on its full meaning. If we are to address this as scholars, we need to stop thinking about cultures solely as unified national blocks or monoliths.

While such 'new' forms of interculturality are often not recognised as such, there is also a risk that academic discourse promoting a more fluid vision of cultures and interculturality also misses its target when it comes to analysing the influence of national and other cultures which are more often identified and labelled as such in everyday interactions. After spending several years trying to widen students' perspectives beyond the national level of culture, I have also come to realise that this perspective is not sufficient in itself, since it risks ignoring the social context in which discourse about interculturality is being produced. It is true that macro-level generalisations cannot be applied directly on the microsocial level because they ignore the way people actually communicate and adapt to one another, based on the identities, groups, or categories which they ascribe to one another. However, this same social categorisation, which is fundamental to the way people relate to each other, is often based on cultural differences as a social construct. People see each other as belonging to different national, religious,

20 *Alexander Frame*

ethnic, generational groups, etc., generally linked to more-or-less stereotyped representations of those groups, based on more-or-less fantasised or realistic behavioural patterns which are seen to constitute social norms in those groups. As such, the representations that 'Germans behave like this' or 'young people behave like that', however factually and contextually inaccurate they may turn out to be, are part of our expectations of individuals we assign to social groups different to our own, and may shape our behaviour towards them and the way we interpret what they say and do. Critical approaches to cross-cultural communication and management have also underlined the way in which these differences may be constructed strategically, in order to seek to perpetuate or to challenge power differentials between ingroups and outgroups (Dervin & Machart, 2015a; Nakayama & Halualani, 2010; Primecz et al., 2016). Another challenge today is thus to take into account this discourse around national and other cultures, the consciousness of 'interculturality' which changes the frame of analysis (Frame, 2015) and to understand how this *also* affects the way people relate to one another.

When it comes to teaching and learning about interculturality, this vision has led me to distinguish three phases through which learners can usefully be accompanied in order to gradually build up a complex understanding of the phenomenon. These can also be indexed on the four research paradigms in cross-cultural management identified by Laurence Romani and her colleagues (Romani et al., 2018). The three phases, which will be further developed and applied to intercultural management in a later section, are summarised in Table 2.1.

Interculturalising interculturality

Although these three phases of learning about interculturality aim to gradually complexify the learners' understanding of the phenomenon, we could argue that they do not go very far in 'interculturalising interculturality', as Dervin and Jacobsson (2022) and the editors of this collective volume invite us to do. On

Table 2.1 Three phases of learning about interculturality

Phase	Paradigm	Type of understanding
1: Decentring	Positivist	Overcoming ethnocentrism and learning about potential macro-level cultural differences between social groups as a shared source of predictability in interpersonal communication.
2: Fluidifying	Interpretivist	Learning about the negotiation of cultures and identities in contextualised, micro-level interactions: the emergent dimension of cultures as intersubjective processes.
3: Re-categorising	Postmodern, Critical	Taking into account representations of other social groups as discursive constructs impacting behaviour and understanding, related to intergroup dynamics and power differentials.

one level of understanding, this expression invites scholars to try to overcome a traditional 'Western-centric' focus in the field of intercultural communication education. It is highly paradoxical that this should be necessary in a field which is supposed to reflect on how to better take into account diversity. As an English-speaking scholar who has grown up and lived all my life in Western Europe, I understand and appreciate the need to avoid adopting a solely 'Western' approach to interculturality in order to try to engage with other perspectives and other voices. It is something that I strive to promote when designing courses about interculturality. From a scientific standpoint, however, this is no simple feat, since it would entail a major upheaval of the current sociological structures of scholarship: peer-reviewed journals, criteria for funding allocation, publication-based criteria for recruitment, promotion, etc. The sociology of international academia not only uses English as a lingua franca but tends to reinforce the expression of Western views and ideas through its implicit or explicit editorial norms and the peer-review process. Non-Western scholars often have their work reviewed by 'peers' from the West who collaborate with scientific journals, and as a result find themselves having to compose with Western terms, concepts, and references in order to 'improve' their work to reach the 'international standard' required to have it published in these journals which are taken as references for the international scientific community. They may themselves feel obliged to 'prove their credentials' by respecting these unquestioned norms in their writing, twisting and adapting them to fit into the Western epistemological mould.[3]

The project to make audible other voices and perspectives in the field of interculturality is thus a very necessary one. But to succeed it would require far more than an affirmative-action-style approach foregrounding scholars of non-Western national origins. Indeed, it is important to avoid the other extreme, which would result in essentialising views of interculturality based on the national or ethnic origin of the person speaking. This is reminiscent of situations in which anti-essentialist, fluid approaches to interculturality meet the preservationist heterocentrism[4] of cultural studies. On the one hand, an anti-essentialist, *laisser-faire* attitude can lead to the most powerful groups imposing hegemonic cultural norms to the point of excluding diverse voices. This is arguably the case currently in the field of intercultural communication. On the other hand, a posture of anti-anti-essentialism (Gilroy, 1993) can result in pressures to (artificially) preserve a supposed cultural 'purity' – itself a very utopian, essentialising idea – with the risk of inventing or promoting voices for the sake of their supposed (constructed) difference. I believe that we can collectively make progress on this if we have a dose of sensitivity to issues of power and privilege, and if we can raise awareness of the underlying Western-centric normativity of the field, by publicly discussing questions such as those raised by Dervin and Yuan (2021).

I also believe that interculturalising interculturality should not just be about national cultures or transnational cultures associated with regions of the globe such as the West, the East, the Global South, and so on. We should also think about all of the other cultures which affect the way we communicate. As a communication studies scholar, my main focus remains on the way people actively use cultures and identities to try to make sense of one another and for one another. These cultures and identities are numerous and cover both what Adrian Holliday calls 'small cultures' (Holliday, 2000; Holliday et al., 2016) and larger ones. When thinking about organisations, for example, it is important to put into the equation the influence of organisational cultures, professional cultures, local departmental cultures, communities of practice, and so on. When we communicate, depending on the situation and how well we know one another, we may also draw on our family cultures, our religious cultures, cultures linked to our leisure activities and interests, to our friendship groups and political ideas. As previously outlined, we may encounter very different worldviews even with people with whom we share very similar sociological profiles, due to algorithmic isolation. Interculturalising interculturality can thus also be about challenging dominant representations by multiplying the disciplinary and epistemological perspectives on interculturality, bringing all of these elements into the frame, in order to better understand the way that interculturality functions as a phenomenon, shaping and shaped by our communication.

Teaching about interculturality applied to communication and management

This section discusses how I seek to apply the three phases of teaching and learning about interculturality, introduced in Table 2.1, to the MA course in intercultural management (ICM) at the University of Burgundy.[5] The course is taught face to face over two years to a group of around 15 graduate students recruited internationally and coming from all parts of the world. As an English-taught 'international master's' degree, students pay a specific annual course fee of €4000. Typically, students joining the course have a degree in the liberal arts, which they have either completed recently or prior to five to ten years of professional experience. Some have previous knowledge of the classic theories of interculturality, and several years of working internationally, while others are moving into a more-or-less unfamiliar field. Their stated aims when choosing this course are typically to increase their soft skills linked to interculturality and to obtain a diploma allowing them to begin working or move on in their career in the fields of international project management, diversity and inclusion, intercultural training or coaching, global mobility, international human resources or international marketing, among others.

The programme is composed of four semesters of study. The first two semesters, lasting 13 weeks each, take place in Dijon. It is over the course of this first year of study that the concept of interculturality is discussed from different perspectives, encouraging the students to build up a complex view of the phenomenon. The second year is dedicated to a specialisation through study abroad in a partner university in semester 3, a short semester 4 in Dijon and a four- to five-month internship. The exchange semester typically allows the students to concentrate on and specialise in a particular area of the course, such as critical interculturality, culture and area studies, business and management, geopolitics, or migration studies, as well as improving their language skills in the language of the host country. The seven-week-long fourth semester is dedicated to finalising the two-year MA thesis, French language certification, some optional specialisation subjects, and guest lectures. It ends with the long internship which gives the students a chance to apply what they have learnt in an organisational setting, build their curriculum vitae (CV) through practical experience, and frequently to move directly into employment in the same organisation at the end of the course.

The MA programme is coordinated by two full-time academics (myself and David Bousquet) and taught jointly by a team of around 40, composed of academics (≈40%; approximately half from the University of Burgundy and half from other universities), teachers (≈30%, typically for language classes), and professionals working in the field (≈30%). The ICM programme is structured around three pillars: *interculturality*, *language teaching*, and *management*. Although the cultural dimension underlies all of these, I will concentrate in this chapter on the way that we teach interculturality in particular. However, regarding the other parts of the course, one of the difficulties we have encountered as course coordinators is to manage the different perspectives on interculturality among the teaching staff, and namely the uncritical positivist approaches of many non-specialist teachers and academics who teach classes on languages or various aspects of management, approaches which are shared by some established intercultural trainers. We discuss perspectives on interculturality when recruiting new staff members, and explain the critical and complex approach which the course as a whole presents to the students, in the hope that teachers adapt to or adopt this. However, where they are not familiar with such perspectives, and if they see their subject as only indirectly related to interculturality, they do not necessarily embrace this complexity. In such cases, depending at what point in the two years their class takes place, the students can be quite vocal in underlining what they have come to see as the limits of sweeping national-level generalisations, and quite critical towards the classes in question.

The classes specifically dealing with interculturality can be more-or-less closely associated with the three phases of learning about interculturality identified earlier (Table 2.1) and with the four paradigms listed by Romani and colleagues (Romani et al., 2018). They are presented in this way in Table 2.2.

Decentring the intercultural gaze

The course begins with what I have described as the 'decentring phase'. This involves difference-based approaches aiming to overcome ethnocentrism and deals with material covered in the majority of intercultural communication training courses, focusing on macro-level, collective representations, and the differences between national groups. The Introduction to Intercultural Communication class covers definitions of the key concepts and the main theories and models in the field, both comparative and more communication-based (including anxiety and uncertainty management theory and communication accommodation theory, as well as the development model of intercultural sensitivity, acculturation theory,

Table 2.2 The three phases of learning about interculturality in the ICM MA course

Phase	Paradigm(s)	Class	Hours	Semester
1: Decentring	Positivist	Introduction to Intercultural Communication	12	1
1: Decentring	Positivist	Culture Shock and Mobility	10 & 8	1 & 2
1: Decentring	Positivist	Culture and Area Studies	6 & 6	1 & 2
1: Decentring	Positivist, Postmodern	Cultural Differences Seminar	12 & 12	2 & 4
2: Fluidifying	Interpretivist, Critical	Managing Diversity	10	1
2: Fluidifying	Interpretivist, Postmodern, Critical	Anthropology & Ethnography	6	2
2: Fluidifying	Interpretivist, Postmodern, Critical	Cultures in Organisations	6	2
2: Fluidifying	Interpretivist	Interpersonal Communication	8	2
3: Re-categorising	Postmodern, Critical	Intercultural Communication Theory	12	2
3: Re-categorising	Interpretivist, Postmodern, Critical	Intercultural Management	12	2
3: Re-categorising	Interpretivist, Postmodern, Critical	Thesis Seminar	12 & 12	2 & 4

and culture shock). This is done to ensure that students are aware of these key references and to begin a more critical discussion of them, situating the models in their epistemological tradition and underlining their limits and biases. One two-hour session is dedicated to the Hofstede model, covering the dimensional model itself and criticism of it. In general, the classes use the 'flipped learning' model: students are given reading to do before class, and then this is discussed during class, linked to slides and group exercises. The class also involves debates on underlying questions, which the students prepare and perform in teams: universalism vs particularism applied to culture, and the social vs biological definitions of the concept of race.

Alongside this introductory module, taught over the first six weeks of semester 1, the Culture Shock and Mobility class gives the students a chance to act as trainers for other students interested in interculturality. They are invited to plan and facilitate five online workshops designed to encourage non-specialist students to think about interculturality, in order to help the latter prepare for study mobility in a partner university. The classes are devoted to helping the ICM students plan their workshops, and then to debriefing and troubleshooting. They are thus required to think from a trainer's perspective about how other students approach cultures and how they can moderate sessions on interculturality. The classes in the second semester go further in thinking about how to develop non-essentialist approaches to cultures through training, as well as having the ICM students film and work on their moderation techniques.

The Culture and Area Studies classes were a later addition to the ICM programme, corresponding to a repeated request from the students to learn more about specific 'cultural zones'. Originally, as programme coordinators, we did not wish to include anything so potentially essentialising, especially given the limited amount of class time which could reasonably be devoted to this. The teachers are academic or professional 'specialists' of different geographical zones (Africa, Australasia, China, India, the Middle East, etc.) who are encouraged to present in a non-essentialising way, moving between national-level and other types of important social groupings (e.g. religious, ethnic, professional) which can form the basis of meaningful identifications for individuals in the regions concerned. This 'area studies' approach in the first two semesters is completed with the Cultural Differences Seminar in semesters 2 and 4. The second-year students are invited to present various national cultures to the first years, based on their experiences abroad during the exchange semester, but also their personal experiences of growing up and living in different countries. They are encouraged to present macro-level differences while remaining sensitive to the generalising nature of the exercise, resulting from individual rationalisation and sensemaking, and to underline the limits of such generalisations, apparent contradictions, confusions, and situations in which behaviour observed could not be explained by such projected regularities. Given that the students base their accounts on their own experiences and refer to the multiple identities which may become salient, as well as focusing on the inherent ambiguity they may encounter, I consider that this class alternates between the positivist and the postmodern paradigms, thus opening onto more complex conceptualisations of cultures and identities.

The marked shift away from more simplistic positivist approaches since the 1990s, because of their potentially essentialising nature, raises the question of whether we should (still) be teaching and learning about them today. However, given the continued importance of the positivist approach to interculturality in social and media discourse in general, I could not imagine not including it in the course: I believe that students need to be aware of the models and theories, as well as their limits, and they need to learn how to deal with people who do define interculturality through the prism of imagined national cultural differences. Others might feel that the vicious circle needs to be completely broken, though personally I would find it hard to imagine specialists of interculturality who were not somewhat familiar with these approaches. However, I feel strongly that interculturality should not be about *strengthening* perceptions of difference, any more than it should be about *denying these perceptions*, which are very common and which affect our behaviour towards one another. What is needed is a greater degree of complexity: understanding that the supposed macro-level distinctions are a necessary part of interpersonal communication, alongside other identities, and taking them into account as such.

Fluidifying approaches to cultures and identities

The second phase in learning about interculturality thus aims to shift the perspective from macro-level similarities and differences to the micro-level processes which govern the way we use different cultures in our communication to make sense of ourselves and others. In the ICM course, we do this through various classes which introduce the interpretivist but also the critical and postmodern paradigms. Since diversity, equity, and inclusion (DE&I) is about managing different identities and cultures within an organisation, the class Managing Diversity, taught in the first semester, already addresses intergroup dynamics, power, and privilege, and raises the question of how we take into account our multiple, intersectional identities and cultures in our behaviour towards one another.[6] It is thus a first approach in the programme to these questions, paving the way for more intensive discussions of the underlying processes in the second semester.

The second-semester classes begin with an introduction to anthropology and ethnography, which is then developed through a semester-long research seminar and project in which the students carry out participant observation and ethnographic analysis. Unlike the seminar, the introductory classes figure in Table 2.2 because of the associated reading and discussions centre on deconstructing the concept of culture. Starting from discussions in the field of anthropology, the students are introduced to critical literature on culture, which questions both its use and its usefulness as a concept. They are invited to debate this collectively and to position themselves both for and against the continued use of the term, in the light of discussions of liquid and solid approaches to cultures. This in turn underlines the need to conceptualise communication in terms of multiple identities, multiple levels of common expectations (cultures), and the interpersonal contexts in which we communicate. It introduces discussions of small cultures and cultures as building blocks, repertoires, or toolboxes.

These subjects are then picked up first in the class Cultures in Organisations and then in Interpersonal Communication. The former deals with the multiple identities and cultures which are found in any organisational context, their interplay through interactions, and the 'negotiated cultures' (Brannen & Salk, 2000) which result from sensemaking processes in everyday working situations (Weick, 1995). It explicitly introduces the postmodern paradigm with reference to work by Joanne Martin (1992, 2004), as well as critical approaches to national identifications in the context of joint ventures or international projects, from cross-cultural management literature (Van den Ende & Van Marrewijk, 2015; Ybema & Byun, 2009). The Interpersonal Communication class uses a symbolic interactionist perspective to explain the way that we employ different identities and cultural references in our everyday interactions, and introduces the 'semiopragmatics model of communication' (Frame, 2012) as a way of thinking about interculturality by articulating macro-level and micro-level perspectives.

Re-categorising perceptions in the light of intergroup dynamics

The third phase of learning about interculturality concerns the need to take into account social discourse and people's beliefs about interculturality itself. This involves coming to terms with what Fred Dervin calls the 'simplexity' (see Dervin, 2016; Dervin & Gross, 2016) of the concept: even if culture is complex, people don't tend to see it that way, and use various identity labels in a 'solid', essentialising and thus simple fashion. One of the keys to understanding this and including it in analyses of interculturality is to pay attention to the way cultures are constructed in discourse: 'they are doing things that way, because it is their culture', 'they are not respecting our traditions and values', etc., whoever 'they' and 'we' happen to be in the circumstances. Critical scholars have shown how this process of rationalising behaviour in cultural terms, thereby using 'cultures' as a pretext, as an excuse, can lead us to manipulate identities to try to keep others out, to maintain privilege, to stigmatise, or to assert our rights (Dervin & Machart, 2015b; Holliday, 2015).

In the ICM course, many of these ideas are introduced within the discussions of the interpretivist approach: thinking about the way that cultures are negotiated and multiple identities are taken into account in interactions also tends to spur reflections on which identities are being used in a given context, and how, which in turn leads to considerations of power relations and intergroup dynamics. Many of the aforementioned classes thus also deal with these questions. However, other classes go more deeply into the specifics of power and privilege. Intercultural Communication Theory deals with post-colonial and cultural studies approaches to interculturality, from a textual point of view where power is often mediated through language, but also gives students a chance to explore and discuss the links between interculturality and the algorithms which shape today's digital public sphere. Intercultural Management combines critical approaches to cross-cultural management, in the form of case studies looking at how inequality and discrimination are created and perpetuated in the workplace through language and organisational structures, and discussions of working practices in virtual teams and how to avoid potential problems stemming from inequalities linked to the online medium. Finally, the thesis seminars in both the first and second years (semesters 2 and 4), plus the individual thesis tuition throughout the course, deal with both methodological and theoretical questions, aiming to help students avoid the traps of methodological determinism and apply multiple perspectives to their research questions.

In the case of a programme such as ICM, which caters for specialists, sufficient time is available to develop in-depth understanding of these different perspectives, through a variety of pedagogical activities. These include interactive discussions of readings, theories, and ideas, relating them where possible to students' own experiences, or to videos, role-plays, or games designed to simulate the phenomena in question. What can be interesting is not just the exercises themselves, but the vision of interculturality that they implicitly portray. For example, as well as shorter exercises on stereotyping or group dynamics,

I use both a version of the intercultural training game Barnga and an exercise in 'intercultural negotiation', which I ask the students to review critically once completed, taking into account different perspectives on interculturality. Moreover, repetition is important. As described earlier, the fact that different subjects cover complementary topics and perspectives, that students are able to make links between cases seen in different classes and with different colleagues, helps reinforce their grasp on and confidence in using the various models in new contexts. Having the students carry out ethnographic research themselves over an extended period shapes and sharpens the way they consider social phenomena. Having them keep a journal for self-reflection on the different identities they use, and when and how they use them, helps raise awareness of otherwise implicit social phenomena.

However, as previously mentioned, such courses for specialists are relatively scarce and do not represent the majority of teaching about interculturality. MA programmes in other countries are often less 'tubular' than they are in France, with less compulsory modules. Classes for non-specialists often leave teachers and learners considerably less time in which to develop a complex understanding of the phenomenon. In this domain, a little knowledge can be counterproductive if it leads to reinforcing stereotypes or representations of difference. In a short time frame, it is challenging to complete the three phases of learning about interculturality, and even if this is possible, the lack of time may limit the effectiveness of such teaching. Indeed, it is important for students to be able to think about, discuss extensively, and apply the different paradigms to different examples in order to truly assimilate them and be able to themselves employ or propose multiple perspectives in a given situation (Kokkonen et al., 2022).

Conclusion

The current period is a particularly critical one for teaching and learning about interculturality. Societal debates (or the lack thereof) about immigration, cultural appropriation, wokism, cancel culture, diversity, equity and inclusion, or the side effects of the digital revolution on the way cultural knowledge and references circulate online are all hot topics for interculturalists. Although the field has been encountering what some scholars have described as 'theoretical turbulence' (Poutiainen, 2014), this has largely not filtered beyond the closed doors of academia: in the media but also among many professional trainers, positivist approaches to interculturality remain dominant, with a quasi-exclusive focus on national cultures and cultural differences, and often little concern for how the term 'culture' is used as a concept.

Although this context makes it harder to think outside the box and to apply complex approaches to better understand the phenomenon commonly described as interculturality, this is exactly the challenge for the next generation of thinkers and citizens of the world. They need to be able to contextualise and question overly-simplistic implicit models; to be aware of multiple identities, of negotiated cultures, and of the way these structure our communication in particular contexts; and also of power issues and the way cultural identities can be instrumentalised through discourse. They should develop the capacity to bring new perspectives to societal debates centred on culture or identity-related phenomena, contributing to these debates with a balanced and critical view.

The three phases of learning about interculturality outlined here can help learners achieve a sufficient degree of competency in applying various perspectives to analyse phenomena described as 'intercultural' in an appropriate and complex way. The discussion of the MA programme in intercultural management at the University of Burgundy illustrates how we have sought to implement these three phases through the programme design.[7] Despite the fact that the three phases aim to develop the complexity of learners' understanding of interculturality, it is important that teaching about the topic does not become excessively theoretical and abstract. As far as possible, teachers should seek to combine the conceptual and the practical, bringing in practice-based teaching postures and experiential learning, as a complement to readings and abstract discussions.[8] However, it is important not to propose exoticising activities with no conceptual depth, designed simply to highlight the difference. This can be a particular risk in shorter courses for non-specialists, notably with an international group of participants. Activities should be designed to encourage learners to engage with the ideas being discussed, and the limits of the activities themselves can also be a topic of conversation. Ideally, discussions should allow learners to make links with ongoing societal debates or current affairs, applying different perspectives to these. Many media texts relating to questions of immigration, politics, foreign travel, etc. make cultural or identity-based distinctions, and it can be interesting to question the vision of interculturality which shapes them.

In terms of its necessary societal impact, the field of interculturality still faces several major challenges to overcome in the next few years. Through the courses we teach, we should try to dispel the widespread (mis)conception that reduces interculturality to national cultures and to difference. It should not be about glamorising folklore and traditions, reinforcing the idea that we all belong in our own boxes. Interculturalising the field itself will involve overcoming the Western-centric stance, as well as the sole focus on national differences, while avoiding the risk of conceptual relativism and essentialising exoticism. Algorithmic isolation and the fragmentation of the online public sphere are remapping social structures along affinity-based lines, leading to new and unanticipated representational divides in society, which can usefully be analysed in terms of identities and cultural references. Finally, critical approaches and complexity require considerably more cognitive engagement than stereotypes and generalisations. This makes it all the more important that we find appropriate methods and learning activities to ensure that the (critical) courses we teach about interculturality have a significant impact on learners, so that they themselves then become the multipliers of these ideas and help redefine the way we talk about these important questions in society as a whole.

Notes

1 Interestingly, this research from the 1980s already touched on many of the questions which have recently been foregrounded through neuroscience approaches to interculturality, although the latter do not currently refer to the earlier French-language scholarship.
2 In reality, several forms of cultural differentiation are involved in this process: exposure to a limited set of representations, but also pressures linked to in-group and out-group differentiation.
3 Even when identified as a French scholar, I have received negative reviews for a proposed text in English, claiming that my work on political communication in France uses predominantly French references whose 'quality cannot be verified' (presumably meaning that the reviewer does not have this competence). The reviewer also stated that 'a simple Google Scholar search of the keywords shows multiple references in English which are not acknowledged in the text', and proceeded to list a few examples of these important English-language references, including one of my own books!
4 Jonas Stier (2010) reminds us of the dangers of exoticising 'heterocentrism' (the obsession with difference) and 'xenocentrism' (the obsession with the Other) in the field of intercultural communication.
5 https://blog.u-bourgogne.fr/mastericm/about-us/. Page accessed on 29 July 2022.
6 The topic is clearly increasing in importance in organisations in general, spreading from North America to other parts of the world. I believe that this reflects the growing importance of identities and identification in society in general, which has been underlined by sociologists for many years (Bauman, 2011; Featherstone, 1995; Weber, 1905). But it is also a less essentialist way of framing interculturality, which recognises the discursive, identity-based nature of perceived difference, and relates this to questions of management. As such, I see it as a key area of development for interculturalists.
7 Since different learners react differently to the teaching materials and activities proposed, and given the fact that the programme involves multiple teaching staff, who may all have slightly different conceptions of and ways of teaching about the different perspectives, the programme design may differ somewhat from its execution and from what different learners actually take away from it. Since these elements were beyond the scope of this chapter, and would naturally require further investigation, no claims are being made about the programme's actual impact.
8 A recent book by Robert Gibson (2021), an intercultural trainer and consultant, offers many useful exercises and case studies applied to business and management, which are compatible with a complex view of interculturality, going beyond the positivist paradigm.

References

Altheide, D. L. (2013). Media logic, social control, and fear. *Communication Theory*, 23(3), 223–238. https://doi.org/10.1111/comt.12017.

Barmeyer, C., & Franklin, P. (2016). *Intercultural Management: A Case-Based Approach to Achieving Complementarity and Synergy*. London: Palgrave.

Bauman, Z. (2011). *Culture in a Liquid Modern World*. Cambridge: Polity Press.

Blumer, H. (1969). *Symbolic Interactionism: Perspective and Method*. Berkeley, CA: University of California Press.

Brachotte, G., Frame, A., Gautier, L., Nazarov, W., & Selmi, A. (forthcoming). Les discours complotistes sur Twitter à propos de la vaccination contre la COVID-19 en France: Communautés et analyse sémio-linguistique des #. *Mots*.

Brannen, M. Y., & Salk, J. E. (2000). Partnering across borders: Negotiating organizational culture in a German-Japanese joint venture. *Human Relations, 53*(4), 451–487. https://doi.org/10.1177/0018726700534001.

Burke, P. J., Owens, T. J., Serpe, R. T., & Thoits, P. A. (Eds.). (2003). *Advances in Identity Theory and Research*. Dordrecht: Kluwer Academic/Plenum Publishers.

Burke, P. J., & Stets, J. E. (2009). *Identity Theory*. Oxford: Oxford University Press.

Dacheux, E. (1999). La communication: Point aveugle de l'interculturel? *Bulletin de l'ARIC, 31*, 1–2.

Demorgon, J. (1989). *L'exploration interculturelle: Pour une pédagogie internationale*. Paris: Armand Colin.

Dervin, F. (2016). *Interculturality in Education*. London: Palgrave Macmillan.

Dervin, F., & Gross, Z. (2016). Towards the simultaneity of intercultural competence. In F. Dervin & Z. Gross (Eds.), *Intercultural Competence in Education: Alternative Approaches for Different Times* (pp. 1–10). London: Palgrave Macmillan.

Dervin, F., & Jacobsson, A. (2022). *Intercultural Communication Education: Broken Realities and Rebellious Dreams*. London: Springer.

Dervin, F., & Machart, R. (Eds.). (2015a). *Cultural Essentialism in Intercultural Relations*. London: Palgrave Macmillan.

Dervin, F., & Machart, R. (2015b). Introduction: Omniscient culture, omnipotent cultures. In F. Dervin & R. Machart (Eds.), *Cultural Essentialism in Intercultural Relations* (pp. 1–11). London: Palgrave Macmillan.

Dervin, F., & Yuan, M. (2021). *Revitalizing Interculturality: Chinese Minzu as a Companion*. London: Routledge.

Featherstone, M. (1995). *Undoing Culture: Globalisation, Postmodernism and Identity*. London: Sage.

Frame, A. (2012). Cultures, identities and meanings in intercultural encounters: A semiopragmatics approach to cross-cultural team-building. In V. Carayol & A. Frame (Eds.), *Communication and PR from a Cross-Cultural Standpoint: Practical and Methodological Issues* (pp. 31–42). Bern: Peter Lang.

Frame, A. (2014). On cultures and interactions: Theorizing the complexity of intercultural encounters. In S. Poutiainen (Ed.), *Theoretical Turbulence in Intercultural Communication Studies* (pp. 29–44). Newcastle: Cambridge Scholars Publishing.

Frame, A. (2015). Étranges interactions: Cadrer la communication interculturelle à l'aide de Goffman? In P. Lardellier (Ed.), *Actualité d'Erving Goffman, de l'interaction à l'institution* (pp. 79–96). Paris: L'Harmattan.

Frame, A., & Boutaud, J.-J. (2010). Performing identities and constructing meaning in interpersonal encounters: A semiopragmatics approach to communication. *Mémoires de la société néophiliologique de Helsinki LXXXI*, 85–96.

Gibson, R. (2021). *Bridge the Culture Gaps: A Toolkit for Effective Collaboration in the Diverse, Global Workplace*. Boston, MA: Nicholas Brealey Publishing.

Gilroy, P. (1993). *The Black Atlantic: Modernity and Double Consciousness*. Boston, MA: Harvard University Press/Verso.

Hepp, A. (2015). *Transcultural Communication*. London: Wiley.

Holliday, A. (2000). Culture as constraint or resource: Essentialist versus non-essentialist views. *Iatefl Language and Cultural Studies SIG Newsletter, 18*, 38–40.

Holliday, A. (2015). Afterword. In F. Dervin & R. Machart (Eds.), *Cultural Essentialism in Intercultural Relations* (pp. 198–202). London: Palgrave Macmillan.

Holliday, A., Kullman, J., & Hyde, M. (2016). *Intercultural Communication: An Advanced Resource Book for Students*. London: Routledge.

Kaluža, J. (2021). Habitual generation of filter bubbles: Why is algorithmic personalisation problematic for the democratic public sphere? *Javnost - The Public*, 1–17. https://doi.org/10.1080/13183222.2021.2003052.

Keyes, R. (2004). *The Post-Truth Era: Dishonesty and Deception in Contemporary Life*. London: Macmillan.

Kokkonen, L., Jager, R., Frame, A., & Raappana, M. (2022). Overcoming essentialism? Students' reflections on learning intercultural communication online. *Education Sciences*, *12*(9), 579. https://doi.org/10.3390/educsci12090579.

Ladmiral, J.-R., & Lipiansky, E.-M. (1989). *La communication interculturelle*. Paris: Armand Colin.

Lewandowsky, S., Ecker, U. K., & Cook, J. (2017). Beyond misinformation: Understanding and coping with the "post-truth" era. *Journal of Applied Research in Memory and Cognition*, *6*(4), 353–369.

Lipiansky, E.-M. (1992). *Identité et communication*. Paris: PUF.

Martin, J. (1992). *Cultures in Organizations: Three Perspectives*. Oxford: Oxford University Press.

Martin, J. (2004). *Organizational Culture* (Research Paper Series no. 1847). Stanford, CA: Stanford Graduate School of Business.

Mathews, G. (2000). *Global Culture/Individual Identity: Searching for Home in the Cultural Supermarket*. London: Routledge.

Nakayama, T. K., & Halualani, R. T. (Eds.). (2010). *The Handbook of Critical Intercultural Communication*. London: Wiley-Blackwell.

Poutiainen, S. (Ed.). (2014). *Theoretical Turbulence in Intercultural Communication Studies*. Newcastle: Cambridge Scholars Publishing.

Primecz, H., Mahadevan, J., & Romani, L. (2016). Why is cross-cultural management scholarship blind to power relations? Investigating ethnicity, language, gender and religion in power-laden contexts. *International Journal of Cross Cultural Management*, *16*(2), 127–136. https://doi.org/10.1177/1470595816666154.

Romani, L., Barmeyer, C., Primecz, H., & Pilhofer, K. (2018). Cross-cultural management studies: State of the field in the four research paradigms. *International Studies of Management & Organization*, 1–17. https://doi.org/10.1080/00208825.2018.1480918.

Romani, L., & Frame, A. (2020). Les études critiques en gestion interculturelle. *Communication & Organisation*, *58*(2), 25–40. Cairn.info. https://doi.org/10.4000/communicationorganisation.9201.

Spencer-Oatey, H., & Franklin, P. (2009). *Intercultural Interaction: A Multidisciplinary Approach to Intercultural Communication*. London: Palgrave Macmillan.

Stier, J. (2010). The blindspots and biases of intercultural communication studies: A discussion on episteme and doxa in a field. *Journal of Intercultural Communication*, *24*(3). http://www.immi.se/intercultural/nr24/stier-24.htm.

Stryker, S. (1980). *Symbolic Interactionism: Social Structural Version*. Amsterdam: Benjamin/Cummings Pub. Co.

Stryker, S., & Burke, P. (2000). The past, present, and future of an identity theory. *Social Psychology Quarterly*, *63*(4), 284–297.

Swidler, A. (1986). Culture in action: Symbols and strategies. *American Sociological Review*, *51*(2), 273–286. https://doi.org/10.2307/2095521.

Van den Ende L., & Van Marrewijk, A. (2015). The social construction of cultural differences in a Siberian joint-venture megaproject. *Journal of Strategic Contracting and Negotiation*, *1*(2), 168–185. https://doi.org/10.1177/2055563615598164.

Weber, M. (1905). *The Protestant Ethic and the Spirit of Capitalism*. London: George Allen & Unwin.
Weick, K. E. (1995). *Sensemaking in Organizations*. London: Sage.
Ybema, S., & Byun, H. (2009). Cultivating cultural differences in asymmetric power relations. *International Journal of Cross-Cultural Management*, 9(3), 339–358. https://doi.org/10.1177/1470595809346600.

3 Unity in diversity

Exploring intercultural teaching and learning practices in secondary education and teacher training in Austria

Jasmin Peskoller

Introduction

Processes of globalisation and international migration "have resulted in an opening up of new spaces and resources for identity construction and negotiation" (Baker, 2015: 239). Hence, contemporary societies are characterised by a growing scope of linguistic and cultural diversity and life designs have become highly heterogeneous and fluid. Describing society as a "network of perspectives" (Risager, 2012: 106), Risager (2018: 25) also argues that "culture, society and the world, and also the classroom itself, are seen as a multitude of individual and group perspectives and identities". As they constitute direct mirrors of society (BMB, 2017), classrooms at a global day and age demonstrate an increasingly multilingual and multicultural student population. This development can, for instance, be observed in the educational context of Austria, a country located in central Europe. Over the past ten years, the share of learners with another L1 than German, the official language of instruction for the major part of Austria, has increased by 60%, so that the proportion of students using a different language than German at home amounted to 29.3% in lower secondary education in the school year of 2020/2021 (Statistik Austria, 2021a). Reporting on linguistic diversity, these numbers can be indicative of the presumed cultural diversity present inside Austrian classrooms today. But how can culture and interculturality be conceptualised? How can intercultural teaching and learning be implemented in education?

My empirical study on Indigenous perspectives in Australian education (Peskoller, 2021) and my research on the implementation of intercultural learning in Austrian EFL (English as a foreign language) classrooms (e.g. Peskoller, 2022) have shaped my understanding of culture and interculturality. Moreover, my approach towards these two concepts was influenced by my experience as an EFL/mathematics teacher and teacher trainer as well as by two years of educational work with refugee students from over ten different countries. This contribution thus starts with a delineation of my understanding of culture and interculturality. I then proceed to conceptualise the classroom as a meaningful meeting place and fruitful starting point for intercultural learning before discussing selected policy documents informing the Austrian educational context. Adopting a practical lens, I present my ideas and experience in connection with teaching (about) interculturality

DOI: 10.4324/9781003345275-4

looking both at secondary education and (language) teacher training and discuss related objectives, approaches, and challenges. I conclude by summarising core concerns and outlining directions for future discussions.

Culture and interculturality

Fundamentally, scholars such as Volkmann (2010) have highlighted a persistent lack of clarity in connection with the concept of culture, while Brunsmeier (2016) pronounced the field of interculturality in education a *conceptual jungle*. In light of these impediments, I regard it essential for anyone working in the field of interculturality to outline their underlying understanding and conceptualisation of the used constructs. Hence, this chapter aims at meeting this requirement.

A university lecturer on Indigenous Australian perspectives used the term "ways of knowing, being, and doing" (Power et al., 2015: 441) to refer to the complex construct of culture. Consistent with common conceptualisations and proposed models for intercultural competence, this expression reflects the concept's tripartite nature consisting of cognitive, affective, and action-oriented dimensions. Based on this foundation, I understand culture as a highly individual, dynamic, and transnational construct, and support a late modernist and Cultural Studies, hence non-essentialist, view in my work as a teacher, language teacher educator, and researcher. Specifically, I believe that culture encompasses aspects such as "individual emotions, memories, habits of thought and behaviours" (Kramsch, 2009: 235) rendering every person "unique in his or her experience-based, socially influenced perspective" (Risager, 2012: 106). Considering Risager's (2018; 2012) work on *linguaculture*, culture has transcended national borders and has become a dynamic, hybrid, and intersecting construct (Blell & Doff, 2014; Kramsch, 2009). At a global day and age, nationality has become one among numerous other dimensions such as class, gender, language, religion, or sexuality that can play a part in identity construction (Svarstad, 2021; Baker, 2015). This approach has rendered the former notion of one country equating one culture obsolete and problematised the essentialist view of culture as a means to explain people's practices, products, or values (Risager, 2018). Contrary to fixed affiliations, culture "is constructed and shaped minute by minute by speakers and hearers in their daily verbal and non-verbal transactions" (Kramsch, 2009: 234) through "processes of identification of self and Other" (Risager, 2018: 130). Therefore, Ferri (2018: 27) comprehensibly identifies individuals as "dialogic entities constantly evolving through interaction". This reality again emphasises the dynamic nature of culture as being shaped, contested, and redefined through encounters (Risager, 2018). In this regard, Byram (1997: 40) highlights that it is not language or culture systems but individuals that meet, negotiate meaning, and "bring to the situation their own identities and cultures" (Byram, 2021: 51). Hence, Liddicoat and Scarino (2013: 21) summarise:

> Cultures are therefore dynamic and emergent – they are created through the actions of individuals and in particular through the ways in which they use

language. This means that meanings are not simply shared, coherent constructions about experience but rather can be fragmented, contradictory, and contested within the practices of a social group because they are constituted in moments of interaction. Culture in such a view is not a coherent whole but a situated process of dealing with the problems of social life. Cultures thus are open to elements that are diverse and contradictory, and different interpretations may be made of the same events by individuals who may be considered to be from the same culture.

Based on such an open, dynamic, and highly individualised understanding of culture, I subsequently regard interculturality as the multitude of dimensions in which human beings can show commonalities and differences and which (can) play a role for (successful) interaction and collaboration. Among others, these may include individuals' experiences and stories, opinions and viewpoints, life designs, values, or approaches. Specifically, I support Svarstad (2021) in regarding interculturality an "active engagement with diversity" (41) as well as a non-essentialist umbrella concept encompassing discourses on identity, subjectivity, inclusion, and various forms of intercultural encounters in different domains (Risager & Svarstad, 2020; Lütge, 2019). Similarly, Dervin and Jacobsson (2021: 16) understand interculturality as a critical framework "to analyse how discourses of culture are activated by different people in different contexts and for different purposes".

Fundamentally, interlocutors will never exhibit commonalities *only* but will share more or less similarities with their counterparts in an interaction. Hence, the latter can be understood to take place on a continuum ranging from many to few (perceived) commonalities between individuals, with most of them remaining undetected during conversations or playing an insignificant role for the successful outcome. Thus, in essence, every encounter constitutes an intercultural encounter.

In the German-speaking research context, some scholars have adopted the concept of *transculturality* to counter an all too rigid understanding of culture, which the intercultural discourse was frequently accused of. Despite the received criticism of the prefix, I use the terms *inter*cultural and *inter*culturality in my elaborations, as encounters always take place *between* individuals. Concurrently, my work and understanding is based on an open, postmodernist view of culture and identity as outlined in this chapter.

Finally, I discuss the idea of *interculturalising interculturality* as proposed by Dervin and Jacobsson (2022) and supported by the editors of this volume, and derive implications for teaching and research practice. To me, the term signifies a *practise what you preach* for anyone involved in the field of interculturality. Interculturalising interculturality means entering a dialogue to reflect, rethink, and revise our conceptualisations and understandings of interculturality. The integration of different perspectives and voices does justice to the dynamic nature of the field and can promote progress. Overall, critically rethinking, reshaping, redefining, reassessing, and reviewing multiperspectivity constitutes an intercultural process that should present a standard course of action in any academic discipline or educational context. In the upcoming chapter, I proceed to discuss the intercultural nature of classrooms and any (learning) group.

Classrooms as intercultural meeting places

Looking more closely at educational realities, Australian educator Lo Bianco (2009: 113) manifests that the "strongest indicator of the transformed realities of contemporary education in a globalised world is the depth of cultural, racial and linguistic diversity in schools". Relating to this development, I also want to share one of Gorski's (2016: 222) statements: "All students are culturally and linguistically diverse relative to one another: No student is culturally and linguistically diverse on her or his own without being compared to somebody else." Thus, Grünewald et al. (2011) designate classrooms as ideal places to explore different voices and stories, relativise personal viewpoints and experiences, and build empathy. With Rogge (2014) speaking of an elusive complexity of potential encounters and conversations among learners, the (language) classroom becomes a *hybrid space* (Hallet, 2002) in which students are intercultural agents as they negotiate meanings, values, and perspectives (Freitag-Hild, 2018).

Based on my view of interculturality, I thus regard classrooms as intercultural meeting places that provide meaningful starting points to be harnessed for intercultural learning. This notion also becomes apparent in fundamental educational policy documents relevant for the Austrian context, which I investigate in the next section.

The intercultural educational context of Austria

Located in the centre of Europe with a population of 8.8 million (Statistik Austria, 2021b), "Austria has a long tradition as a country of immigration and emigration" (Hintermann et al., 2014: 80). Since 2010, people from almost all countries of the world have been living in Austria, Germany, and Switzerland, which has led to a strong increase of linguistic, cultural, and social heterogeneity (Gogolin, 2016: 61). In 2021, 25.4% of Austria's inhabitants indicated to have a background of migration predominantly associated with former Yugoslavian countries or Turkey. The respective value amounted to 18.8% in 2011 implying a growth of nearly 7 percentage points in 10 years (Statistik Austria, 2021a, 2021b).

Looking into Austrian schools, one can observe an increasing share of learners with other first languages than German. Juxtaposing data from the school years of 2009/10 and 2019/20, the overall proportion of students predominantly using a different language than the language of instruction increased by almost 10 percentage points from 17.8% to 27.0% (Statistik Austria, 2021c: 45). Specifically, in the school year of 2020/21, 29.3% of learners in lower secondary education indicated to have a different first language than German (Statistik Austria, 2021a). Specific data on the language varieties predominantly used by learners in Austria is only available for elementary levels: the most frequent first languages among four- to five-year-olds in Austria in 2021 were Turkish, Bosnian/Croatian/

Serbian, Rumanian, and Arabic (Statistik Austria, 2021b: 47). Aside from German as the official language, six recognised autochthonous minorities hold special rights to secure language and culture preservation in determined regions of Austria. For instance, there are bilingual primary schools and secondary schools that use Hungarian, Slovenian, or Croatian as additional languages of instruction (Bundeskanzleramt, 2022).

The national school curriculum for secondary education as well as the fundamental decree on intercultural education constitute two policy documents that inform contemporary education in Austria and directly address intercultural matters. Particularly, intercultural learning has featured as the second of ten fundamental, interdisciplinary teaching principles in the Austrian curriculum for secondary education since 1992. According to the document, the construct encompasses comprehending, experiencing, and actively co-creating cultural values through learning together. Thereby, fostering in-class cohesion, inviting an open and respectful discussion on different viewpoints, and investigating cultural backgrounds in an equality-driven approach are central (BMBWF, 2022: 12–13). In addition, the third teaching principle in the curriculum, multilingualism, also shows references to intercultural matters. Specifically, this section emphasises the importance of language(s) in a world characterised by increasing linguistic and cultural diversity. Furthermore, it identifies linguistic sensitivity and intercultural understanding as the basis of a democratic society. Lastly, the fourth interdisciplinary teaching principle, diversity and inclusion, also outlines the relevance of a constructive handling of the increasing plurality among learners through fostering individual skills and potentials independent from affiliations. The necessity to create non-discriminatory spaces for learning and development for children from 'different backgrounds' is also emphasised (BMBWF, 2022: 13–14). Moreover, the syllabus highlights the special role of foreign language education (FLE) in connection with intercultural learning as these subjects contribute to the familiarisation with and deliberate perception of foreign or unknown dimensions. As stated in the policy document, students can develop a deeper understanding of the diversity of life designs as well as an increased sensitivity for cultural commonalities and differences through addressing intercultural topics, discussing related questions, and reflecting on their personal experiences (BMBWF, 2022: 55–56).

In order to increase the implementation of intercultural learning in classroom practice and to enhance educators' conceptual understanding, the Austrian ministry of education released a fundamental decree on intercultural education in 2017 (BMB, 2017). The document delineates cultural diversity inside classrooms as an enrichment for learning and is based on an open understanding of culture as well as a dynamic concept of identity. Connecting to learners' diverse biographies, lives, and experiences, intercultural education contributes to a learning atmosphere grounded in appreciation and respect. From a practical perspective, the decree commends educators to encourage their students to question stereotypes, prejudice, and ethnocentrism as well as identify and react to excluding, racist, or sexist statements and actions. Through activities such as reflection, critical analysis, and perspective changing, learners' empathy, openness, respect, and tolerance for ambiguity can be fostered (BMB, 2017).

In spite of this foundation, the large-scale Teaching and Learning International Study (TALIS) indicated only 13.6% of teachers in Austrian lower secondary education felt (well-)prepared to work in a multicultural classroom setting in 2018. In addition, approximately 49% of the surveyed educators identified the adjustment of their methodological approaches to the needs of the culturally diverse student population as a daily challenge (Schmich & Itzlinger-Bruneforth, 2019).

Based on these insights into the Austrian educational context, I discuss intercultural education in connection with objectives, approaches, and challenges I believe to be central to the discourse henceforth.

Implementing intercultural education in teaching practice

With linguistic and cultural diversity constituting characteristics of societies and classrooms in a global day and age, the "multicultural world has made intercultural teaching necessary" (Sobkowiak, 2016: 697). In my elaborations, I make use of the term *intercultural education* to refer to processes of intercultural teaching and learning. I favour these expressions over *teaching (about) interculturality* as the latter suggests a rather external, observing position regarding interculturality exclusively as a topic or content matter. On the contrary, it is vital to integrate the methodological dimension of intercultural education and regard teachers and learners as contributors to the interculturality of the classroom setting. Also, teaching and learning should not be discussed in isolation, as these processes are inherently connected.

Hence, this chapter sheds light on objectives, approaches, and challenges in connection with the implementation of intercultural education focusing on secondary education and (language) teacher training in Austria.

Objectives of intercultural education

Broadly speaking, intercultural education should contribute to countering discrimination, exclusion, and racism (Fäcke, 2019; BMB, 2017) by regarding diversity as an enrichment that can provide new possibilities (Bär, 2017). In particular, a core objective of intercultural teaching and learning lies in the development of learners' awareness of "different sociocultural perspectives and identities and their implications for intercultural communication and understanding, empathy and collaboration" (Risager, 2018: 25). In this regard, the construct of intercultural competence emerged, which Liddicoat and Scarino (2013: 24) define as "being aware that cultures are relative […] that there is no one 'normal' way of doing things, but that all behaviors are culturally variable". Conceptualised in a transnational and global frame, intercultural competence thus assists learners to "navigate in a world characterised by cultural flows mainly caused by transnational migrations, and representations of the moving world" (Risager, 2009: 29). Hence, the construct is closely connected with the global and intercultural citizenship discourse aiming to prepare learners for participation in a multilingual and multicultural society (Hammer, 2012; Byram, 2008).

In this regard, I want to refer to two frameworks that provide a useful overview of core aims and concerns in the discourse of interculturality. To start, the OECD (2018) published a model for the multidimensional construct of *global competence* strongly connected with the sustainable development goals (United Nations, 2019). The model entails dimensions such as the analysis of local, global, and intercultural challenges, understanding and appreciating various viewpoints and worldviews, participating in open, adequate, and effective interactions, and includes attitudes such as openness, respect for people with different backgrounds, appreciation of diversity, and a willingness to act (OECD, 2018: 9–18). Similarly, connecting the discourses of global and intercultural citizenship education, the *Reference Framework for Competences for Democratic Culture* (Council of Europe, 2018) constitutes another interdisciplinary model that I regard both relevant and useful. The framework demonstrates cognitive, action-oriented, and two affective dimensions of values and attitudes, and outlines the "competences that need to be acquired by learners if they are to participate effectively in a culture of democracy and live peacefully together with others in culturally diverse democratic societies" (Council of Europe, 2018: 11). Among others, these include open-mindedness, awareness of diversity, respect for otherness, reflectivity, empathy, critical approach as well as a willingness to act (Council of Europe, 2018: 38).

While Fäcke (2019) argues that all facets of interculturality shape FLE, I now proceed to investigate selected intercultural aims in foreign language education. Sercu (2000: 389) highlights that FLE should promote "learners' acquisition of the attitudes and skills required for interacting with people from differing cultural and linguistic backgrounds". While Byram (2021: 29) proposes that FLE "should have an impact on how learners see their own culture, that they should be able to critique it and view it differently". In this context, intercultural communicative competence is still regarded a key dimension in FLE (Schumann, 2019a) and learners should be supported in becoming critical intercultural speakers (Martinez, 2019; Byram, 1997). Through an awareness of the existence of the "multiple, ambivalent, resourceful, and elastic nature of cultural identities in an intercultural encounter" (Guilherme, 2002: 125), critical intercultural speakers problematise identities and concepts connected with essentialism, nationalism or ethnicity and are aware that "the development of identities involves a constant negotiation" (Risager, 2018: 133).

As expressed by the two preceding models, in educational policy documents, as well as in the work of various authors in the field, fostering learners' open-mindedness, empathy, and respect for diversity as well as strengthening their reflective capabilities and willingness to act constitute central objectives in intercultural education integrating cognitive, affective, and action-oriented dimensions. While these constructs are polysemous and require precise definitions, what remains undeniable is the need for educators to continuously strive to develop and strengthen these competences themselves in order to promote the respective dimensions in their learners. Moreover, teachers ought to be self-critical and reflective towards their own views and approaches and need to be familiarised with strategies to harness the existing diversity in their classrooms as a vital resource and starting point for intercultural learning.

Having outlined key objectives in connection with intercultural education, a main question for pre- and in-service teachers concerns the implementation of the concept in teaching practice, which I address in the upcoming section.

Approaches to intercultural education

As indicated before, I believe interculturality needs to be viewed both from a methodological perspective and a potential teaching and learning content. After discussing these two dimensions and presenting a criteria catalogue for intercultural education (Peskoller, 2022) that can assist teachers with its educational implementation, the section concludes with two practical examples from my material fund.

From a methodological viewpoint, intercultural education follows the principles of multiperspectivity, dialogue, and reflection (Freitag-Hild, 2018: 168) while integrating the dimensions of subjectivity, process orientation, and interaction (Schumann, 2009: 214–215). I believe that intercultural education fundamentally emanates from the existing diversity inside classrooms and support Kramsch's proposal to thematise and openly discuss learners' "culturally diverse representations, interpretations, expectations, memories, and identifications" in class (2009: 236). Moreover, scholars have identified awareness-building, perception training, analysing and comparing, interpreting, and role-play as core methodological building blocks of an intercultural pedagogy (Schumann, 2019a, 2009; Freitag-Hild, 2018; Blell & Doff, 2014). Specifically, the added value of working with different types of literature such as post-colonial writings and works of fiction has frequently been emphasised (e.g. Matos & Melo-Pfeifer, 2020; Lütge, 2018) and was designated an intensively researched dimension in intercultural pedagogy (Dalton-Puffer et al., 2019). Developing Liddicoat and Scarino's (2013: 60) interacting processes of intercultural learning with its four stages of noticing, comparing, reflecting, and interacting further, Risager and Svarstad's (2020: 49) cycle model includes specifications for the individual dimensions and proposals for their implementation, "knowledge and critical cultural awareness" (Risager & Svarstad, 2020: 49) at the centre of their model. Connecting to Byram's (1997, 2021) model of intercultural communicative competence, the authors position.

Based on a literature review combining theoretical-conceptual work, previous empirical research, and relevant educational policy documents for the Austrian context, a criteria catalogue for intercultural learning (Peskoller, 2022) emerged using Freitag-Hild's (2018) seven-dimensional typology for intercultural tasks in language education as a framework. While the catalogue itself needs to be critically reflected and reviewed, it can provide stimuli and

Table 3.1 Criteria catalogue for intercultural learning activities

Warming up
Is learners' previous knowledge included?
Are learners' cultural experiences included?

Self-reflection
Are learners encouraged to analyse their personality or personal life stories?
Are learners encouraged to express and share their opinions, perspectives, or personal experiences?
Are learners encouraged to reflect on their opinions, perspectives, or personal experiences?

Interpretation and change of perspective
Are learners encouraged to empathise with other points of view and relativise their own cultural viewpoints?
Are learners encouraged to change, discuss, or coordinate different perspectives?
Are learners encouraged to relate new aspects or topics to familiar ones?
Are learners encouraged to interpret visual and verbal cultural representations?

Analysis and reflection
Are learners encouraged to explore cultural dimensions or collect culture-related information?
Are learners encouraged to compare cultural dimensions by stating commonalities and differences?
Are learners encouraged to reflect on differences?
Are learners encouraged to analyse or reflect on racism, prejudice, or stereotypes?
Are learners encouraged to analyse or reflect on critical incidents or identify causes for misunderstandings in interaction?

Negotiation and participation
Are learners encouraged to hold a discussion?
Are learners encouraged to do a roleplay?
Are encounters with another culture addressed?

Contextualisation
Is a personal relation established by connecting to learners' interests or *Lebenswelt*?
Are learners encouraged to recognise or explore the diversity of backgrounds, perspectives, or experiences in the classroom?
Are learners encouraged to identify ethnocentric perspectives in their own or other contexts?

(Meta-)Reflection
Are learners encouraged to reflect on their intercultural learning process?

Source: Peskoller, 2022.

guidance for educators to assist in implementing different dimensions of intercultural education (see Table 3.1). The criteria can not all be easily realised in a single activity, but they can be combined in various ways to ensure that different dimensions are regularly integrated in classrooms discourse. Though the items emerged from a comprehensive literature review, integrate various perspectives, and were revised multiple times on the basis of research talks, culture and interculturality are more complex than can ever be mapped by checklists. Thus, the categories naturally still reflect my subjective understanding of the constructs (Cortazzi & Jin, 1999).

Aside from the methodological dimension, interculturality also needs to be made explicit in education. For teaching about intercultural content matters, authors (e.g. Schumann, 2009) have listed aspects such as rituals, symbols, self-images, perceptions of others, migration, transcultural identities, culture contact, and culture conflict. Others have suggested working with and reflecting on (virtual) encounters and critical incidents (Heringer, 2019; Müller-Hartmann & Schocker-von Ditfurth, 2015). Furthermore, Svarstad (2021: 50) proposes dealing with current topics and political debates such as the #MeToo or the Black Lives Matter movement, climate change, Indigenous peoples, terrorism, or gay pride.

Furthermore, contemplating questions of intersectionality and multiperspectivity (Dervin, 2016: 83), the topics of equality, diversity, discrimination, justice, stereotypes, prejudice, and racism need to feature as the contents of education. While all these topics and ideas are valuable and can be harnessed for intercultural education, I want to note the inherent danger of essentialising, which I will turn to in an upcoming section.

For implementing intercultural education, different types of media such as texts, images, or videos can be didacticised (see Table 3.1) and used as facilitators. In this regard, three print resources have particularly fascinated me in my practice both at school and university. Firstly, the (German) reflection cards on diversity, anti-discrimination, and anti-racism by Mengis and Drücker (2019) provide stimuli for discussions and reflections on the basis of factual statements and the description of thought-provoking situations. Secondly, the collection of self-reflection activities provided in *Allyship in Action* (Sauseng et al., 2020) include inspiring ideas to promote a critical analysis, reflection, and discussion in class. Finally, the resource *Let's Talk* (Teaching Tolerance, 2019) contains detailed and staged instructions to facilitate critical conversations among learners and create the necessary foundations for an adequate and respectful learning environment.

To conclude this section, I provide two practical examples from my own material collection to demonstrate how I endeavour to implement intercultural teaching and learning both at methodological and content level. I illustrate my approach by explicitly working with stereotypes in the EFL classroom using slightly adapted extracts from a city guide to Innsbruck, Austria (InfoEck, 2018), in the first example and a video clip (Tanaka, 2013) in the second. In Figure 3.1 and Figure 3.2, I outline how these and other resources can be harnessed as starting points for intercultural learning processes encouraging fruitful discussions, analyses, and reflections.

While the material can naturally be used in a variety of ways, the designed activities strive to integrate different dimensions of intercultural learning as demonstrated in Table 3.1. More precisely, learners are encouraged to critically analyse and interpret the document "Act like a local" (InfoEck, 2018) by exploring their own and others' practices, reflecting on their experiences, changing perspectives, and relativising their personal viewpoints. After the activity, I often invite learners to share their findings and ideas in plenum and initiate an open discussion

City guide to Innsbruck: "Act like a local"
Read the extracts from a city guide to Innsbruck and discuss <u>three</u> of the following bullet points with a partner:
- What do you think is the aim of this section of the map? Who is meant by *we*?
- Who would want to *act like a local* and why?
- Would you argue that the information is useful? Why (not)?
- Which of these aspects are true for you? Would you argue that this information holds true for all people living in Innsbruck? Why (not)?
- If you had to write a brochure on the city you are living in, how would you go about it? What would you (not) include and why?
- What might be problematic about these extracts from the city guide?

ACT LIKE A LOCAL

WE EAT A LOT
If you go to a restaurant, be careful how much you order. We do love to eat and normally serve good portions of sumptuous food. Sometimes the soup is already enough for an entire meal. Also be careful with dessert – a Kaiserschmarrn is totally worth trying, but you should still be hungry when ordering it.

PLAY CARDS
We learned playing the card game "Watten" from our grandpas, still play it with our friends and will one day teach it to our grandchildren. It involves cards called "Ober" and "Unter", colours like leaves and acorns and a lot of swearing.

YOU ARE NOT IN GERMANY
Even though we definitely speak German, we are proud to be Austrian. Some places are packed with Germans, so it can seem like you are in Germany – but you are not. Please don't mistake us for Germans – we will be really offended.

SAY HELLO!
At an altitude of about 900m, we drop the anonymity of the city and surprisingly start greeting everyone we meet. When hiking, don't be shy and say: "Griass di" (sing.), "Griass eich (plur.) or "Servas".

WEAR SHOES
There seems to be some kind of myth in other countries that you can climb a mountain shoeless or in flip-flops. Our mountains are powerful. They are steeper and the rocks are harder than in most other places. You can definitely not climb them in flip-flops. It's not safe at all, so please don't do it!

ODER?
We like to end sentences with "oder", oder? It's similar to the English "right". We don't expect to get an answer. It's just a bridge to our next sentence, oder?

IDENTIFY THE MOUNTAINS
You will blend in perfectly if you can identify the surrounding mountains. Knowing where the Nordkette (mountain range to the north) is really helps with orientation.

FIND A LOCAL
You can recognise locals quite easily, as they're the people who don't take photos of the mountains and the Old Town. Actually, during summer days or the Christmas Market you won't find them in the Old Town anyway. It's just too packed with tourists. This map will give you new perspectives and holds secret insider tips for exploring our wonderful city.

ALWAYS READY TO SKI
We love to go skiing and snowboarding. You can always see us carrying around our equipment – at university, on the bus and in the streets. This is especially entertaining during spring. Watch out for locals in sneakers on their bike with skis on the way up the mountain.

INNSIDER*
We are constantly talking about the water level of the Inn river. We notice things like: "Oh, look how high it is!" when the snow is melting in spring and: "Wow, the Inn got brown! And what is floating over there?" after heavy rains.
*puns with "Inn" are very popular.

Figure 3.1 Addressing stereotypes in the EFL classroom – example 1

on all six bullet points. Also, learners can be asked about the reasons for their choice of bullet points as well as their approach to the selection process.

Alternatively, I often approach the topic of stereotypes in my EFL classrooms using audiovisual material like YouTube clips. Figure 3.2 thus demonstrates the integration of different facets of intercultural learning using the resource "What kind of Asian are you?" (Tanaka, 2013). The video shows an encounter between two runners in the countryside leading to a short conversation in English.

The proposed questions accompanying this video clip require learners to decidedly change and coordinate perspectives to interpret the individuals' feelings and behavioural patterns. Moreover, students are encouraged to critically analyse the conversation individually before they share and reflect their viewpoints with a partner mapping similarities and differences.

Overall, when teaching *about* interculturality teachers ought to embed different topics in a methodological framework that encourages a critical analysis,

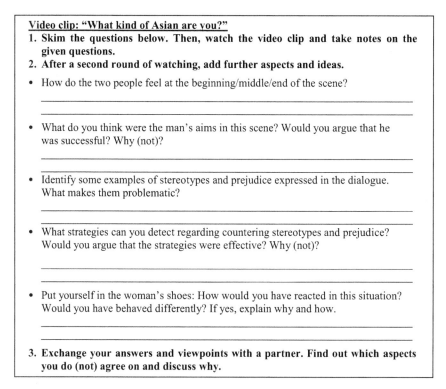

Figure 3.2 Addressing stereotypes in the EFL classroom – example 2

reflection, and discussion. I believe that the methodological dimension of interculturality particularly needs to be strengthened so that stereotyping, othering, or an essentialist understanding of culture and identity are not (unintentionally) expressed and solidified, but actively deconstructed. This alludes to the different impediments in the discourse of interculturality, which is the focus of the next section.

Challenges in intercultural education

Building on the previous sections, I now discuss selected challenges that I regard central to the discourse on interculturality and intercultural education. As before, these elaborations derive from my personal viewpoint and experience as a teacher, teacher educator, and researcher in language education.

To me, the greatest obstacle at the interface of interculturality and classroom practice constitutes essentialist and nationalist conceptions of culture and identity and actions based thereon. This entails educators' understanding of culture as a static, separable, and homogeneous entity, attributing it a descriptive and explanatory role, and conceptualising it through shared norms, values, products, and practices (Risager, 2018). Holliday (2010: 4) clarifies that essentialism "presents people's individual behaviour as entirely defined and constrained by the cultures in which they live so that the stereotype becomes the essence of who they are". This issue is frequently connected with a focus on nationalities and the conviction of one country equating one culture, often termed the *national paradigm* (Risager, 2021, 2018; Grünewald, 2012; Kramsch, 2009). On the contrary, as previously outlined, seeing culture as a highly dynamic, hybrid, and fluid entity, the "national community is only one of the many cultures an individual participates in" (Kramsch, 2009: 235). Against the backdrop of the increasing linguistic and cultural diversity in societies and classrooms, essentialist and nationalist approaches need to be problematised and contested (Blell & Doff, 2014; Kramsch, 2009).

While Holmes and Dervin (2016: 6) argue that the "over-emphasis on 'cultural difference' and (national?) 'culture' in the 'intercultural' [...] is increasingly becoming a thing of the past", I still observe these tendencies among in- and pre-service teachers. For instance, I frequently notice educators treating non-German L1 learners as experts for a specific country without inquiring about the relevance of this country for their lives and perhaps being unaware of the fact that learners may have never been to their relatives' country of origin. This could be a testimony of many teachers' lack of intercultural competence and sensitivity towards their learners' cultural diversity as well as an ignorance about the underlying emotionality of certain topics. I consequently advocate for teachers to reflect on their used terminology, methodology, and materials accordingly. Thereby, the perhaps well-intentioned but certainly problematic activity of an intercultural lunch to which everybody brings food from their alleged 'home country' can easily be modified into an intercultural lunch to which everybody brings their favourite dish.

In foreign language education, even though the focus on 'target language cultures' has been contested through work on linguae francae and international languages, efforts towards a late modernist understanding of culture, and the emergence of the critical intercultural speaker, the national paradigm is still present in educational practice (Grünewald, 2012; Kramsch, 2006; Cortazzi & Jin, 1999). Specifically, culture in FLE is frequently limited to providing learners with factual knowledge on the history, politics, and social framework connected with target cultures (Schumann, 2019b; Müller-Hartmann & Schocker-von Ditfurth, 2015). In this regard, Grünewald (2012: 55) argues that the reduction of interculturality to the so-called *Landeskunde* stems from a prevailing insecurity among educators in connection with the theoretical conceptualisation and practical implementation of the complex construct of intercultural education. As Kumaravadivelu (2008: 172–173) explains:

> [I]n most formal systems of language education, the learning and teaching of culture have been confined to the learning and teaching of the cultural beliefs and practices associated with the members of the target language (TL)

community, that is, the community of people speaking the second or foreign language (L2) that the learners are studying.

On the contrary, drawing on a transnational, late modernist, and open understanding of culture and with languages being used for communication internationally, the expression 'target culture' needs to be challenged and may have become obsolete as "no plurality and diversity is expressed" (Boeckmann, 2006: 12). In addition, the exclusive focus on certain countries "not only treats contemporary cultural challenges inadequately but it also neglects the L2 learners' need for developing global cultural consciousness" (Kumaravadivelu, 2008: 173). In the case of EFL, Syrbe and Rose (2018: 152) have also emphasised that learners are more likely to use the language as a lingua franca than in conversations with L1 speakers. Consequently, Kramsch (2009: 235) advocates "revisit[ing] the traditional teaching of culture in foreign language education" which should start with reconceptualising "culture as an open, fluid ('hybrid') and individual (yet non-arbitrary) construct" (Blell & Doff, 2014: 81). Thus, a wider perspective and the inclusion of various viewpoints is required (Sercu, 2000) to adequately do justice to the complexity of a diverse, globalised world (Lütge, 2019). Moreover, the inclusion of affective and action-oriented dimensions of intercultural education needs to be strengthened to counter the prevailing focus on cognitive aspects and move beyond *Landeskunde* (Grünewald, 2011).

Furthermore, I consider processes of othering, stereotyping, and the perpetuation of the self-other dichotomy highly problematic in teaching practice. This relates to previously addressed aspects such as the used teaching materials and applied methodology which can reinforce othering and exclusion (Hintermann et al., 2014). Albeit perhaps unintentional and well-meaning, the following scenario is not an observed singularity in secondary education: A learner is put in the spotlight and asked the complex, emotional, and certainly highly uncomfortable question: "Since you are black, what do you think about racism in Austria? Are we all racists and treat you badly here?" When inquired about their underlying aim, the educator explained that they do not shy away from cultural diversity and complex topics but want to make them explicit. This clear lack of empathy and critical self-reflection of one's own teaching practices and foregrounding of differences calls for improved professional development. In connection with the emergence and solidification of stereotypes, Hintermann et al. (2014) have also criticised certain words and phrases used in the Austrian context, such as 'Black Africa', "whose use runs the risk of reinforcing pupils' existing stereotypes" (Hintermann et al., 2014: 92). In addition, the uncritical and unreflective use of certain activities included in textbooks can bear the danger of solidifying instead of deconstructing stereotypes and reinforcing othering processes (e.g. Peskoller, 2022). On the contrary, education in a context of plurality needs to criticise and abandon dynamics of ethnocentricity and exclusion (Lütge, 2019: 203). Therefore, documents such as the *Autobiography of Intercultural Encounters* (Council of Europe, 2022), in which critical incidents are explicitly addressed and reflected on, need to be handled with care. Despite the fact that the authors declare that intercultural encounters can take many shapes and forms, all the examples provided in the text's rationale refer solely to different countries (Council of Europe, 2022: 3). As Ferri (2018: 26) remarks,

> the danger in analysing and labelling encounters and experiences as 'intercultural' is rooted in the implicit reproduction of power relations in which the subject positions of the participants are assigned according to the prevalent discourses of a given socio-political context, albeit hidden behind the label of cultural difference.

As I believe all encounters to be intercultural encounters, they can indeed constitute meaningful starting points for intercultural learning but need to be accompanied by critical analyses, (self-)reflection and discussion activities; if learners are not invited to "critically scrutinize stereotyped identities" (Hintermann et al., 2014: 99), othering might be encouraged instead of dismantled.

Lastly, ignoring the existing in-class diversity and treating students as linguistically and culturally homogeneous (Martinez, 2019) constitutes a final issue in teaching practice I want to highlight. The results from the aforementioned TALIS revealing that only a small share of the surveyed teachers indicated to feel (well-)prepared to work in a multicultural classroom setting (Schmich & Itzlinger-Bruneforth, 2019) provide a possible albeit shocking explanation for this observation. Hence, Gogolin's (2008) demonstrated monolingual habitus of a multilingual school seems to apply to intercultural dimensions as well. As a result, both pre- and in-service teachers need to receive proper training in connection with multilingual and intercultural education to receive guidance for its implementation and to develop the required competences and sensitivity themselves.

Looking at the syllabus for pre-service teacher education at Austrian universities, however, courses with a focus on interculturality and diversity remain rare and are mostly offered as electives. While in-service teachers should, ideally, already possess the respective capabilities to implement intercultural teaching and learning, TALIS has shown that this is not necessarily the case in the Austrian context. Moreover, I find the following two observations in connection with professional development for teachers in Austria alarming: On the one hand, there are only a few courses available that tackle intercultural matters and those that do frequently fall through due to insufficient registrations. On the other hand, the offered courses' contents and methodology often fail to adopt a critical and reflexive approach towards interculturality that is essential today (Dervin & Jacobsson, 2021) but adhere to rather dated, essentialist concepts of culture. Hence, teacher education and professional development are urgently called upon to address these shortcomings and provide adequate training in connection with interculturality (Svarstad, 2021).

Conclusion and outlook

In this chapter, I have outlined my understanding of culture and interculturality and conceptualised the classroom as a meaningful meeting place and valuable starting point for intercultural learning. Having looked at relevant educational policy documents in Austria, I proceeded to map out what I consider significant aims and challenges in the discourse and attempted to provide ideas for the implementation of intercultural education both from a content and a methodological perspective.

Among other aspects, I have highlighted the need to move past the prevailing overemphasis on nationalities and countries. In language education, this entails expanding the focus to include various perspectives and explore different contexts in which the language is used, particularly against the backdrop of English as a lingua franca (Baker, 2015; Holmes & Dervin, 2016). More broadly, as learners (and teachers) demonstrate a virtually infinite number of categories in which they can show commonalities and differences, with their nationality being only one of them, the emphasis should be put on the diverse and complex nature of identities. Unreflectingly referring to learners' (presumed) country of origin and making assumptions and attributions about their identities and culture(s) promotes othering processes and can do great harm to students' well-being and readiness to learn.

Hence, I believe that educators face a balancing act in their daily teaching practice: On the one hand, ignoring differences and treating learners as a homogeneous group denies them access to their diverse identities, experiences, and opinions, and goes against contemporary educational objectives suitable for a pluralistic, globalised world. On the other hand, overemphasising differences and heterogeneity among learners can reinforce othering processes and the emergence or solidification of stereotypes inside classrooms. What is necessary for teachers is to constantly reflect on their practices through critically evaluating their materials and methodology, and questioning and deconstructing possible pre-established notions and solidified images. (Language) educators should not be intimidated by the complexity and impediments connected with interculturality, but can and should adopt an intercultural pedagogy and make intercultural topics explicit inside their classrooms. Getting to know one's learners and their stories and acknowledging the existing diversity inside any group is vital, but has to be approached with utmost sensitivity and care. Creating a safe and comfortable learning environment and empowering learners in their dynamic identities, all students can be invited to share their experiences and exchange opinions without pressure or an immanent threat of being singled out. Thus, educators from all fields need to interculturalise their approaches through entering a dialogue with teachers from the same or differing subjects, levels, or educational institutions to receive other perspectives on interculturality and intercultural teaching practices.

My elaborations thus demonstrate rigorous demands for teacher education such as the need for interculturality to become a central element of teacher training and professional development (Dervin et al., 2020; Dervin & Jacobsson, 2021; Svarstad, 2021). Assigning intercultural matters an enhanced role in curricula and assessing the quality of offered courses in teacher education is pivotal, as high-quality intercultural education can only be integrated through interculturally competent educators. Thus, if teachers are not adequately prepared for the global classroom and dated approaches to culture and interculturality are perpetuated, students will not be adequately prepared for global citizenship, as a consequence. Also, teacher education needs to be interculturalised in itself, which involves processes of critical analysis, reflection, and discussion regarding redesigning its contents, aims, and approaches moving towards a critical interculturality and critical teacher education (Banegas & Gerlach, 2021; Dervin & Jacobsson, 2021, 2022).

Based on an open, dynamic, and highly individual understanding of culture, identity, and interculturality, I have argued that, essentially, every encounter between individuals is an intercultural encounter. Consequently, terms such as 'culture clash' or 'culture shock' need to be questioned and problematised as they suggest a static, closed, and negative view of culture that does not do justice to the complex and heterogeneous realities present in societies and schools today. Intercultural matters need to be addressed explicitly, on a content level, and included implicitly, on a methodological level, by harnessing the existing in-class diversity as a meaningful starting point for intercultural learning. Thereby, the development of open, respectful, and empathetic global citizens as a central goal in contemporary teaching practice can be decisively promoted.

We are all different in different ways which makes the world so colourful and interesting. If we show a willingness to relativise our own viewpoints, engage in a dialogue with others, and cherish multiperspectivity, we can learn a lot from and with each other and grow together.

Let's celebrate: Unity in diversity.

References

Baker, W. (2015). *Culture and Identity Through English as a Lingua Franca. Rethinking Concepts and Goals in Intercultural Communication.* Berlin and Boston, MA: De Gruyter Mouton (Developments in English as a Lingua Franca, 8).

Banegas, D. L., & Gerlach, D. (2021). Critical language teacher education: A duoethnography of teacher educators' identities and agency. *System*, *98*, 102474. https://doi.org/ 10.1016/j.system.2021.102474.

Bär, M. (2017). Auf dem Weg zur inklusiven Schule. Mögliche Implikationen aus fremdsprachendidaktischer Perspektive. In E. Burwitz-Melzer, F. G. Königs, C. Riemer, & L. Schmelter (Eds.), *Inklusion, Diversität und das Lehren und Lernen fremder Sprachen. Arbeitspapiere der 37. Frühjahrskonferenz zur Erforschung des Fremdsprachenunterrichts* (pp. 10–20). Tübingen: Narr Francke Attempto.

Blell, G., & Doff, S. (2014). It takes more than two for this tango: Moving beyond the self/other-binary in teaching about culture in the global EFL-classroom. *Zeitschrift für Interkulturellen Fremdsprachenunterricht*, *19*(1), 77–96.

Boeckmann, K. (2006). Dimensionen von Interkulturalität im Kontext des Fremd- und Zweitsprachenunterrichts. *Zeitschrift für Interkulturellen Fremdsprachenunterricht*, *11*(3), 1–19.

Brunsmeier, S. (2016). *Interkulturelle Kommunikative Kompetenz im Englischunterricht der Grundschule. Grundlagen, Erfahrungen, Perspektiven.* Tübingen: Narr.

Bundeskanzleramt. (2022). Volksgruppen. https://www.bundeskanzleramt.gv.at/themen/volksgruppen.html.

Bundesministerium für Bildung (BMB). (2017). *Interkulturelle Bildung: Grundsatzerlass.* https://bildung.bmbwf.gv.at/ministerium/rs/2017_29.html.
Bundesministerium für Bildung, Wissenschaft und Forschung (BMBWF). (2022). Bundesrecht konsolidiert: Gesamte Rechtsvorschrift für Lehrpläne – allgemeinbildende höhere Schulen. https://www.ris.bka.gv.at/GeltendeFassung.wxe?Abfrage=Bundesnormen&Gesetzesnummer=10008568.
Byram, M. (1997). *Teaching and Assessing Intercultural Communicative Competence.* Clevedon: Multilingual Matters.
Byram, M. (2008). *From Foreign Language Education to Education for Intercultural Citizenship: Essays and Reflections.* Clevedon: Multilingual Matters.
Byram, M. (2021). *Teaching and Assessing Intercultural Communicative Competence: Revisited.* Clevedon: Multilingual Matters.
Cortazzi, M., & Jin, L. (1999). Cultural mirrors: Materials and methods in the EFL classroom. In E. Hinkel (Ed.), *Culture in Second Language Teaching and Learning* (pp. 196–219). Cambridge: Cambridge University Press.
Council of Europe. (2018). *Reference Framework of Competences for Democratic Culture: Context, Concepts and Model* (Vol. 1). Strasbourg: Council of Europe Publishing.
Council of Europe. (2022). *Autobiography of Intercultural Encounters* (2nd ed.). Strasbourg: Council of Europe.
Dalton-Puffer, C., Boeckmann, K.-B., & Hinger, B. (2019). Research in language teaching and learning in Austria (2011–2017). *Language Teaching, 52*, 201–230.
Dervin, F. (2016). *Interculturality in Education: A Theoretical and Methodological Toolbox.* London: Palgrave Macmillan.
Dervin, F., & Jacobsson, A. (2021). *Teacher Education for Critical and Reflexive Interculturality.* Cham: Palgrave Macmillan.
Dervin, F., & Jacobsson, A. (2022). *Intercultural Communication Education: Broken Realities and Rebellious Dreams.* Singapore: Springer.
Dervin, F., Moloney, R., & Simpson, A. (Eds.). (2020). *Intercultural Competence in the Work of Teachers: Confronting Ideologies and Practices.* Milton: Routledge.
Fäcke, C. (2019). Interkulturalität und interkulturelles Lernen. In C. Fäcke & F.-J. Meißner (Eds.), *Handbuch Mehrsprachigkeits- und Mehrkulturalitätsdidaktik* (pp. 179–184). Tübingen: Narr.
Ferri, G. (2018). *Intercultural Communication: Critical Approaches and Future Challenges.* Cham: Palgrave Macmillan.
Freitag-Hild, B. (2018). Teaching culture—Intercultural competence, transcultural learning, global education. In C. Surkamp & B. Viebrock (Eds.), *Teaching English as a Foreign Language: An Introduction* (pp. 159–175). Stuttgart: J.B. Metzler.
Gogolin, I. (2008). *Der monolinguale Habitus der multilingualen Schule.* Münster: Waxmann Verlag.
Gogolin, I. (2016). Folgen der Migration für Bildung und Erziehung. In E. Burwitz-Melzer, G. Mehlhorn, C. Riemer, K. Bausch, & H. Krumm (Hg.), *Handbuch Fremdsprachenunterricht* (6th ed., pp. 60–64). Tübingen: A. Francke Verlag.
Gorski, P. (2016). Rethinking the role of 'culture' in educational equity: From cultural competence to equity literacy. *Multicultural Perspectives, 18*(4), 221–226. https://doi.org/10.1080/15210960.2016.1228344.
Grünewald, A. (2011). Förderung der Interkulturellen Kompetenz in Französisch- und Spanischlehrwerken. *Fremdsprachen Lehren und Lernen, 40*(2), 64–82.
Grünewald, A. (2012). Förderung interkultureller Kompetenz durch Lernaufgaben. *Fremdsprachen Lehren und Lernen, 41*(1), 54–71.

Grünewald, A., Küster, L., & Lüning, M. (2011). Kultur und Interkulturalität. In F.-J. Meißner & U. Krämer (Eds.), *Spanischunterricht gestalten. Wege zu Mehrsprachigkeit und Mehrkulturalität* (pp. 49–80). Seelze: Klett/Kallmeyer.

Guilherme, M. M. (2002). *Critical Citizens for an Intercultural World*. Clevedon: Multilingual Matters.

Hallet, W. (2002). *Fremdsprachenunterricht als Spiel der Texte und Kulturen. Intertextualität als Paradigma einer kulturwissenschaftlichen Didaktik*. Trier: WVT (ELCH, 6).

Hammer, J. (2012). *Die Auswirkungen der Globalisierung auf den modernen Fremdsprachenunterricht. Globale Herausforderungen als Lernziele und Inhalte des fortgeschrittenen Englischunterrichts; are we facing the future?* Heidelberg: Winter.

Heringer, H. J. (2019). Critical incidents. In C. Fäcke & F.-J. Meißner (Eds.), *Handbuch Mehrsprachigkeits- und Mehrkulturalitätsdidaktik* (pp. 481–484). Tübingen: Narr.

Hintermann, C., Markom, C., Weinhäupl, H., & Üllen, S. (2014). Debating migration in textbooks and classrooms in Austria. *Journal of Educational Media, Memory, and Society*, 6(1), 79–106. https://doi.org/10.3167/jemms.2014.060105.

Holliday, A. (2010). *Intercultural Communication and Ideology*. London: Sage.

Holmes, P., & Dervin, F. (Eds.). (2016). *The Cultural and Intercultural Dimensions of English as a Lingua Franca*. Bristol, Buffalo, and Toronto: Multilingual Matters.

InfoEck. (2018). *Welcome to Innsbruck*. Innsbruck: InfoEck.

Kumaravadivelu, B. (2008). *Cultural Globalization and Language Education*. New Haven, CT: Yale University Press.

Kramsch, C. (2006). *Context and Culture in Language Teaching*. Oxford: Oxford University Press.

Kramsch, C. (2009). Cultural perspectives on language learning and teaching. In B. Seidlhofer & K. Knapp (Eds.), *Handbook of Foreign Language Communication and Learning* (pp. 219–246). Berlin: Mouton de Gruyter.

Liddicoat, A. J., & Scarino, A. (2013). *Intercultural Language Teaching and Learning*. London: Wiley-Blackwell.

Lo Bianco, J. (2009). Dilemmas of efficiency, identity and worldmindedness. In J. Miller, A. Kostogriz, & M. Gearon (Eds.), *Culturally and Linguistically Diverse Classrooms: New Dilemmas for Teachers* (pp. 113–131). Bristol: Multilingual Matters.

Lütge, C. (2018). Digital, transcultural and global? Reconsidering the role of literature in the EFL Classroom. In A.-J. Zwierlein, J. Petzold, K. Boehm, & M. Decker (Eds.), *Anglistentag 2017 Regensburg: Proceedings* (pp. 299–309). Trier: WVT Wissenschaftlicher Verlag Trier.

Lütge, C. (2019). Von der Egalitätshypothese zur Global Education. In C. Fäcke & F.-J. Meißner (Eds.), *Handbuch Mehrsprachigkeits- und Mehrkulturalitätsdidaktik* (pp. 200–204). Tübingen: Narr.

Martinez, H. (2019). Strategien und ihre Förderung im Rahmen interkultureller Ansätze. In C. Fäcke & F.-J. Meißner (Eds.), *Handbuch Mehrsprachigkeits- und Mehrkulturalitätsdidaktik* (pp. 231–238). Tübingen: Narr.

Matos, A. G., & Melo-Pfeifer, S. (Eds.). (2020). *Literature and Intercultural Learning in Language and Teacher Education*. Berlin: Peter Lang.

Mengis, E., & Drücker, A. (2019). *Antidiskriminierung, Rassismuskritik und Diversität. 105 Reflexionskarten für die Praxis*. Weinheim: Beltz Juventa.

Müller-Hartmann, A., & Schocker-von Ditfurth, M. (2015). *Introduction to English Language Teaching*. Stuttgart: Klett.

OECD. (2018). *Preparing our Youth for an Inclusive and Sustainable World: The OECD PISA Global Competence Framework*. Paris: OECD.

Peskoller, J. (2021). *The Multicultural Classroom. Learning from Australian First Nations Perspectives*. Stuttgart: ibidem-Verlag.

Peskoller, J. (2022). Interkulturelles Lernen als Grundlage nachhaltiger Bildung. Einblicke in eine Lehrwerksanalyse für das Fach Englisch. In C. Sippl & E. Rauscher (Eds.), *Kulturelle Nachhaltigkeit Lernen und Lehren* (pp. 411–424). Innsbruck, Wien: Studienverlag.

Power, T., Virdun, C., Sherwood, J., Parker, N., Van Balen, J., Gray, J., & Jackson, D. (2015). REM: A collaborative framework for building indigenous cultural competence. *Journal of Transcultural Nursing, 27*(5), 439–446.

Risager, K. (2009). Intercultural competence in the cultural flow. In A. Hu & M. Byram (Eds.), *Intercultural Competence and Foreign Language Learning: Models, Empiricism, Assessment* (pp. 15–30). Tübingen: Gunter Narr Verlag.

Risager, K. (2012). Linguaculture and transnationality: The cultural dimensions of language. In J. Jackson (Ed.), *The Routledge Handbook of Language and Intercultural Communication* (pp. 101–115). London: Routledge.

Risager, K. (2018). *Representations of the World in Language Textbooks*. Bristol and Blue Ridge Summit, PA: Multilingual Matters.

Risager, K. (2021). Language textbooks: Windows to the world. *Language, Culture and Curriculum, 34*(2), 119–132. https://doi.org/10.1080/07908318.2020.1797767.

Risager, K., & Svarstad, L. K. (2020). *Verdensborgeren og den interkulturelle læring. Inspiration og nytænkning til sprogfagene og andre fag*. Frederiksberg: Samfundslitteratur.

Rogge, M. (2014). Going beyond the limitations of one's own culture – Inter- und transkulturelle Lernerfahrungen in fremdsprachlichen Begegnungsprojekten. In F. Matz, M. Rogge, & P. Siepmann (Eds.), *Transkulturelles Lernen im Fremdsprachenunterricht. Theorie und Praxis* (pp. 153–165). Frankfurt a.M: Peter Lang.

Sauseng, J., Prugger, D., & Kübler, L. (2020). *Allyship in Action*. Innsbruck: Universität Innsbruck.

Schmich, J., & Itzlinger-Bruneforth, U. (2019). *TALIS 2018 (Band 1): Rahmenbedingungen des schulischen Lehrens und Lernens aus Sicht von Lehrkräften und Schulleitungen im internationalen Vergleich*. Graz: Leykam. https://www.iqs.gv.at/_Resources/Persistent/d3b0c71d9d54f150311e8267eb3916782560fc2e/TALIS-2018_Gesamt_final_Web.pdf.

Schumann, A. (2009). Förderung interkultureller Bildung und Kompetenzen. In A. Grünewald & L. Küster (Eds.), *Fachdidaktik Spanisch. Tradition, Innovation, Praxis* (pp. 213–225). Stuttgart: Klett Sprachen.

Schumann, A. (2019a). Interkulturelle Kommunikation. In C. Fäcke & F.-J. Meißner (Eds.), *Handbuch Mehrsprachigkeits- und Mehrkulturalitätsdidaktik* (pp. 184–188). Tübingen: Narr.

Schumann, A. (2019b). Landeskunde im Kontext von Mehrkulturalität und Globalisierung. In C. Fäcke & F.-J. Meißner (Eds.), *Handbuch Mehrsprachigkeits- und Mehrkulturalitätsdidaktik* (pp. 192–195). Tübingen: Narr.

Sercu, L. (2000). *Acquiring Intercultural Communicative Competence from Textbooks: The Case of Flemish Adolescent Pupils Learning German*. Leuven: Leuven University Press.

Sobkowiak, P. (2016). Critical thinking in the intercultural context: Investigating EFL textbooks. *SSLLT, 6*(4), 697–716. https://doi.org/10.14746/ssllt.2016.6.4.7.

Statistik Austria. (2021a). Schülerinnen und Schüler im Schuljahr 2020/21, für die Deutsch nicht die erstgenannte im Alltag gebrauchte Sprache ist (Schulstatistik). https://www

.statistik.at/wcm/idc/idcplg?IdcService=GET_PDF_FILE&RevisionSelectionMethod=LatestReleased&dDocName=029650.

Statistik Austria. (2021b). *Statistisches Jahrbuch: Migration & Integration*. Wien: Statistik Austria.

Statistik Austria. (2021c). Bevölkerung mit Migrationshintergrund seit 2008. https://www.statistik.at/wcm/idc/idcplg?IdcService=GET_PDF_FILE&RevisionSelectionMethod=LatestReleased&dDocName=069443.

Svarstad, L. K. (2021). A cultural studies approach to interculturality in ELT. In V. Mabel & S. Chittima (Eds.), *Interculturality and the English Language Classroom* (pp. 27–54). Cham: Palgrave Macmillan.

Syrbe, M., & Rose, H. (2018). An evaluation of the global orientation of English textbooks in Germany. *Innovation in Language Learning and Teaching, 12*(2), 152–163. https://doi.org/10.1080/17501229.2015.1120736.

Tanaka, K. [helpmefindparents]. (2013, May 23). "What kind of Asian are you?" [Video]. YouTube. https://youtu.be/DWynJkN5HbQ.

Teaching Tolerance. (2019). *Let's Talk: A Guide to Facilitating Critical Conversations with Students*. Montgomery: The Southern Poverty Law Center.

United Nations. (2019). *Sustainable Development Goals*. https://www.un.org/sustainabledevelopment/sustainable-development-goals/.

Volkmann, L. (2010). *Fachdidaktik Englisch: Kultur und Sprache*. Tübingen: Narr.

4 Teaching in intercultural classrooms
An Italian perspective

Agostino Portera

Challenges in time of globalisation and interdependence

The world has dramatically changed. Today, the whole humanity is facing multiple, complex, and interdependent transformations on local, regional, national, and global levels. We live in an era of 'nowist culture' and 'hurried culture' (Bertman, 1998), of the obsessive search for something new, of the renegotiation of meaning and fundamental references. The current liquid modern 'consumer society' evidences the transition from "linear time to pointillist time" (Bauman, 2016: 21). Increasingly, we are witnessing the advent of 'new myths' that generate simple ideas "that are comfortable, do not create problems, facilitate judgment, in a word, reassure us" (my translation) (Galimberti, 2009: 11). Globalisation and planetary interdependence seem to generate a growing attention to economic, political, and technological aspects, to the detriment of sociocultural or environmental implications. We are witnessing the emergence of a single market on a world scale, the concentration of capital and persistent 'economic wars' between nation States, which have generated an imbalance of wealth at the international level, with consequences both of a political and social nature (Bauman & Portera, 2021).

As result, new challenges arise, which involve not only opportunities, but also risks and crises in the cultural, economic, environmental, political, social, and technological sectors. In particular, schools are involved in a very serious way. The presence of scholars and students with differences in terms of ethnicity, languages, values, religions, and behaviours demand new aims and methodologies. In addition, teachers and principals increasingly experience *neoliberalism*, considered as "a drift towards lifestyles", that has transformed more and more schools and universities from spaces of education, culture, and democratic organisation to places of "performance and efficiency" (Giroux & Giroux, 2006: 24). Neoliberalism promotes excessive individualism (loss of the ability to perceive oneself as part of a social group with common humanity), indifference (towards the needs and sufferings of plants, animals, and other human beings), competition (at the expense of cooperation), reductionism of complex phenomena and problems (experts in details, unable to grasp connections and links), standardisation (little or no consideration of individual and social differences and inequalities), and promotion of a culture of 'I don't care'. As a consequence, in almost all

DOI: 10.4324/9781003345275-5

countries there is economic turmoil due to greed and excess on the part of some people to the detriment of others. Environmental degradation and social conflicts increase, as well as exclusion and racism (Ball, 2009; United Nations, 2019). The United Nations (UN); the United Nations Educational, Scientific and Cultural Organization (UNESCO); and the Council of Europe (CoE), along with several scholars (e.g. UNESCO, 2006; Barrett, 2013; CoE, 2014; Portera, 2022) have identified intercultural education (IE) as one of the most appropriate approaches to address these challenges, to promote equity in education, and to facilitate the full development of every human being.

Intercultural education as one of the most appropriate answers

In 2019 the 193 UN member States came to an agreement and formulated the UN 2030 Agenda for the 17 Sustainable Development Goals (UN, 2019), as a universal call to action to combat the rise of poverty, protect the planet, improve the lives and prospects of 'everyone, everywhere'. In this document world leaders call for a decade of action for sustainable development, committing to mobilising funding, improving strategies, and strengthening institutions to achieve some specific targets in the decade 2020–2030. Quality of education is considered one of the main goals.

Awareness of this scenario was previously evident in the UNESCO (1994) document *Integrated Framework of Actions for Peace, Human Rights and Democracy*, signed by the Ministers of Education in 1994, as well as in the International Implementation Programme for the *United Nations Decade of Education for Sustainable Development for 2005–2014*. Both these texts also placed education at the centre of essential intervention strategies to be adopted and identify a holistic, transdisciplinary and integrated, value-based approach to education that takes into account sociocultural, economic, and environmental aspects, and focuses on sociopolitical issues such as equity, poverty, democracy, and quality of life (De Leo, 2010). In addition, the International Implementation Scheme (UNESCO, 2005) identified three spheres of action for sustainable development (all interconnected through culture): economics, environment, and society (and politics). In this model, the role of intercultural understanding and respect for cultural diversity is highly significant. In a different publication, UNESCO (2006) further specified the role of IE for facing these challenges.

In Europe, significant impulses for developing an intercultural approach have come specifically from the Council of Europe. At a meeting of the Ministers' Deputies on 2 February 2022, a new *Recommendation of the Committee of Ministers to member States on the importance of plurilingual and intercultural education for democratic culture* (CoE, 2022) was adopted. This recommendation addresses the importance of the cognitive, linguistic, and social benefits of learning several languages, and promotes plurilingual and intercultural competence in schools to enhance educational success, inclusion, and democracy. The central role of IE is further clarified in the *White Paper on Intercultural Dialogue: Living Together as Equals in Dignity* (CoE, 2008), which clearly goes beyond a limited understanding of 'multiculturalism' and provides theoretical and methodological support for an intercultural approach. The document considers that, in order to manage democratically growing cultural diversity, it is urgent (1) to overcome societies of segregated groups, marked by the coexistence of majorities and minorities; and (2) to work to establish a "vibrant and open society", characterised by the inclusion of all resident citizens and full respect for human rights. Moreover, the White Paper (2008: 64) states that a common future depends on the promotion of mutual understanding through the "capacity to safeguard and develop human rights, democracy and the rule of law".

Transcultural, multicultural, and intercultural education in Europe

In human history, migration is a very old phenomenon. The most likely scenario is a permanent network of cultural (and genetic) exchanges between different people. According to paleontological, archaeological, historical, genetic, and linguistic studies (e.g. Lewontin, 1984; Cavalli Sforza, 1993), the common origin of *all* human beings can be traced to an area between North-Eastern Africa and the Middle East. So, if we are aware of the common origin of *all* human beings (we share a common genesis and compatible DNA) and that migration and diversities are not the exception but the rule, we should erase the false premise (and a scientific mistake), regarding the existence of several distinct races (often based on different skin colours or features). *The only race on Earth is the human race.* If it is true that human beings are *all relatives*, it is also true that we are *all different*: In the course of history, people have developed different somatic features, languages, and cultural standards. The origins of life and human existence are founded on difference.

Historically the main problems seem to have originated from differences. Although migration is a primordial phenomenon, the word 'foreign' is commonly associated with negative or even threatening connotations, and the issue of coexistence remains an unresolved one. An overview of the meetings (and/or clashes) of people with different cultural, ethnic, linguistic, and religious characteristics demonstrates (see also Portera, 2017):

- The most notorious example has been the ruthless *suppression* through violence of the numerically, militarily, or economically weak.
- Another widespread method is *assimilation* (a foreigner will be 'absorbed' into the dominant culture).
- The methods of *segregation* or *ghettoisation* have also frequently been employed (people with different cultural, ethnic, linguistic, religious features are segregated, and thus they become 'harmless' to the dominant group).
- Another model is *fusion* or the so-called *melting pot* (cultural differences are combined and 'melted' to form a single culture).

- *Universalism* can also be defined as a pattern (on the basis of universal values, aspects in common to all human beings are emphasised, whereas all differences are omitted or neglected).
- The method of peaceful coexistence or *multiculturalism* (human beings with ethnic, cultural, and religious differences are educated in living together in mutual respect and understanding).

At school and in educational sectors, it is first and foremost necessary to reject models like suppression (violence can never help human development, instead problems escalate and become unsolvable), assimilation (it is impossible to force a person to change their identity), segregation (also a kind of violence; walls never stop humans from communicating), and fusion (it is impossible to 'lose' or 'renounce' one's own identity even if based on a "democratic decision"[1]). Close attention needs to be paid to the universalism (related to transcultural education) and to the multicultural approach.

The concept of universalism is inherent in transcultural theory and is applied in the fields of cross-cultural psychology (Shiraev & Levy, 2020) and transcultural psychiatry (Cox, 1986). Universalism refers to common cultural elements, spreading through lands, culture, and people. Educational strategies are aimed at the development of universal and common elements of formal values (e.g. respect, honesty, autonomy) and goals (e.g. peace, justice, and environmental protection). This approach is supported by cultural universalism theory, which is rooted in Emanuel Kant's (1922) cosmopolitan education, in the universal principles of the French revolution affirming the dignity of all human beings, and e.g. in Norberto Bobbio's (2006) studies on education aimed at 'universal values'. This educational model, called *Educazione alla mondialità* in Italy, *Erziehung zum Weltbürger* in German, and *global education* in the USA, might be possible to understand as 'additional', i.e. as other values, roles, and principles, are added to one's own identity. It offers the chance of realising educational interventions based on the recognition and respect of common, universal values, norms, and rules. Although there are many advantages (education to similarities and communities among all human beings, from common values and human rights to human needs), several objections could be raised to its rather improbable unitary vision of the world, which is in reality fragmented and not homogeneous. Since universalism has origins in the European context and is coupled with the supremacist position of Western countries and their economic power, the risk of dominating the rest of the world in a monopolistic control of culture is paramount. Who in fact decides which laws, rules, and values are universal? By focusing on the common elements of different cultures, several important and different aspects of cultural life are neglected. It also overemphasises stability and permanence, whereas movement and the ongoing processes of change in cultural systems are not taken into consideration. Teachers might also be tempted to disregard salient cultural differences, and develop interventions based on the assimilation of minorities.

The concept of multiculturalism, deeply rooted in the multi- or pluricultural approaches, refers to the existence of diverse cultural standards. It is based on the principle of cultural relativism (Lukes, 2003) that claims that all cultural traditions are equally good, and the choice of one or another is only a matter of free choice. This principle aims for a peaceful coexistence of cultures, and also implies the concepts of uniqueness and unsettled cultural differences, as well as the right to personal autonomy. Multicultural educational aims are acknowledgement and respect of cultural diversity. This epistemology arose between the two World Wars as a result of criticisms of positivist approaches, Cartesian dualism, and the rationalist paradigm, by scholars such as E. Husserl (1859–1938) in philosophy, C. Saussure in linguistics (1857–1913), and F. Boas (1858–1942) in anthropology. The first treatise in which the notion of cultural pluralism emerged (suggesting the value of diversity and the acknowledgement of otherness) was written in 1580 by M. E. Montaigne in his essays *Of Cannibals and Coaches* (Montaigne, 2003). However, the modern foundations were laid between 1720 and 1740, above all by G. B. Vico, whose book *Principi di Scienza Nuova* (1959) is regarded as one of the first texts of multicultural epistemology.

In the US, multicultural education became a topical issue in the early 1970s as the scholarly focus moved from ethnic studies. The first academic publications were authored by, e.g., James Banks, Carlos Cortès, Geneva Gay, and Carl Grant as a result of increased attention paid to the education of African Americans and other students of colour (Nieto, 2009). As a consequence of the melting pot ideology, which continued at schools and universities until the end of the 1960s, researchers' awareness of genuine ethnic and cultural differences was rather low, and the assimilationist ideology was dominant, which obviously benefitted White ethnic groups. Therefore, during the 1970s, cultural contrasts and conflicts persisted and were compounded by the Civil Rights and Ethnic-Revival movements as well as the struggles against racial segregation in schools and discrimination in society at large. African Americans promoted the motto 'Black is beautiful' and proudly began to affirm their origins and to study their roots. Some ethnic groups demanded educational and structural inclusion and the right to retain many of their culture standards, like language, religion, and other characteristics and symbols (Sleeter & Grant, 2007; Banks, 2009).

In some parts of Europe, multicultural education has come to mean recognising diversity and respecting it 'as is', without attempting to modify it. In countries like Germany and France, this approach led to the development of a kind of pedagogy for foreigners (*Ausländerpädagogik*, or *Pédagogie d'accueil*), which is very similar in its objectives and methods to, e.g., the special education pedagogy for students with disabilities. In German schools, multicultural pedagogy (with the impossibility of respecting all diversities) has become a pedagogy of assimilation into the majority (Nieke, 1995: 12–17). For teachers, applying a multicultural approach has the advantage of considering contemporary circumstances, the presence of many different cultures in classrooms, and pursues the educational aims of acknowledging and respecting cultural diversities. However, although this model is largely appreciated, some scholars (e.g. Abdallah-Pretceille, 1986; Perotti, 1996; Allemann-Ghionda, 1999; Gundara, 2000; Portera, 2011; Barrett, 2013) have identified its limitations, including (a) a static and rigid idea of culture and identity (i.e. cultures are to be understood and to be respected and should not be changed; individuals are moulded in an unchangeable and immutable identity), which stands in contrast to the aim of education itself; (b) *epochè*, or the suspension of political and moral judgement (i.e. modern anthropologism); (c) *organicism*, where each culture is perceived as a single, indivisible organisation (as mostly associated with the nation state); (d) *absence of evaluation*, or the idea that cultures cannot be compared (i.e. the ideas of anthropologists are accepted, but cannot be sustained from an educational point of view); and (e) educational strategies that aim at peaceful coexistence as if in a condominium. As a result, educational interventions have been often limited to folksy or exotic presentations that have inevitably and increasingly constrained immigrants to their so-called 'native culture', to patterns of behaviour that are outdated even in their countries of origin (see also Portera, 2011).

Considering all the previous models, one of the best answers to cope with ethnic and cultural diversity is viewed in the concept of intercultural education. In the European educational field this constitutes a potential Copernican revolution. Concepts like identity and culture are no longer approached rigidly, but rather *dynamically* and in constant evolution (not only for immigrants but also for the autochthonous population). Otherness, emigration, and life in a complex and multicultural society are not seen as risk factors or potentially harmful features, but as opportunities for personal and common enrichment. Epistemologically, a specific take on the intercultural model was first introduced in the context of educational studies. Among the pioneers, one finds Louis Porcher, a sociologist, and Martine Abdallah-Pretceille (1986), who, after her experience as a teacher, in 1985 wrote a PhD dissertation on the topic under the supervision of Porcher at the University of Sorbonne in Paris. The intercultural approach is positioned between *universalism* (education of all human beings, regardless of skin colour, language, culture or religion; Secco, 1999) and *relativism* (everybody should have the opportunity to assume and to show their own cultural identity; right of equality in difference; Shaw, 2000). It takes into consideration opportunities and limitations from both perspectives. Further it transcends them and builds a new synthesis, with improved opportunities for genuine dialogue, exchange, and interaction. Whereas multiculture evokes descriptive elements, with people from different cultures living peacefully side by side, the prefix *inter-* implies relations, interaction, and exchange of two or more elements (Abdallah-Pretceille, 1986). Consequently, IE rejects immobility and human hierarchy, and encourages dialogue and relationships on equal terms, so that people do not feel constrained to sacrifice significant aspects of their own cultural identity.

For teachers, applying intercultural strategies involves both acknowledgement and respect of relevant differences, and also the recognition of similarities and the promotion of common roles and norms. In addition, in classrooms there are also increased opportunities for real encounters, dialogue, exchanges, and interactions between students with different cultural backgrounds. In this sense, the intercultural approach enhances opportunities of growth and enrichment, beyond egocentrism and ethnocentrism. This dynamic view of culture allows dialectical relationships, and the opportunity for change and development of the identities of all the people involved (see also Rey, 2011). In light of this situation, IE requires and promotes a new *formae mentis*. It cannot be taught separately or in a special project. Instead intercultural perspectives must be included in all disciplines and in all planned activities. Teachers should not adopt a cumulative approach (additional lessons about immigrant children, further history or geography lessons) or work out ad hoc plans or particular projects in addition to or in place of curricula.

Intercultural education in schools. Example from Italy

Historically, Italy has been a country affected by emigration and the phenomenon of immigration has become salient only from the end of the 1970s. Therefore, teachers were able to profit from the experiences and mistakes made abroad. Schools and universities are generally led from the principles of IE to promote equity (equal access to educational opportunities), the right of hospitality (*accoglienza*), and inclusion. The dissemination and popularity of IE in Italy are perhaps one of the highest in Europe and even in the world, not only in the scientific literature, but also within school curricula and ministerial documents (see Zoletto, 2012; Catarci & Fiorucci, 2015; Portera, 2022).

The most significant documents and publications of the Italian Ministry of Education include:

- C.M. (*Circolare Ministeriale*) No. 301 of 8 September 1989, *Integration of Foreign Pupils Into Compulsory Education. Promotion and Coordination of Initiatives for the Exercise of the Right to Study*, focused on the need to become aware of the challenges of the presence of students of non-Italian nationality. The aim concerned their right to study, the learning of the Italian language, and helped to promote an open cultural awareness.
- C.M. No. 205 of 22 July 1990, *Compulsory Schooling and Foreign Pupils: Intercultural Education*, officially introduced IE as a form of intervention and affirms the principle of involving Italian students in an interactive relationship with foreign students. In this document, IE is also defined as the highest and most comprehensive form of prevention and fights against racism and all forms of intolerance.
- The National Education Council (*Consiglio Nazionale della pubblica istruzione*) subsequently issued two important documents. The first document from 23 April 1992, *IE in Schools*, identified some of the needs of the school system (also the reform of school curricula for including intercultural perspectives, the policy for the initial training of teachers at all school levels, institutional spaces, sufficient time and resources to deal effectively with intercultural education). The second document from 24 March 1993, *Racism and Anti-Semitism Today: The Role of School*, reiterates the urgency to take IE into a systemic way, supporting the autonomy of schools, and establishing the presence of intercultural mediators for promoting the process of integration of foreign pupils.

- C.M. No. 73 of 2 March 1994, *Intercultural Dialogue and Democratic living Together*, promoted the process of economic and political integration in the European context. In schools, disciplines and programmes were organised through an intercultural perspective.
- C.M. No. 24 of 1 March 2006, *Guidelines for the Reception and Integration of Foreign Students*, is one of the most important and mature documents on issues related to IE at school. It states that "Italy has chosen the full integration of all in school and IE as its cultural horizon". In addition, the document offers a concrete handbook to manage the difficulties arising from the school inclusion of pupils of foreign origin, stressing that IE is the background for training courses for foreign students while aiming at action for all students.
- The document *La Via Italiana per la Scuola Interculturale e l'Iintegrazione Degli Alunni Stranieri* (Italian way of intercultural school and the integration of foreign students), issued in October 2007 by the National Observatory for the Integration of Foreign Pupils and Intercultural Education, established at the Ministry of Education in December 2006. This important document presents a model of integration to be implemented through fundamental actions such as some practices of inclusion in school; Italian as a second language; enhancement of multilingualism; intercultural perspectives in the disciplines; and the role of teachers, principals, and non-teaching staff.
- C.M. No. 2 of 8 January 2010 established a ceiling of 30% for the presence of students with non-Italian citizenship in school classes of all levels. In this document, which aims to combat school segregation, there is a shift from the term 'integration' (which focuses on students' effort and agency) to the term 'inclusion' (which underlines the responsibility of teachers and schools).
- The D.M. (*Direttiva Ministeriale*) from 27 December 2012, *Intervention Tools for Pupils with Special Educational Needs and Territorial Organization for School Inclusion*, in which foreign pupils can (but must not) have the opportunity to benefit from measures for children with special educational needs (e.g. an individualised educational plan).
- In 2014 the *New Guidelines for the Reception and Inclusion of Foreign Students* were issued, which offered a distinction between the many types of pupils of foreign origin, and operational indications on their distribution in schools, their reception, the involvement and participation of families, evaluation, guidance, the teaching of Italian as a second language, schools with a strong presence of foreign pupils, the training of school staff, and adult education.

Thanks to these initiatives and the establishment of an intercultural approach in Italian schools and universities, many steps forward were made on the issues of inclusion. However, gaps and criticisms still remain. The last Invalsi Report (2021) showed that, especially for students from migrant backgrounds, the COVID-19 pandemic has led to new levels of fragility and the deepening of disparities and inequalities. Relevant actions to counter this negative development include the *Orientamenti Interculturali. Idee e Proposte per l'Integrazione di Alunni e Alunne*

Provenienti da Contesti Migratori (Intercultural guidelines. Ideas and proposals for the integration of pupils from migrant backgrounds) (Miur, 2022), published in March 2022 by the Ministry of Education. The guidelines aim to provide Italian teachers with more precise indications for interventions related to the presence of students with a migrant background. Building on the guidelines of 2006 and 2014, this document underlines, for example, the urgency of specific interventions related to students ages 0–6 years or to over 14 years (second generation) who were not covered in precedent versions. Students with a migration background are viewed as in need of specific kind of measures for bridging the initial language gap or other obstacles related with the migratory experience. For those students, the right to personal curricula is recognised. Like pupils with special educational needs, schools must endorse intercultural learning measures for promoting inclusion and success. For schools, the guidelines aim to act in two directions: (a) *specific integrative proposals*, e.g. the right to study, language learning, intercultural mediation, counselling, prevention of early school leaving, and relations in class and in extracurricular time; and (b) *universality of IE* for all students, which in classrooms means citizenship education, mutual respect, enhancement of linguistic and cultural diversity, promoting multilingualism, or curricula open to cultures and civilisations other than European and Western.

Despite these advances, some problems with implementation still exist in Italy. There is a lack of a specific professional figure (it is not required by law) responsible for cultural diversity management in schools. Effective and efficient training courses in Intercultural Competence (IC, hereafter) and diversity management for teachers are not widely accessible (Milani, 2017; Balloi, 2021). The most concrete risk is, as Colombo (2016: 14) has also stated, that all foreign students may be included in the special education category, or, on the contrary, that diversities are neglected – this problem was previous noted for Italian students in Germany by Portera (1995).

Need for intercultural competences in schools

A survey promoted by the European Commission (2017) has drawn a comparative framework of EU member countries (including Italy) on how new teachers are educated for diversity management competence, especially for contrasting xenophobic and local interest. The research focused on the teacher as an agent of change and assumed that there is no coherent European policy since each national system (and sometimes also particular territorial areas) can choose to train its teachers differently. The hypothesis was that the national training policy for teachers may be more oriented to cultural diversity as *deficit* by stimulating compensatory school interventions to help disadvantaged pupils, instead of underlining the advantages of diversity and by encouraging teachers to bring out the best from the diverse cultures present in their classrooms. This research has shown that there is no common policy framework for training and recruitment of teachers in the field of IE. The teaching staff has been seen to be ambivalent towards diversity and to show poor preparation for operating effectively with children with immigrant backgrounds. Finally, the research also underscores the absence of teachers with migratory backgrounds.

In Italy until 2015, it was possible to become a teacher without having passed an examination on IE, without a certificate of proficiency in a European language higher than B2, and without having any certification for teaching of Italian as a second language. In the reform of schools (L. 107 of 2015) and the Note Miur (5 November 2015), a new cycle of training was established as compulsory for 64,000 newly recruited teachers in which social inclusion and intercultural dynamics are rendered explicitly required among the eight areas of training priorities. Despite this effort, in Italy and in many other European countries paying more attention to this topic (such as Denmark, Spain, Sweden, and Portugal), the inclusion of IC in teacher training is definitely scarce and is still considered secondary to other areas (e.g. information technology and disability). This has led Colombo (2016: 18) to conclude: "No wonder the professional category of teachers reveals, overall, a widespread unpreparedness (so admit the same samples of teachers interviewed) and a perception of the Other full of anxieties and contradictions."

Given increasing diversities (not just in Italy or in Europe, but all over the globe), for teachers there is an urgent need of acquiring IC. A lack of IC can exacerbate the difficulties that teachers have with classroom management, since human relationships, ways of teaching and learning, and appropriate behaviour are culturally influenced. Additional conflicts occur when teachers and students come from different cultural backgrounds. Hence some scholars have proposed a *culturally responsive classroom management* (CRCM) system (see e.g. Weinstein et al., 2014).

The personality of the teacher is also essential. Vallone et al. (2022) explored the influence of five 'universal' personality traits (cultural empathy, open-mindedness, social initiative, emotional stability, flexibility) in predicting the management styles adopted by teachers (integrating, obliging, compromising, dominating, avoiding) from five European countries (Austria, Belgium, Germany, Italy, Spain) to deal with cultural conflict in classrooms, with and between students. The data from 589 secondary school teachers revealed that teachers who were more open-minded reported greater adoption of the integrating and obliging styles when managing cultural conflicts with and between students. Teachers who were less culturally empathic and flexible were more likely to adopt the dominating style. Those who possessed lower social initiative and flexibility were more likely to adopt the avoiding style. Teachers with lower levels of emotional stability showed greater adoption of the obliging style.

Another issue concerns the IC of principals and its influence on school policies. A literature review on the development of educational leadership, administration, and management has identified the central role of principals and school policies for promoting democratic values (Tian & Huber, 2020). In order to transform schools into equity-driven professional communities, leaders need to incorporate democratic values, trust, professional efficacy, and shared responsibilities (Tschannen-Moran, 2009). Fullan (2009) reviewed large-scale educational reforms in Canada, England, Finland, and the USA prior to 1997, between

1997 and 2002, and between 2003 and 2009. In these countries he found a positive shift from leader-centred perspectives with a competitive culture to new leadership practices with a distributive perspective promoting a collaborative culture. Other authors (Ball, 2008, 2009; Bush, 2008) have criticised neoliberal politics, privatisation, and marketisation in the public management era and educational policies and reforms, which are based on incorporating business efficiency models to measure educational performance, growth, and competitiveness, and to promote collaboration with consultancy companies to formulate educational policies and engage private providers in the education 'market'. Marketisation also arises in consumers' choices, performance-based accountability, and quasi-market competition (Branson, 2008), and also by introducing business practices and a free market into educational administration and using private schools to compete with public schools (Gunter & Fitzgerald, 2013).

Final reflections

Finally, we turn to some short considerations to stimulate further reflections, encounters, and dialogues.

1. In globalisation, (school-based) education has a preeminent role to play, also in schools. In the awareness of current uncertainties, crises, and diseases, it is necessary to recognise the paramount role of education: "Many of our most worrying and serious social problems could be alleviated if we knew how to educate our young people", wrote Postman (1995: 7), referring to the multicultural reality of the United States. This is especially relevant in democratic, industrialised and pluralistic societies, at a time when all the human sciences are forced to give space and visibility to disciplines associated with economic profit (Nussbaum, 2010). It is urgently necessary to revitalise education not only in theory, but also through studies and research with appropriate scientific methodologies, above all in school practice.
2. Education (also in schools) must consider the various new challenges, risks, and opportunities related to, e.g., globalisation, interdependence, neoliberalism, and climate change. In addition to focusing on practical intervention, I am strongly convinced that teachers need to reflect upon how they engage with a given approach. As such, it is necessary to clarify the language that we choose. Due to the fact that words are never neutral (Freire, 1998), it is urgent to reach a consensus on many levels: semantics, theoretical frameworks, and practical applications. *Multicultural*, *transcultural*, and *IE* have their merits and can be viewed as complementary. On the other hand, given the semantic misunderstandings and confusion across nations and disciplines, it is necessary to promote a dialogue to find a shared language and accurate understanding. My proposal is to use 'multicultural' in descriptive terms (societies are multicultural; see also Gundara, 2000), and 'multicultural education' to describe ways of improving knowledge about and respect for ethnic and cultural diversities. 'Transcultural education' should be used to

refer to recognising, developing, and respecting common rules and values (like the Universal Declaration for Human Rights). 'Intercultural' should be applied only in reference to interventions. What is more, in my opinion, the term 'interculturality', which is used by many scholars around the world, can lead to misunderstanding, because effective intercultural interactions seldom occur spontaneously. IE should be considered as an activity, an impulse for practitioners to overcome the condominium view of culture (coexistence; living peacefully side by side), and should be used to refer to education that considers both similarities and differences between students, and (when opportune or feasible) promotes contact, encounters, dialogue, interaction, and conflict management.

3. Regarding the future of IE and the issue of 'interculturalising interculturality' as proposed by Dervin and Jacobsson (2021, 2022), and central in the present volume, like any theory the intercultural model is strongly rooted culturally (North Europe, North America). Some scholars (e.g. Aman, 2017) consider IE as a colonial approach, which merely reflects Western norms and values. Therefore, today it is also urgent to move beyond the first stage of reflections and launch a truly international prospective (including also Asia, Arabic countries, First Nations, etc.). In addition, I consider it appropriate to further extend the meaning of the word 'culture'. It is necessary to overcome linguistic, national, and ideological barricades, and start taking into account all forms of diversity. In my opinion, IE leads to an education which considers and tries to face all types, forms, and manners of diversity which may be present in the classroom: not only linguistic, cultural, and ethnic, but also, for example, related to gender, political or sexual orientation, social status, power, (dis)abilities, and economic differences. After having clarified its semantic meaning and after having become aware of the many limitations, it will still be also essential to rethink and expand the adjective 'intercultural'.

Next to become more rooted in education (not only but primarily at school level), IE should be also spread in all areas of potential application (healthcare, factories, the economic domain, law, counselling, mediation), and politics (also relationships between national states), and in the civil societies.

4. Regarding teaching in the field of IE, teachers, principals, and other school personnel should acquire intercultural competences in their teacher training through specialised courses. The Centre for Intercultural Studies in Verona has carried out research on the IC needed in education, counselling, and mediation (Portera, 2017). As a result, a model of IC was developed, which underlines interactive aspects (see the graphic model in Portera, 2017). The Area of the Self, which contains *attitudes* (like openness, sensitivity, decentralisation, curiosity, humility, flexibility, respect, responsibility, critical thinking, acceptance, empathy, and congruence), is positioned at the heart of the model. Around the Area of the Self one finds the categories of *knowledge* (awareness of the cultural self, knowledge of one's own culture and the culture of others; verbal-linguistic, nonverbal, and paraverbal knowledge; disciplinary, multidisciplinary, and interdisciplinary knowledge) and *skills* (e.g.

linguistic and communicative skills, observation, analysing and interpreting subjective reality, establishing positive relationships, building stable and trustful relationships). In a subsequent study (Portera, 2020) an attempt was made to validate the first model by means of the Delphi method and a practical application in a master's programme. A new dynamic, interactive model of IC was developed, which transcends the Eurocentric or North American conceptualisation of IC and include competences rooted in Eastern traditions, mentioned in the philosophies of Taoism (e.g. the importance of not rigidly dividing the world and persons) and Chakra (also considering aspects such the divine, emotions, or be rooting in the reality).

In times of globalisation, neoliberalism, and interdependence, besides acquiring specific competences regarding the most solid theories, principals, teachers, and school professionals need to be *educated* (I intentionally avoid the word 'trained', which is more related to military or sport proficiencies) for facing real encounters and dialogues with foreigners and 'alterities'. The new challenge in schools is to face diversities and manage conflict adequately, without using authoritarian (hidden or visible) forms of control and power. The aim should be to promote education practices for fostering a stronger and more robust democratic civilisation worldwide, by encouraging dialogue and overcoming dictatorships, religious fundamentalism, and practices that violate basic human rights. This is the current challenge for the field of intercultural education.

Note

1 For more details about the process of identity building in multicultural context, see Portera (1995) and Bauman and Portera (2021).

References

Abdallah-Pretceille, M. (1986). *Vers une pédagogie interculturelle*. Paris: Institut de Recherche Pédagogique.

Allemann-Ghionda, C. (1999). *Schule, Bildung und Pluralität*. New York, Bern: Peter Lang.

Aman, R. (2017). *Decolonising Intercultural Education: Colonial Differences, the Geopolitics of Knowledge, and Inter-Epistemic Dialogue*. New York: Routledge.

Ball, S. (2008). The legacy of ERA, privatization and the policy ratchet. *Educational Management Administration & Leadership*, 36(2), 85–199. https://doi.org/10.1177/1741143207087772.

Ball, S. J. (2009). Privatising education, privatising education policy, privatising educational research: Network governance and the 'competition state'. *Journal of Education Policy*, 24(1), 83–99. https://doi.org/10.1080/02680930802419474.

Balloi, C. (2021). La diversità nei luoghi di lavoro. In C. Balloi, S. Premoli, & D. Crespi (Eds.), *Prendersi cura delle persone e dell'azienda. La consulenza organizzativa tra identità, cultura e apprendimento* (pp. 121–144). Milan: Franco Angeli.

Banks, J. A. (Ed.). (2009). *The Routledge International Companion to Multicultural Education*. New York: Routledge.

Barrett, M. (Ed.). (2013). *Interculturalism and Multiculturalism: Similarities and Differences*. Strasbourg: Council of Europe Publications.

Bauman, Z. (2016). Liquid modern challenges to education. In P. Portera & P. Dusi (Eds.), *Neoliberalismo, educazione e competenze interculturali* (pp. 21–39). Milan: Franco Angeli.

Bauman, Z., & Portera, A. (2021). *Education and Intercultural Identity*. London: Routledge.

Bertman, S. (1998). *Hyperculture: The Human Cost of Speed*. Santa Barbara: Praeger.

Bobbio, N. (2006). *Liberalism and Democracy*. London: Verso Books.

Branson, C. M. (2008). Achieving organisational change through values alignment. *Journal of Educational Administration, 46*(3), 376–395. https://doi.org/10.1108/09578230810869293.

Bush, T. (2008). From management to leadership: Semantic or meaningful change? *Educational Management Administration & Leadership, 36*(2), 271–288. https://doi.org/10.1177/1741143207087777.

Catarci, M., & Fiorucci, M. (Eds.). (2015). *Intercultural Education in the European Context: Theories, Experiences, Challenges*. London: Ashgate.

Cavalli Sforza, L., & Cavalli Sforza, F. (1993). *Chi siamo. La storia della diversità umana*. Pioltello: Mondadori.

Council of Europe. (2008). *White Paper on Intercultural Dialogue: Living Together as Equals in Dignity*. Strasbourg: Council of Europe Publications.

Council of Europe. (2014). *Developing Intercultural Competences Through Education*. Strasbourg: Council of Europe Publications.

Council of Europe. (2022). *Recommendation CM/Rec 1 of the Committee of Ministers to Member States on the Importance of Plurilingual and Intercultural Education for Democratic Culture*. Strasbourg: Council of Europe Publications.

Colombo, M. (2016). Cultural diversity management nella scuola: come vengono preparati gli insegnanti italiani? *OPPInformazioni1, 21*, 10–21. http://hdl.handle.net/10807/98380.

Cox, J. L. (1986). *Transcultural Psychiatry*. New York: Routledge.

De Leo, J. (2010). *Reorienting Teacher Education to Address Sustainable Development: Guidelines and Tools–Education for Intercultural Understanding*. Paris: UNESCO Publishing.

Dervin, F., & Jacobsson, A. (2021). *Interculturaliser l'interculturel*. Paris: L'Harmattan.

Dervin, F., & Jacobsson, A. (2022). *Intercultural Communication Education: Broken Realities and Rebellious Dreams*. London: Springer.

European Commission, Directorate-General for Education, Youth, Sport and Culture. (2017). *Preparing Teachers for Diversity: The Role of Initial Teacher Education: Final Report*. Brussels: EC Publications Office. https://data.europa.eu/doi/10.2766/637002.

Freire, P. (1998). *Pedagogy of the Oppressed*. Upper Saddle River, NJ: Prentice-Hall.

Fullan, M. (2009). Large-scale reform comes of age. *Journal of Educational Change, 10*(2), 101–113. https://doi.org/10.1007/s10833-009-9108-z.

Galimberti, U. (2009). *I miti del nostro Tempo*. Milan: Feltrinelli.

Giroux, H. A., & Giroux, S. S. (2006). Challenging neoliberalism's new world order: The promise of critical pedagogy. *Cultural Studies – Critical Methodologies, 6*(1), 21–32. https://doi.org/10.1177/1532708605282810.

Gundara, J. (2000). *Interculturalism, Education and Inclusion*. London: Paul Chapman.

Gunter, H. M., & Fitzgerald, T. (2013). New public management and the modernisation of education systems. *Journal of Educational Administration and History, 45*(3), 213–219. https://doi.org/10.1080/00220620.2013.796914.

Invalsi. (2021). *Gli alunni con cittadinanza non italiana*. Roma: Ministero dell'istruzione.
Kant, I. (1922). *Kritik der reinen Vernunft*. Herausgegeben von A. Görland. Berlin: Cassirer.
Lewontin, R. (1984). *La diversité génétique humaine*. Paris: PUF.
Lukes, S. (2003). *Liberals and Cannibals*. London: Verso.
Milani, M. (2017). *A scuola di competenze interculturali*. Milan: Franco Angeli.
Montaigne, M. (2003). *Complete Essays 1533–1592*. London: Penguin Books.
MIUR-Ministero dell'Istruzione. (2022). *Orientamenti Interculturali. Idee e proposte per l'integrazione di alunni e alunne provenienti da contesti migratori*. Rome: MIUR.
Nieke, W. (1995). *Interkulturelle Erziehung und Bildung*. Leverkusen: Leske und Budrich.
Nieto, S. (2009). Multicultural education in the United States: Historical realities, ongoing challenges, and transformative possibilities. In J. A. Banks (Ed.), *The Routledge International Companion to Multicultural Education* (pp. 79–95). New York: Routledge.
Nussbaum, M. C. (2010). *Not for Profit: Why Democracy Needs the Humanities*. Princeton, NJ: Princeton University Press.
Perotti, A. (1996). *Migrations et société pluriculturelle en Europe*. Paris: L'Harmattan.
Portera, A. (1995). *Interkulturelle Identitäten. Faktoren der Identitätsbildung Jugendlicher italienischer Herkunft in Südbaden und Süditalien*. Wien: Bohlau Verlag.
Portera, A. (2011). Multicultural and intercultural education in Europe. In C. A. Grant & A. Portera (Eds.), *Intercultural and Multicultural Education: Enhancing Global Interconnectedness* (pp. 12–32). New York: Routledge.
Portera, A. (2017). Intercultural competences in education. In A. Portera & C. A. Grant (Eds.), *Intercultural Education and Competences for the Global World* (pp. 23–46). Newcastle: Cambridge Scholars Publishing.
Portera, A. (2020). Intercultural competences: Different models and critical reflections. In A. Portera, R. Moodley, & M. Milani (Eds.), *Intercultural Mediation, Counseling and Psychotherapy in Europe* (pp. 31–55). Newcastle: Cambridge Scholars Publishing.
Portera, A. (2022). *Educazione e pedagogia interculturale*. Bologna: Il Mulino.
Postman, N. (1995). *The End of Education: Redefining the Value of School*. New York: Alfred A. Knopf.
Rey, M. (2011). The intercultural perspective and its development through cooperation with the Council of Europe. In C. A. Grant & A. Portera (Eds.), *Intercultural and Multicultural Education: Enhancing Global Interconnectedness* (pp. 33–48). New York: Routledge.
Secco, L. (1999). Preliminari della pedagogia interculturale come pedagogia dell'essere. *Studium Educationis*, 6(4), 620–632.
Shaw, S. (2000). *Intercultural Education in European Classrooms*. London: Trentham Books.
Shiraev, E. B., & Levy, A. D. (2020). *Cross-cultural Psychology* (7th ed.). New York: Routledge.
Sleeter, E., & Grant, C. A. (2007). *Making Choices for Multicultural Education* (5th ed.). New York: Wiley.
Tian, M., & Huber, S. G. (2020). Mapping educational leadership, administration and management: Research 2007–2016. Thematic strands and the changing landscape. *Journal of Educational Administration*, 58(2), 129–150. https://doi.org/10.1108/JEA-12-2018-0234.
Tschannen-Moran, M. (2009). Fostering teacher professionalism in schools: The role of leadership orientation and trust. *Educational Administration Quarterly*, 45(2), 217–247.

UN. (2019). *Agenda 2030 for the 17 Sustainable Development Goals (SDGs)*. New York: UN Publishing.
UNESCO. (1994). *Integrated Framework of Actions for Peace, Human Rights and Democracy*. Paris: UNESCO Publishing.
UNESCO. (2005). *Draft International Implementation Scheme for the United Nations Decade of Education for Sustainable Development*. Paris: UNESCO Publishing.
UNESCO. (2006). *Guidelines for Intercultural Education*. Paris: UNESCO Publishing.
Vallone, F., Dell'Aquila, E., Dolce, P., Marocco, D., & Zurlo, M. C. (2022). Teachers' multicultural personality traits as predictors of intercultural conflict management styles: Evidence from five European countries. *International Journal of Intercultural Relations*, *87*, 51–64. https://doi.org/10.1016/j.ijintrel.2022.01.006.
Vico, G. B. (1959). *Principj di scienza nuova* (in Opere, a cura di Rossi P). Milano: Rizzoli.
Weinstein, C. S., Tomlinson-Clarke, S., & Curran, M. (2014). Toward a conception of culturally responsive classroom management. *Journal of TeacherEducation*, *55*(1), 25–38. https://doi.org/10.1177/0022487103259812.
Zoletto, D. (2012). *Dall'intercultura ai contesti eterogenei*. Milan: Franco Angeli.

5 Teaching through learning about intercultural difference(s)

Autoethnographic experiences of a teacher aide in an Australian regional secondary school

P. A. Danaher

Introduction

The scholarly field of interculturality continues to grow apace, and in doing so it reflects a crucial diversity of viewpoints, and it manifests productive debates and dialogues. These debates and dialogues have elicited specific groupings of approaches to defining and understanding interculturality. For instance, Elias and Mansouri (2020) differentiated between interculturalism (IC) and intercultural dialogue (ICD), and, despite asserting that both paradigms are "largely constrained by a lack of conceptual clarity and theoretical precision", they concluded that "IC provides the conceptual foundations that enable an ICD articulation around intercultural exchange and dialogue across differences" (p. 490). From a different perspective, and reflecting an avowedly politicised apprehension of the intercultural, Guilherme (2019: 2) highlighted the indissoluble interdependence of the intercultural, the critical and the decolonial – for example, by stating baldly that "the critical and the intercultural are inescapably intertwined", and also by posing the foundational questions "how intercultural must critique be?" and "how decolonial should critique be?" Yet another position was expressed by Dervin and Simpson (2021: 27–28), who, with characteristic precision, distilled fundamental insight into several of the key ingredients of current comprehension of interculturality when they propounded:

> At the interpersonal level, interculturality is based on (endless) negotiations, [and] reflexive and critical dialogues. The very word interculturality contains the prefix inter-[,] which refers to *between, mutually, reciprocally, together*. The dialogues between the self and the other are thus continuous and always in the making. However, the false assumption that *we are free to be or act interculturally* is omnipresent in research and education (amongst others)[.]

From this it emerges that the intercultural is complex, contested, and contextualised, with considerable diversity of approaches to conceptualising and analysing manifestations of interculturality. Those characteristics certainly apply to

DOI: 10.4324/9781003345275-6

accounts of the vital question of how can and should we teach (about) the intercultural, the focus of this volume. Both the importance and the difficulty of engaging with this question were reflected in a typical response, which holds that "an intercultural approach is where people of different cultures have engaging interactions with each other. They develop strong relationships through the sharing of ideas and values and show mutual respect and understanding" (Melbourne Polytechnic, 2018: n.p.). This response also elaborated four "steps" in such an approach:

1. Admit uncertainty
2. Challenge assumptions
3. Practice empathy
4. Embrace diversity. (Melbourne Polytechnic, 2018: n.p.)

On the one hand, there is commendable clarity evident in this evocation of interculturality and of strategies to enhance it. On the other hand, these strategies lack specificity and perhaps inevitably assume a linearity of sequencing that belies the reality of many if not most intercultural encounters. Moreover, and again perhaps inevitably, such strategies appear to eschew the complex, contested, and contextualised character of the intercultural enunciated earlier.

My contribution to this volume is focused on my retrospective analysis of a set of autoethnographic experiences in the first quarter of 2022 in my role as a part-time teacher aide or teaching assistant working in a large secondary school in regional Queensland, Australia. As I elaborate in the following text, I frame that analysis in terms of interpreting the experiences as diverse kinds of intercultural encounters in order to discern their educational foundation and to extrapolate the potential broader lessons for teaching of such encounters.

The chapter has been structured as follows. The next section presents a combined focused literature review, philosophical propositions, and research design. Then I provide an account of my selected autoethnographic experiences in the school, followed by identified implications for conceptualising and understanding intercultural difference(s). These implications in turn generate particular wider lessons, clustered around three proposed principles, for teaching directed at the intercultural.

Literature review, philosophical propositions, and research design

Given this chapter's analysis of my autoethnographic experiences in a school, the focused literature review component of this section of the chapter concentrates on specific studies of interculturality in schools and schooling. Against that backdrop, and resonating with Guilherme's (2019) elaboration of the interdependence of the intercultural, the critical, and the decolonial, Pineda et al. (2020: 1175) explored what they saw as a fundamental dissonance between "[t]he educational agenda of indigenous groups" and "the expansion of schooling" in Colombia. Blackmore et al. (2022) adopted a similarly critical stance to analysing the construction of a policy of "internationalisation-at-home" pertaining to intercultural relationships between international and domestic students in two Australian schools. More generally, Müller et al. (2020) used their very comprehensive systematic literature review of tools to assess social, emotional, and intercultural competences to highlight the overreliance on self-reports among those tools, and to argue that very few tools assess all three competences together.

On the other hand, Barrett (2018) presented a more optimistic view of the capacity of schools to promote the intercultural competence of young people. A similarly optimistic perspective was shared by Piipponen and Karlsson (2019), based on their research with children using the storycraft storytelling technique to share stories about intercultural learning with other students in different European countries (see Piipponen, Chapter 15, this volume). Intriguingly, given the focus on inclusive education in the next section, Sorkos and Hajisoteriou (2021) developed a pedagogical model that they named "sustainable intercultural and inclusive education", and that they asserted was capable of bridging what they decried as "the dichotomy between intercultural and inclusive education" (p. 517). Likewise, Puente-Maxera et al. (2020) argued that playing games from around the world was an effective approach to promoting intercultural education through sport education in a secondary school in northern Spain.

Several published studies have helped to canvass intercultural education and its variations in different schools and school systems in diverse countries. This is important to ensuring an appropriately geographically variegated coverage of the inherently localised manifestations of global education phenomena (see also Norberg-Hodge, 2022). For instance, Idris (2020) explored the intercultural competence of a sample of government or state junior high school English teachers in Yogyakarta, Indonesia, which they rated as being generally high. Berglund and Gent (2019) highlighted the agency of Muslim students in English and Swedish schools in mobilising intercultural synergies between Qur'anic studies and 'mainstream' religious education. By contrast, Thumvichit (2018) identified a dissonance between Thai secondary school teachers' willingness to embrace English language teaching (ELT) and a general lack of coverage of localised cultural contexts in the reading-focused activities in available ELT coursebooks. Tsang (2022) conducted research with students in a multicultural tertiary education institution in Hong Kong and emphasised the importance of on-campus intercultural experiences, as well as greater intercultural competence being exhibited by multilingual than by bilingual students. Turning from students to teachers, Hajisoteriou et al. (2019) created a participatory intercultural development course for teachers in Greece focused on challenging cultural stereotypes, and they contended that "it is only through participatory, collaborative, critical and action-research models of professional development that we may achieve change in teachers' attitudes and practices, and, in turn, facilitate school improvement" (p. 166).

In varied ways, the foregoing focused literature review has demonstrated anew the complex, contested, and contextualised character of interculturality highlighted earlier in the chapter, specifically with regard to the intercultural and schools and schooling. This character is also evidenced in my reflections on my selected autoethnographic experiences as a part-time teacher aide presented in the next section. Those reflections are also framed by an emergent philosophising about intercultural encounters informed by my experiences. At this point, I outline some philosophical propositions that build on the preceding focused literature review, and that also resonate with the meaning-making that I elaborate later based on my reflections on my autoethnographic experiences.

More specifically, those philosophical propositions have been derived from what has been termed the "Buber–Levinas debate on otherness" (Skrefsrud, 2022; see also Danaher & Danaher, 2019). Martin Buber and Emmanuel Levinas were well-known and influential philosophers with several convergences in their thinking. As Friedman (2001: n.p.) noted: "Both are solidly rooted in Judaism. Both are philosophers who have broken with the central thrust of philosophy from Plato to Heidegger in favor of a radical relation to otherness, alterity. Both are centrally concerned with ethics." While a great deal has been written about these convergences, my interest here lies in how these convergences can help to extend my understandings of the intercultural encounters described later.

Viewed from that perspective, much of Buber's writing was concerned with diverse kinds of relationships, including those among humans, and between humans and God. For Buber (1937), "Relation is mutual. My Thou affects me, as I affect it. We are moulded by our pupils and built up by our works. ... We live our lives inscrutably included within the streaming mutual life of the universe" (pp. 15–16). Hintze et al. (2015) synthesised Buber's ethical standpoint in his well-known statement that "all real living is meeting" (1970: 6):

> This distillation of the primacy of human relationships and our interactions with one another is authentic Buber and truly only underscored by everything else he wrote. Taking this idea – that life is defined by our coming together with one another – together with the notion of *mutuality* ..., Buber is most concerned with how we meet and treat one another; how my *I* interacts with *You*. That we are compelled to respond, with words or actions, when approached (met) by the Other, is what creates our responsibility to the Other. It is only through dialogue that I and You can relate and fully meet.

Likewise, Hintze et al. (2015: 6) observed that a vital corollary of Buber's thought was that

> to invest one's self in the Other means to lose a measure of control over the ensuing dialog and its direction. To take this risk is to embrace living, as Buber defined it; it is to accept that when we invest in the Other – when we care – we accept a measure of moral responsibility for that Other in a way that can never be predetermined by rules or procedures.

By contrast, given Levinas's writings about phenomenology and transcendence, Hintze et al. (2015: 7) posited that "Levinas ... conceive[d] of an approach to ethical behavior that was grounded in *relational experience* that had nothing to do with control, prediction, or manipulation. ... That relational experience was defined by Levinas as the face-to-face meeting". Hintze et al. evoked some memorable metaphors in elaborating the consequences of such experience:

> The asymmetrical nature of this relationship is worth noting, with the "defenceless nudity" of the Other's face on one side and my position, will, and ability to choose my actions on the other. I can indeed choose to respond to the obligation his [*sic passim*] need places on me by refusing to see it or taking a tranquilizer. I can desensitize myself and deny that there is humanity behind the face of the Other, no matter my initial reaction. ... The greater the asymmetry of the relationship (the greater my power with respect to the other whether socially, economically, or physically), the greater is my obligation to him, to treat him in a way that is not based on control, prediction, or manipulation: to engage in my side of our implicit dialogue with respect before we even begin to speak.

There is considerable resonance between Buber's and Levinas's work about relationality and otherness. At the same time, there is a burgeoning scholarship about the nuanced and subtle differences between their ideas. My particular interest in that scholarship pertains to necessarily selective aspects of relationality and otherness that for me constitute elements of the Buber–Levinas debate with important implications for understanding intercultural encounters. One perspective on that debate was afforded by the Jewish political researcher Neve Gordon (2004: 98):

> Levinas's critique of Buber's notion of reciprocity ... [contrasted] with the prominent place of the "other" in Levinas's thought. ... Buber's thought does not lend itself to an ethical relation that commences with the other, or to an ethical relation founded upon the other.

Furthermore:

> It is clear that Levinas rejects the attempt to construct a world from the ego, a tendency that in the past informed the oppression of the colonies by the West, and today is reflected in the economic subjugation of the Third World. Levinas's assertion that the other should not be appropriated by the ego points to the integrity of the other. The emphasis on the other and the prominent place it receives in Levinas's writings reveal the origin of Levinas's assertion that there is an inherent discrepancy between Buber's notion of reciprocity and an ethical relation.
>
> (Gordon, 2004: 99)

Another perspective on this crucial yet complex Buber–Levinas debate was provided by the British ethics researcher Stephen Wigmore (n.d.: 10), who contended that, for Levinas, Buber's I–You relationship "is a formal relation incapable of carrying the significant content that Levinas considered essential for a true rendering of the significance of interpersonal encounter". Moreover, "the I–You relation primarily emerges from the 'I' and only reaches out to the 'You'. ... [T]he emphasis is on the action and stance of the self, rather than the Other" (Wigmore, n.d.: 11). More broadly, according to Wigmore (n.d.: 20):

> Buber and Levinas were essentially attempting to achieve different things through their philosophy. Levinas' philosophy had the clear aim to supply a basis for ethics and replace ontology. Buber, on the other hand, aimed to give a more pure description of human relation, whether with man, God, nature or Art, rather than to use the description of inter-personal encounter for wider philosophical work. Levinas, however, considered this problem of Ethics to be more important than the more obviously relational aspects Buber was concerned with.

By contrast, Lisbeth Lipari (2004), a United States communication scholar, redressed somewhat the balance in the Buber–Levinas debate, observing that "many scholars ... read Buber through the lens of Levinas, thereby tending to favor Levinas's reading of Buber" (pp. 123–124), and adding that some contributions to this debate

> [rely] on Levinas's contested reading of Buber, ... [and] also ... [privilege] Levinas's philosophical project over Buber's. ... Because Buber never published his own reading of Levinas's work, however, his writings on Levinas pertain only to the latter's reading of him, which, he insisted, was a misreading.
>
> (p. 124)

More widely, Lipari (2004: 123)

> [read] these textual encounters between Levinas and Buber in an effort to explore the ethical implications of the failure to listen for the other, that is, to listen without stealing our interlocutor's possibilities and horizons of meaning. Beyond warning of the danger of the failure to make strange and see the other as wholly other, the story of the encounter between Levinas and Buber highlights a relation somewhat in shadow: the connection between listening and responsibility.

Crucially, Lipari (2004: 123) used this reading to discern a fundamental implication for understanding intercultural encounters:

> Perhaps more than anything, this failed dialogic engagement suggests that the relation of alterity to responsibility may be enacted primarily through the process of listening – through the gifts of reception, attention, and presence to the other and through the concomitant renunciation of attempts to "control and master" the other.

The Buber–Levinas debate has been taken up in different forms across a range of disciplines, including communication studies (Arnett, 2004), feminism (Butler, 2011), international relations (Warner, 1996), and philosophy (Bernasconi, 2004). Despite that wider perspective, my intention here was to trace the broad contours of this debate in order to present two key philosophical propositions about intercultural encounters: firstly, that such encounters involve, to varying degrees and with varied effects, particular manifestations of difference(s) and otherness; and, secondly, that (as reflected in the Buber–Levinas debate) there are appropriately diverse understandings of those manifestations in specific such encounters.

Finally, in this section of the chapter, with regard to the research design underpinning the chapter, I have drawn on the principles and procedures of autoethnography (Anteliz et al., 2023, in press) to select and analyse the experiences portrayed in the next section. In particular, I have been attentive to autoethnography as a rigorous and systematic method of inquiry that has entailed considerable reflexivity on my part in communicating and deriving meaning from those experiences (see also Throne, 2019). I have also been acutely aware of my ethical obligations and responsibilities, which have been increased rather than diminished by my reporting my experiences through my frame of reference, rather than seeking to calibrate them against others' recollections (see also Edwards, 2021).

Selected autoethnographic experiences of intercultural encounters as a teacher aide

This section of the chapter takes up and extends, and is in some ways a sequel to, an earlier autoethnographic account of 2022 as a year of personal and professional transition (Danaher, 2023). For instance, that earlier account referred to three job interviews in which I participated in the week from 17 to 21 January 2022. My experiences as a teacher aide derived from a subsequent job interview to those three that occurred on 4 February 2022. Through the kind introduction performed by a mutual friend, on that date I met the head of special education at a large government secondary school who equally kindly offered me the opportunity to work as a teacher aide in the school, initially every Friday for the remainder of the first teaching term of 2022. This offer was made despite my manifest inexperience in special education provision and notwithstanding that I had not been a secondary school teacher since the end of 1990.

I shall always be grateful for this opportunity, which taught me a great deal about myself as well as about the students and teachers with whom I interacted during that teaching term. I have restricted my account here to specific instances of interactions with difference(s), which I analyse more fully in the next section. My work as a teacher aide entailed working under the supervision of the classroom teacher and interacting primarily with one or two students in each of the four lessons of the school day, with those allocated lessons sometimes varying on particular Fridays as the school term progressed. Furthermore, each student with whom I worked exhibited one or more forms of difference – as I did from them – that formed the foundation of highly varied intercultural encounters.

These encounters took place in the context of the school providing an extensive programme of support for students' special needs that involved approximately 50 teacher aides. That programme in turn aligned with, and was informed by, the policy of inclusive education articulated by Education Queensland, the education system governing government or state schools in Queensland. That policy defined inclusive education as follows:

> Inclusive education means that all students can access and fully participate in learning alongside their similar[ly]-aged peers. Teaching and learning strategies are adjusted to meet students' individual needs. Inclusive education encompasses all aspects of school life and is supported by culture, policies, programs and policies.
>
> (Education Queensland, 2021: n.p.)

In common with most education jurisdictions, that same policy identified specific and highly varied student groups with particular respective experiences of difference and hence as being posited to require certain kinds of inclusive education support:

- Aboriginal and Torres Strait Islander [Indigenous Australian or First Nations] students
- students from culturally and linguistically diverse backgrounds
- students who identify as LGBTIQ
- students living in out-of-home care
- students from rural and remote communities
- students with disability
- students with mental health needs
- gifted and talented students.

(Education Queensland, 2021: n.p.)

That is clearly a lengthy list of highly differentiated identified needs and presumed accompanying support strategies. Nearly all the students with whom I worked remained in the regular classroom with the other students; my role was either to assist them to complete the same work as the rest of the class or alternatively to complete tasks requiring a lower level of complexity than those undertaken by the other students. A few times I interacted with students who had been withdrawn from their regular classes in order to work with learning resources that would have been difficult to integrate into the mainstream classroom.

The individual students with whom I interacted traversed a broad range of characteristics and experiences. Some children exhibited learning difficulties that impeded their access to all elements of the mainstream curriculum. With these students, I read and explained the instructions for particular activities, and sometimes I assisted them to complete alternative tasks designed by the classroom teacher. In some cases, it was specific challenges with literacy and/or numeracy that hindered their learning, rather than mastery of the subject matter content. In such situations, my role was somewhat akin to an interpreter or translator, helping the student to decode the text and thereby to unravel what would otherwise remain a mystery.

That same role of interpretation or translation certainly applied to my work with a few migrant and refugee children who had many accomplishments, but who did not yet speak or write the majority language comprehensively. Our conversations sometimes included their sharing information about their birth country and home culture, and about their perceptions of differences between their previous and their present lives, which communicated heightened reflexivity and self-awareness. A couple of these students also had physical challenges that included using a wheelchair, while another student had a visual impairment. I was struck by their determination to succeed in this new environment, and by their intelligent appreciation of their current situation and their aspiration for their future endeavours.

I interacted also with a student who appeared to be gifted, but whose interactions with other students were strained by his family circumstances. Likewise, I found myself unable to work with another student who was oppositionally defiant towards me, and who was silent and withdrawn in her relations with other students in the class.

Understandably, the teachers and fellow teacher aides who worked with the 'special needs' students in the school were themselves highly diverse. Every day that I was at the school, I observed conscientious professionals demonstrating empathy with, and enacting care for, their students against the backdrop of very demanding workloads and increasing pressures on academic performance. Inevitably, on some occasions individual teachers and teacher aides appeared to be succeeding more or less fully at their work, in the same way that the students did, and certainly in the same way that I did. I was offered a full-time position outside the education system at the end of that term, so I was not able to continue my teacher aide role; I came away with an enhanced understanding of and appreciation for the aspirations, efforts, and outcomes exhibited by students and educators alike.

Implications for understanding intercultural difference(s)

This section of the chapter focuses on the meanings that I discerned from the autoethnographic experiences that I presented in the preceding section, specifically in relation to identified implications for understanding intercultural difference(s). To do this, I need to revisit selected conceptualisations of the intercultural from the existing literature.

Some of these conceptualisations are clustered around Dervin's seminal scholarship about interculturality. For instance, Dervin (2017: 1) presented this characteristically productive and provocative evocation of critical interculturality: "understood here as a never-ending process of ideological struggle against solid identities, unfair power differentials, discrimination and hurtful (and often disguised) discourses of (banal) nationalism, ethnocentrism, racism and various forms of -ism". Similarly, Dervin (2017: 14) provided a crucial and timely reminder about the character of difference(s) in relation to interculturality:

> Comparing cultures also sometimes creates false boundaries between people. Because we only look at difference. And yes, there are differences between people. And even between people from within one's own family. But we also have a lot of commonalities. And what I'm interested in, as a scholar working on intercultural competence, is to train people to work within the continuum of similarity and difference. To oscillate between these two, and not just to rush towards difference.

A similarly profound insight into the essence of interculturality was afforded by Simpson in his recently co-authored book with Dervin (Dervin & Simpson, 2021: 50):

> The ways in which people are categorised and labelled in research on the intercultural ('the migrant', 'the refugee', 'the newcomer') represent biases of how the people behind the labels and categories are represented. It can be limited and limiting to view people this way as people become 'boxed in' by static representations. In these instances, seeing people exclusively as an other, through their otherness, negates the dialogues necessary to move beyond surface appearances and representations. If difference in interculturality is only what you want to see, then difference is all you will see.

At this point, I hope that these quotations from the research of Dervin and Simpson help to explain the relevance to a volume about teaching interculturality otherwise of this account of my working as a teacher aide with a highly varied set of secondary school students in regional Queensland, Australia. From that perspective, I have applied (appropriated?) 'culture' as referring to the widely ranging attitudes, backgrounds, behaviours, effects, and outcomes exhibited in, and constituted as framing, the daily school lives of the students with whom I worked. That is, I view culture as the 'ways of being' of individuals and groups manifested as they interact with and experience other individuals and groups and the world at large. This conception of culture is non-essentialist and non-foundationalist (see also Bagg, 2021; Nathan, 2015), and apprehends culture as dynamic, responsive, and shifting rather than as a fixed essence or a predetermined phenomenon.

More broadly, this conception closely aligns with Dervin's (2017: 1) depiction, cited earlier, of "a never-ending process of ideological struggle against solid identities", which accentuated culture as being always in movement and as initiating action in response to others' actions. This understanding of culture also resonates with Dervin's (2017) insistence, also cited earlier, that observing difference(s) should not turn into an ideologically framed refusal to discern similarities among people. This understanding complements as well Simpson's argument, likewise cited earlier from Dervin and Simpson (2021: 50), about the need to move beyond "limited and limiting" stereotypes attached to particular analytical categories, such as "'the migrant', 'the refugee', [and] 'the newcomer'". Precisely the same argument can and should be applied to educationally generated categories such as "students from culturally and linguistically diverse backgrounds", "students with disability", and "gifted and talented students" (Education Queensland, 2021: n.p.).

The conceptualisation of 'culture' outlined here has as its corollary the proposition that in essence 'the intercultural' denotes the interactions and relationships between individuals and groups. These interactions and relationships can be idealised and even reified, in the sense that my encounters with you can be interpreted as equally authentic, generous, and sincere efforts to understand each other. In practice, and as the aforementioned citations of Dervin (2017) and Dervin and Simpson (2021) emphasised, these manifestations of the intercultural are inevitably fraught with mutual misunderstandings and actuated by politicised intentions and actions. These characteristics help to explain why and how difference is accentuated, rather than recognising similarities between individuals and groups (Dervin, 2017), and also why and how the otherness of others is highlighted (Simpson in Dervin & Simpson, 2021), instead of acknowledging that difference and otherness reside in each of us (see also Ferri, 2020).

This understanding of both 'culture' and 'the intercultural', and concomitantly of difference(s) and otherness, helps me to make sense of my selected autoethnographic experiences as a teacher aide presented in the previous section of this chapter. From that perspective, and despite the best efforts of the teachers and other teacher aides at the school, the institutional context in which I interacted with the students was an ideological construction in which every single participant's conceptions and perceptions of her- or himself and of others in the school were highly politicised. This politicisation was evidenced in widely ranging manifestations. These manifestations included the official hierarchy attending school staff members (for instance, the distinction among school leadership, heads of department, and classroom teachers; and the differentiation between teachers and teacher aides), the formal discourses related to 'special needs education' and the particular categories of such needs, and the informal and often implicit and tacit understandings that different groups of students would be more or less successful in their respective educational attainments at the school. In other words, culture, interculturality, difference(s), and otherness abounded and thrived in this environment, sometimes positively, sometimes very negatively, but always interdependently with the influence and impact of these ideologically and politically framed assumptions and apprehensions of individuals and groups, whether directed at the school principal, the head of department, myself as a casually employed teacher aide, or the students.

It is difficult to know the extent to which the people at the school were conscious of these assumptions and apprehensions. Students, teachers, and teacher aides are very busy people, and the unrelenting press of daily school life does not easily afford quiet moments that facilitate consciousness raising. Yet my conversations with the head of special education at the school indicated that she was well aware of the contradictions and tensions framing her colleagues' and her work, and it is likely that others were equally aware. There is considerable stress, as well as a fundamental poignancy, about striving to do well and to act with integrity within a system that one recognises as fundamentally flawed (see also Danaher, 2023). Or, from a different perspective, this dissonance was illustrated starkly by Høy-Petersen and Woodward's (2018) study of professionals and volunteers working in culturally heterogeneous yet not always propitious workplaces with a shared goal of genuinely valuing difference. The authors identified that the participants needed to negotiate "apparently conflicting agendas of ethical openness, self-protection, instrumentalism and parochialism", and they described participants' "cosmopolitan ethical practice [as being] performative and contextual, entangled with a variety of potentially conflicting schemas of evaluation and judgements" (Høy-Petersen & Woodward, 2018: 655).

This section of the chapter has proposed specific understandings of cultural difference(s), derived from the account in the preceding section of my autoethnographic experiences as a teacher aide. In particular, I have used the examples of difference(s) that I encountered as a teacher aide to posit a crucial conceptual relationship among culture, the intercultural, difference(s), and otherness that is broader and more inclusive in character than some other theories of intercultural encounters. I turn now to consider the identified implications for teaching of my experiences outlined earlier of learning about intercultural difference(s).

Lessons and principles for teaching about interculturality

Given this volume's focus on teaching interculturality otherwise, it behoves me in this section of the chapter to draw a contrast between the lessons distilled from my autoethnographic experiences as a casually employed teacher aide in an Australian regional secondary school and some approaches to teaching about the intercultural. From that perspective, DeVoss et al. (2002: 76) elucidated what they called "five challenges in teaching intercultural communication", with "challenges" denoting strategies for enhancing such teaching that were not necessarily easy to implement:

1. focusing on the characteristics of students' own cultures
2. replacing notions of cultural stereotypes (positive and negative) with more fluid, dynamic understandings of tendencies
3. avoiding limiting the guidelines for good intercultural communication to guidelines for good technical communication in general
4. developing a more sophisticated sense of the design considerations necessary for intercultural communication
5. encouraging students to move intercultural communication beyond the classroom[.]

Although the paper by DeVoss et al. (2002) was published more than 20 years ago, many of the less effective strategies for teaching about the intercultural that they disavowed remain in evidence (Zou & Yu, 2021). Yet what can I proffer that might be any different from these existing strategies? After all, 'being intercultural' and 'doing interculturality' are challenging and difficult, and do not admit of straightforward solutions.

Nevertheless, in this section I propose three principles that I contend align with the spirit of interculturality that I outlined earlier. The first principle is to *understand intercultural encounters as fully human interactions*. That is, and with reference to the Buber–Levinas debate elucidated earlier in the chapter, such encounters encapsulate all the complexity and diversity attending human beings and their relationships with themselves and with one another. This principle attaches primacy to the intersection between self and other, and between selfhood and otherness. It also eschews analytical categories and shifting signifiers (such as those referring to ethnicity and gendered identity, for instance) in favour of more comprehensive, and also more nuanced and situated, accounts of individuals and groups.

The second principle is to *direct focused attention at conceptions and implications of difference(s)*. Difference is too easily reduced to outward and external manifestations of variability, with insufficient focus being given to analysing the origins and impacts of theories of diversity, and to what remains as a fundamental ambiguity pertaining to such diversity, and to whether it is celebrated and valued and/or devalued and marginalised in specific contexts in particular communities. This principle also highlights the crucial and still contested relationship between interculturality and difference(s) that warrants further and continuing research.

The third principle is to *locate teaching about interculturality in a wider project of exploring the ideological and politicised constructions of educational provision and attainment*. My autoethnographic experiences as a teacher aide working with highly diverse students in a large Australian regional secondary school evoked their positioning as requiring certain kinds of 'special needs' educational support, which in turn drew attention to their being similarly positioned in particular ways by the broader society. This latter positioning took place despite the conscientious professionalism of the school leaders, teachers, and teacher aides who worked at the school and who sought to generate equitable opportunities for the students in their care. Being attentive to the largely invisible but undeniably powerful forces that frame and constrain all of us in schools – students, teachers, and educational leaders alike – is vital if intercultural education is not to be complicit with the marginalisation of certain learners.

Conclusion

As I have noted elsewhere in this chapter, I remain very grateful to the head of special education at the school where I worked as a part-time teacher aide in the first quarter of 2022. This opportunity prompted me to learn more about myself, and more importantly about the students with whom I worked and about the teachers and other teacher aides who facilitated their learning. I learned also about the complexity and contestation attending the students' highly variegated diversity, as well as their various manifestations of difference(s).

It was really on the basis of that diversity and of those manifestations that I proposed conceptualising interculturality as denoting a broader perspective on culture, and hence on the intercultural, than some other researchers in this scholarly space would allow. Yet that conceptualisation was necessary in my view to engage comprehensively with the full panoply of intentions, actions, experiences, and effects that occur when humans interact with one another. It was equally necessary to accommodate and build on the evidence of difference(s) and otherness that I observed in my teacher aide work. That intentionally more expansive and inclusive perspective was reflected also in the three principles for teaching (about) interculturality that I adumbrated in the final section of the chapter.

Diversity, inclusion, valuing of difference, equipping young people with the knowledge and skills to lead meaningful and productive lives. All of these, and many more, are what are claimed as the purposes and impacts of contemporary schooling. Yet they will come to naught unless careful heed is paid to the fundamental interplay between difference(s) and otherness that is embodied and encapsulated in interculturality. I hope that my reflections on my autoethnographic experiences as a part-time teacher aide during a single term in a large Australian regional secondary school might contribute to the ongoing debate and dialogue about these crucial issues.

Acknowledgements

I am grateful to the book editors for creating this publishing opportunity. In the first quarter of 2022, Ms Rachael Mayers, Deputy Principal (Special Education) at Centenary Heights State High School in Toowoomba, Queensland, Australia, afforded me an encouraging and inclusive welcome as a teacher aide in her department, from whose students and teachers I also learned a great deal. Mr Emilio A Anteliz contributed a comprehensive and thought-provoking literature search to the process of writing this chapter.

References

Anteliz, E. A., Mulligan, D. L., & Danaher, P. A. (Eds.). (2023). *The Routledge International Handbook of Autoethnography in Educational Research*. London: Routledge.

Arnett, R. C. (2004). A dialogic ethic "between" Buber and Levinas: A responsive ethical "I". In R. Anderson, L. A. Baxter, & K. N. Cissna (Eds.), *Dialogue: Theorizing Difference in Communication Studies* (pp. 75–90). New York: Sage Publications.

Bagg, S. (2021). Beyond the search for the subject: An anti-essentialist ontology for liberal democracy. *European Journal of Political Theory*, *20*(2), 208–231. https://doi.org/10.1177/1474885118763881.

Barrett, M. (2018). How schools can promote the intercultural competence of young people. *European Psychologist*, *23*(1), 93–104. https://doi.org/10.1027/1016-9040/a000308.

Berglund, J., & Gent, B. (2019). Qur'anic education and non-confessional RE: An intercultural perspective. *Intercultural Education*, *30*(3), 323–334. https://doi.org/10.1080/14675986.2018.1539305.

Bernasconi, R. L. (2004). "Failure of communication" as a surplus: Dialogue and lack of dialogue between Buber and Levinas. In P. Atterton, M. Calarco, & M. Friedman (Eds.), *Levinas and Buber: Dialogue and Difference* (pp. 65–97). Pittsburgh: Duquesne University Press.

Blackmore, J., Tran, L., Hoang, T., Chou-Lee, M., McCandless, T., Mahoney, C., Beavis, C., Rowan, L., & Hurem, A. (2022). Affinity spaces and the situatedness of intercultural relations between international and domestic students in two Australian schools. *Educational Review.* https://doi.org/10.1080/00131911.2022.2026892.

Buber, M. (1937). *I and Thou* (trans. by R. G. Smith). Edinburgh: T. & T. Clark.

Butler, D. (2011). Disturbing boundaries: Developing Jewish feminist ethics with Buber, Levinas and Fackenheim. *Journal of Modern Jewish Studies, 10*(3), 325–350. https://doi.org/10.1080/14725886.2011.608550.

Danaher, M. J. M., & Danaher, P. A. (2019). Proximity ethics, situated ethics and the Buber–Levinas debate as ethical principles in navigating multiple responsibilities in educational research: Lessons learned from researching with Japanese environmental activists and Scottish fairground families. Unpublished paper.

Danaher, P. A. (2023). Susurrations of a swansong: Autoethnographic sense-making by an Australian professor of education working on identity shift and relationship reshaping. In E. A. Anteliz, D. L. Mulligan, & P. A. Danaher (Eds.), *The Routledge International Handbook of Autoethnography in Educational Research* (pp. 180–196). London: Routledge.

Dervin, F. (2017). *Critical Interculturality: Lectures and Notes.* Cambridge Scholars Publishing.

Dervin, F., & Simpson, A. (2021). *Interculturality and the Political within Education.* London: Routledge.

DeVoss, D., Jasken, J., & Hayden, D. (2002). Teaching intracultural and intercultural communication: A critique and suggested method. *Journal of Business and Technical Communication, 16*(1), 69–84. https://doi.org/10.1177/1050651902016001003.

Education Queensland. (2021). *Inclusive Education Policy.* https://ppr.qed.qld.gov.au/pp/inclusive-education-policy.

Edwards, J. (2021). Ethical autoethnography: Is it possible? *International Journal of Qualitative Methods, 20.* https://doi.org/10.1177/1609406921995306.

Elias, A., & Mansouri, F. (2020). A systematic review of studies on interculturalism and intercultural dialogue. *Journal of Intercultural Studies, 41*(4), 490–523. https://doi.org/10.1080/07256868.2020.1782861.

Ferri, G. (2020). Difference, becoming and rhizomatic subjectivities beyond 'otherness': A posthuman framework for intercultural communication. *Language and Intercultural Communication, 20*(5), 408–418. https://doi.org/10.1080/14708477.2020.1774598.

Friedman, M. (2001). Martin Buber and Emmanuel Levinas: An ethical query. *Philosophy Today, 45*(1), 3–11. https://doi.org/10.5840/philtoday200145137.

Gordon, N. (2004). Ethics and the place of the other. In P. Atterton & M. Calarco (Eds.), *Levinas and Buber: Dialogue and Difference* (pp. 98–115). Pittsburgh: Duquesne University Press.

Guilherme, M. (2019). The critical and decolonial quest for intercultural epistemologies and discourses. *Journal of Multicultural Discourses, 14*(1), 1–13. https://doi.org/10.1080/17447143.2019.1617294.

Hajisoteriou, C., Maniatis, P., & Angelides, P. (2019). Teacher professional development for improving the intercultural school: An example of a participatory course on stereotypes. *Education Inquiry, 10*(2), 166–188. https://doi.org/10.1080/20004508.2018.1514908.

Hintze, D., Romann-Aas, K. A., & Aas, H. K. (2015). Between you and me: A comparison of proximity ethics and process education. *International Journal of Process Education*, *7*(1), 3–19.

Høy-Petersen, N., & Woodward, I. (2018). Working with difference: Cognitive schemas, ethical cosmopolitanism and negotiating cultural diversity. *International Sociology*, *33*(6), 655–673. https://doi.org/10.1177/0268580918792782.

Idris, M. M. (2020). Assessing intercultural competence (IC) of state junior high school English teachers in Yogyakarta. *Indonesian Journal of Applied Linguistics*, *9*(3), 628–636. https://doi.org/10.17509/ijal.v9i3.23213.

Lipari, L. (2004). Listening for the other: Ethical implications of the Buber-Levinas encounter. *Communication Theory*, *14*(2), 122–141.

Melbourne Polytechnic. (2018). *Cultural Awareness: Intercultural Approach.* https://libguides.melbournepolytechnic.edu.au/culturalawareness/interculturalapproach.

Müller, F., Denk, A., Lubaway, E., Sälzer, C., Kozina, A., Vršnik Perše, T., Rasmusson, M., Jugović, I., Lund Nielsen, B., Rozman, M., Ojsteršek, A., & Jurko, S. (2020). Assessing social, emotional, and intercultural competences of students and school staff: A systematic literature review. *Educational Research Review*, *29*, 100304. https://doi.org/10.1016/j.edurev.2019.100304.

Nathan, G. (2015). A non-essentialist model of culture: Implications of identity, agency and structure within multinational/multicultural organizations. *International Journal of Cross Cultural Management*, *15*(1), 101–124. https://doi.org/10.1177/1470595815572171.

Norberg-Hodge, H. (2022). Localisation: The world beyond capitalism. In S. Alexander, S. Chandrashekeran, & B. Gleeson (Eds.). *Post-Capitalist Futures: Alternatives and Futures: Cultures, Practices, Activism and Utopias* (pp. 129–140). London: Palgrave Macmillan.

Piipponen, O., & Karlsson, L. (2019). Children encountering each other through storytelling: Promoting intercultural learning in schools. *The Journal of Educational Research*, *112*(5), 590–603. https://doi.org/10.1080/00220671.2019.1614514.

Pineda, P., Celis, J., & Rangel, L. (2020). On interculturality and decoloniality: *Sabedores* and government protection of indigenous knowledge in Bacatá schools. *Compare: A Journal of Comparative and International Education*, *50*(8), 1175–1192. https://doi.org/10.1080/03057925.2019.1585758.

Puente-Maxera, F., Méndez-Giménez, A., & Martínez de Ojeda, D. (2020). Games from around the world: Promoting intercultural competence through sport education in secondary school students. *International Journal of Intercultural Relations*, *75*, 23–33. https://doi.org/10.1016/j.ijintrel.2020.01.001.

Skrefsrud, T.-A. (2022). The Buber-Levinas debate on otherness: Reflections on encounters with diversity in school. In H. V. Kleive, J. G. Lillebo, & K.-W. Sather (Eds.), *Møter og mangfold – religion og kultur i historie, samtid og skole [Mother and Diversity – Religion and Culture and History, Time and School]* (pp. 229–247). Oslo: Cappelen Damm Akademisk.

Sorkos, G., & Hajisoteriou, C. (2021). Sustainable intercultural and inclusive education: Teachers' efforts on promoting a combining paradigm. *Pedagogy, Culture & Society*, *29*(4), 517–536. https://doi.org/10.1080/14681366.2020.1765193.

Throne, R. (2019). *Autoethnography and Heuristic Inquiry for Doctoral-Level Researchers: Emerging Research and Opportunities.* Hershey, PA: IGI Global.

Thumvichit, A. (2018). Cultural presentation in Thai secondary school ELT coursebooks: An analysis from intercultural perspectives. *Journal of Education and Training Studies*, *6*(11), 99–112. https://eric.ed.gov/?id=EJ1191645.

Tsang, A. (2022). Examining the relationship between language and cross-cultural encounters: Avenues for promoting intercultural interaction. *Journal of Multilingual and Multicultural Development, 43*(2), 98–110. https://doi.org/10.1080/01434632.2020.1725526.

Warner, D. (1996). Levinas, Buber and the concept of otherness in international relations: A reply to David Campbell. *Millennium: Journal of International Relations, 25*(1), 111–128.

Wigmore, S. (n.d.). *Why did Levinas Consider Buber's Philosophy Insufficient as a Theory of Inter-Personal Encounter?* Unpublished paper. https://www.academia.edu/3299338/Why_Did_Levinas_consider_Bubers_philosophy_insufficient_as_a_theory_of_Inter-personal_Encounter.

Zou, T. X. P., & Yu, J. (2021). Intercultural interactions in Chinese classrooms: A multiple-case study. *Studies in Higher Education, 46*(3), 649–662. https://doi.org/10.1080/03075079.2019.1647415.

6 Interculturality and the university

The case of Jagdish Gundara and the Institute of Education Centre for Intercultural Education (UK)

Gary McCulloch

Introduction

Intercultural education (IE) has attracted a growing literature designed to advocate support for its ideals and aspirations (see, e.g., Woodrow et al., 1997; Jain & Savvides, 2019; Rapanta & Trovao, 2021). Understandably, attention has tended to focus more on the ideals and aspirations associated with IE and examples of its key exponents than on the institutional constraints and challenges that it has faced within the social structures of the modern university. This chapter argues that IE belongs to a range of intellectual and social movements that have been obliged to struggle against the grain of the established structures of higher education, and that this helps to account for the limitations and frustrations of its supporters.

In order to address these constraints, it is important to relate IE to the historical development and institutional structures of the modern university. Following a general discussion of these historical and institutional issues, it focuses on the case of Jagdish Gundara and the Centre for Intercultural Education established at the Institute of Education in London (IOE). The Centre for Intercultural Education was established in 1978 under the leadership of Jagdish Gundara with the aim of cutting across the boundaries of the academy. It is possible to appraise the role played by Gundara himself in developing this new centre, and the distinctive ideals of interculturality that it represented, with the help of archival documents held at the IOE. The chapter examines the approach taken to enhance both research and teaching within the centre. The chapter also analyses the further development and the eventual impact of the centre and its ultimate significance for the social and educational practice of interculturality.

Professor Jagdish Gundara (1938–2016) was a highly distinguished and well-respected figure in the global community of IE. He was born in Nairobi, Kenya, with an intercultural family background, then secured university degrees in the USA, Canada, and the UK, and taught in schools in London, England, based in the Inner London Education Authority (ILEA). He was appointed by the IOE in 1978 to take part in its new centre, initially the Centre for Multicultural Education, and led its further development until his retirement in 2006. In 2000, he was awarded the UNESCO Chair in International Studies and Techer Education, which he held at the IOE. According to the obituary by his colleague Richard

Bourne (2016), "Convivial and mischievous, he was never happier than when fulminating against reactionary idiocy with friends over lunch in Bloomsbury." There is no doubt that Gundara was a worthy model as an exponent and 'proselytiser' of IE.

Studies of his contribution, mainly by those who knew and worked with him, have tended to emphasise his intellectual ideals and aspirations, leading to somewhat idealised and uncritical treatments. For example, Namrata Sharma (2022) concentrates on highlighting his role in making the IOE a national and global space for discussions of multiculturalism and diversity in education, his work in making the IOE an attractive place for colleagues and students interested in broadening the field of intercultural studies, and his 'friendly disposition' which "enhanced the culture of the institution as a vibrant community of local-global scholars" (Sharma, 2022: abstract). Similarly, Bash, Coulby, and colleagues seek to build on Gundara's theoretical and political legacies with little consideration of the position of himself and his centre in an institution of higher education (Bash & Coulby, 2016).

The IOE in London was founded in 1902, originally as the London Day Training College and from the 1930s as part of the University of London (Aldrich & Woodin, 2021). In the 1970s it was by far the largest and most prominent university centre for educational studies in the UK, embracing initial teacher education, postgraduate studies in education, and educational research. Its growth had been underpinned by the development of the 'foundation disciplines' of education, comprising in particular sociology, philosophy, psychology, history, and comparative education (McCulloch & Cowan, 2018: chapter 3), giving it a departmental character based on the disciplines (McCulloch, 2014a). Its physical location in central London gave it access to the heart of political power in nearby Westminster, but also placed it in the midst of the educational, social, and cultural and political problems of an urban environment and a world city. It was largely independent with its own funding and governance until it merged with the neighbouring University College London (UCL) in 2014.

Departments and disciplines

The academic disciplines, and the departments that housed them, assumed their modern form in universities in the 19th century, remaining highly resilient to change in the century that followed (Anderson & Valente, 2002). As Andrew Abbott (2002) has argued, the disciplines were themselves social structures, based on the organisational form of university departments, that have withstood assault for many years. They provide models, images, and social practices of coherent discourses in academia. They also prevent knowledge from becoming too abstract or overwhelming, and thus provide a specific tradition or heritage that can be built on (Abbott, 2002). This is an issue that is also taken up by the cultural historian Peter Burke (2012: especially chapter 6), who points out that a new wave of specialised learned journals in the late 19th century accompanied the separation of disciplines and departments.

In the 19th century, the modern research university became firmly established, first in Germany and the USA and then in the UK. Disciplines became institutionalised in the form of separate university faculties, institutes, or departments. The University of Berlin, founded in 1810, was initially organised into the four faculties of philosophy, theology, law, and medicine, but gradually diversified into institutes in different subjects (Burke, 2012: 168). The key period was 1868–1914, as the new disciplines competed for academic recognition and status within the academy. Specialist journals and societies were also founded in rapid succession in Germany (Ruegg, 2003). In the USA, departments began to diversify in the new universities that were being established. Daniel Coit Gilman, the first president of Johns Hopkins University, founded as the first research university in the US in 1876, announced at his inauguration that the criterion for choosing professors would be their devotion to a particular line of study and their eminence in that speciality (Burke, 2012: 169). In the UK, the civic universities of Leeds, Sheffield, and Manchester became established towards the end of the 19th century, while specialised academic subjects became institutionalised even at the traditional universities of Oxford and Cambridge (McCulloch & Cowan, 2018: 13–14).

Becher and Parry (2005) have also emphasised the endurance of the disciplines. They argue that a discipline has both a cognitive and a social aspect. Social factors include incorporation in a typical academic organisation with the provision of courses from the undergraduate stage to an advanced level, a shared set of cultural values, and recognition by the academy at large. Indeed, they insist, "Only when a scholarly community is deemed intellectually acceptable by its peers, is it qualified to achieve disciplinary status" (Becher & Parry, 2005: 134). Nevertheless, disciplines themselves are not stable or unchanging entities, but are in constant change and flux.

These ingrained departmental and disciplinary structures have enabled the growth of research universities around the world. At the same time, they have tended to inhibit and constrain intellectual approaches that go across established departments and disciplines. Knowledge formations that have cut across the grain of academic structures have included combinations of disciplines and cultures, usually described as multidisciplinary and multicultural. Those that have actively challenged and attempted to change these disciplines and cultures, to go across them in a more fundamental way, can be described as *interdisciplinary* and *intercultural*.

One of the leading theorists in this area is the American scholar Julie Thompson Klein, whose 1990 volume *Interdisciplinarity: History, Theory and Practice* set the tone for much detailed work. According to Klein, a subtle restructuring of knowledge has produced new divisions of intellectual labour, collaborative research, team teaching, hybrid fields comparative studies, increased borrowing across disciplines, and new pressures on the traditional divisions of knowledge. All of these trends, she argues, have encouraged a trend towards unity, synthesis and convergence, and the growth of 'interdisciplinarity'.

The British political scientist Wyn Grant has also analysed this general development. With Greaves, he explores the intellectual and practical challenges involved in working across disciplines, especially in teams and in 'thick' interdisciplinary work across the social and natural sciences, but points out the potential rewards in terms of understanding and responding to the large urgent problems of today such as the environment and climate change (Greaves & Grant, 2010). Both Klein and Grant emphasise, moreover, that interdisciplinarity does not necessarily replace the disciplines but indeed depends on disciplinary knowledge for its further development (see also Weingart, 2010).

In terms of institutional initiatives to challenge established departmental and disciplinary structures, those most commonly favoured have been first to create separate and independent institutions at the university level, and then to establish centres that seek to cut across the demarcation lines characteristic of the modern university.

An example of initiatives to create separate and independent institutions to promote new knowledge formations has been that of liberal arts colleges, originally in the USA. These colleges, drawing on the tradition established by Harvard College from 1636, providing a broad four-year undergraduate degree programme, themselves responded to this situation in a range of ways that highlighted the unresolved tensions around new approaches to the curriculum. There are many examples of intercultural courses being established in such colleges, often for international students (e.g. Lewin, 2009; Nishimura & Sasao, 2019). Some commentators have doubts about the future prospects of the liberal arts colleges (see e.g. Koblik & Graubard, 2017). Others are more optimistic, and indeed the basic model has recently been imitated in other parts of the world such as East Asia (e.g. Jung et al., 2016).

Another approach designed to cut across the established structures of the modern university has been to establish centres on particular topics that can draw on a range of interests and perspectives across university departments. In the UK, a prominent example of this type has been the Centre for Contemporary Cultural Studies (CCCS) at the University of Birmingham, from its origins in 1964 until its closure in 2002. CCCS was an avowedly interdisciplinary project from the beginning, and encountered both opportunities and challenges as a direct result of this. On the one hand, it provided a unique forum for academics, students, and interested colleagues from different backgrounds to address common themes and issues. On the other, as it complained, it confronted "the boundaries between disciplines, the division of labour of intellectual work, the awkward problem of relevance and action which flow from truly critical knowledge, the protocols of good academic manners, and the defence of institutional boundaries" (CCCS, 1971). In 1975 it set up an education subgroup, led by Richard Johnson, and this produced a number of interdisciplinary works including *Unpopular Education* (CCCS, 1981). It also harboured transdisciplinary ambitions from a Marxist stance, involving itself in the student protests of the late 1960s and broad educational campaigns in the late 1970s and early 1980s. However, it struggled to survive in the changing political climate of the 1980s and the departmental culture of the academy and was closed in 2002 (see also McCulloch, 2014b; McCulloch & Cowan, 2018: chapter 7).

In general, therefore, the modern research university has been established with strong boundaries in terms of departments and the disciplines, and approaches to support interdisciplinary and intercultural formations have struggled to develop against the grain of these internal barriers. One strategy that has come into use to overcome this institutional structuring has been the creation of interdisciplinary and interdepartmental centres designed to draw on insights across the institution as a whole. These were themselves often prone to difficulties in prospering and surviving over an extended period. It was this type of strategic development that Jagdish Gundara's centre at the IOE sought to provide from 1978.

Gundara and the Centre for Intercultural Education

Gundara was perceptively aware of the structural characteristics of the IOE as an institution of higher education and also of the strategic positioning of his Centre for Intercultural Education (hereinafter, the Centre). He observed in 2000 that "the Centre was set up to cut across the departmental and disciplinary structures of the Institute" (Gundara, 2000: ix). As he noted, it operated through a mechanism that was intended to attract support from around the IOE, irrespective of departmental and disciplinary affiliations: "It worked horizontally across it with a coordinating committee with senior chairpeople and joint Centre and departmental staff appointments" (Gundara, 2000: ix). This was particularly important in his view because of the unique characteristics of IE itself. According to Gundara (2000: ix):

> Intercultural education as such is not a discrete area of study which is appended to the process of mainstream education. It is part and parcel of the educational process. In fact, the assumption here is that educators need to create a culture of intercultural education to be effective.

Indeed, he argued that the Centre at the IOE was unique in national terms in promoting IE in this way, "far in advance of any other higher education institution" (Gundara, 2000: ix). At the same time, it was susceptible to the structural constraints of the IOE. Thus, he concluded, "Its express purpose was to ensure that issues of multiculturalism and anti-racism were integrally part of this large complex institution organised into departments" (Gundara, 2000: ix).

In order to understand the emphasis placed by Gundara on multiculturalism and anti-racism, it is necessary to recall the reasons for the foundation of the Centre in 1978 and the aspirations that were attached to it. The archive of the IOE is helpful in providing documentary evidence of these, including Gundara's own IOE staff file and files relating to the development of the Centre.

The context was a background of rising concern for the relatively poor levels of educational achievement of ethnic minority children in schools. Since the 1950s, immigration from Commonwealth countries including the Caribbean (West Indies), India, and Pakistan had grown, and this led to increasing numbers of ethnic minority children in schools, especially in urban areas. By the 1970s, there was growing evidence that such children were performing less well than their white counterparts, but there was no single authority with the power to address this situation. The Schools Council for the Curriculum and Examinations, which was responsible for discussions of curriculum change (there was no legal national curriculum until 1988) began to consider how to address this problem, while the Inner London Education Authority (ILEA), with an overview of London schools, took an increasingly strong stance in supporting anti-racist policies in education (see, e.g., Dorn & Troyna, 1982). In 1979, a report was commissioned by the Department of Education and Science to examine the education of children from ethnic minority groups. This produced an interim report in 1981 and eventually led to the Swann Report, *Education for All*, published in 1985 (DES, 1985), by which time relations between ethnic groups in urban areas such as London and Birmingham had worsened with riots in the inner cities (see also, e.g., Grosvenor, 1997; Tomlinson, 2019).

As the main university centre for educational studies and research in the UK, and located in the largest urban area associated with the education of ethnic minority children, the IOE was expected to respond to this situation with research and recommendations of its own. Yet its leaders were uncomfortably aware that it had so far provided little support in this area. A Department of Curriculum Studies had recently been established at the IOE under a recognised authority, Professor Denis Lawton, who had now become the IOE's deputy director, but Lawton admitted candidly that its courses lacked material on multicultural education. Existing topics in curriculum studies, he explained, did not seem to lend themselves to this theme, although he could also point to a number of what he described as 'missed opportunities' (Lawton, 1978). One such was the integration into the curriculum of majority cultures for minority children and aspects of minority cultures for all children. With respect to the existing topic of tradition and change in the curriculum, he noted, "One reason for change in the curriculum is the fact that England is now a multicultural society. This should be analysed and stressed" (Lawton, 1978; see also McCulloch & Cowan, 2018: 40–42).

A working party was set up by the IOE's central academic board in spring 1978 with the aim of examining multicultural education and the issue of racism in schools. This initiative was led by Professor Basil Bernstein, recently awarded the Karl Mannheim chair in the sociology of education. The working party met with all the heads of departments to discuss "the integration of Multi-Cultural Educational practice within departmental teaching". It also met with Local Education Authorities (LEAs) to consider the relationship between LEAs and the IOE's provision for the training of teachers in multicultural practice. The working party noted that there was increasing integration of multicultural practice in secondary school courses, including a section on multicultural issues, and that issues of racism and multicultural educational practice were introduced early in the course, with a doubling of provision for students who wished to take the option of studying multicultural education. It also planned to organise a non-residential staff weekend to discuss the issues involved. It was agreed that these activities had raised the awareness of the working party about the possibilities of multicultural education, and that the extension of practice in this area should be both through departmental practice and research, and the creation of an agency for multicultural education (IOE Working Party, 1978a). Despite this activity, a student committee that had already been formed against racism in schools welcomed the initiative but suggested that it had generally been met with 'negativity and apathy' among staff, and called for an interdisciplinary approach led by the director (IOE Student Committee, 1978).

Bernstein was also concerned to maintain a close connection between the working party and the activities of the ILEA, and to ensure that London teachers and the broader ethnic minority community could be represented. Gundara was brought on to the working party for these reasons. He had been working as a lecturer in further and adult education for the ILEA since 1972, completing a PhD on British extraterritorial jurisdiction in 19th century Zanzibar at the University of Edinburgh in 1975. He was a member of the ILEA/community relations councils consultative committee and was now chairman of this group as well as of a new commission of racial equality education forum (Gundara, 1978). Bernstein invited him to join the working party, and by 1979 he had been appointed to be seconded from the ILEA to coordinate a new Centre for Multi-cultural Education (Bernstein, 1978).

A staff weekend was also organised to take place in October 1978. The purpose of this special meeting was to "*begin* a debate, *among themselves*, that address the issues underlying education in a multicultural society" (IOE Working Party, 1978b). The main speaker to begin the weekend was Peter Newsam, ILEA's education officer on 'Multi-cultural studies and teacher training', chaired by Denis Lawton. A set of discussion groups followed, the first being on organisational structure, administration, and admissions. This recognised that the IOE's departmental structure was a problem: "The main discussion focused around the pervasive departmentalism of the Institute and the constraint this imposes on the kind of multidisciplinary work necessary for an effective programme on multi-cultural education" (IOE Working Party, 1978b). This was regarded as being largely a resources issue, which would lead to drawing on 'over-committed' or 'under-employed' staff. It was noted at another discussion group that there were indeed 'two kinds of multiculturalism' at the IOE, in that it had 400 overseas students from many countries, but many fewer from minority cultures in the UK, although it did not know just how many. Another group considered that a non-departmental appointment might be made to work with the directorate and the new agency. It was finally agreed that the existing institutional structure did not allow critical new issues such as racism in schools to be easily raised. A suitable admissions system was also raised as a difficult issue, with no quota system providing a formal mechanism to address the issues involved. Research, it was found, had so far made only a limited contribution to these problems (IOE Working Party, 1978b).

The working party met again to consider the outcomes of the staff weekend, and it was agreed that a new Centre should be created, to be seen and structured as an agency for change rather than as a self-perpetuating body, with a mechanism to be tied in with departments "to encourage interdisciplinary, interdepartmental study and research in multicultural education" (IOE Working Party, 1978c). It noted also that there were 'no grounds for complacency', and that "we must find means to overcome the inertia which inheres to our own practices" (IOE Working Party, 1978c). Every department would also be expected to critically appraise its own teaching, review its teaching programmes, consider contributions to multicultural education, and discuss proposals for possible interdisciplinary teaching and research in the area, which would include a clear research policy (IOE Working Party, 1978d). Some kinds of research would be department based, while "some kinds especially the kinds that demanded an interdisciplinary approach, could be Centre based" (IOE Working Party, 1978d). Once the research was under way, however, departments could 'appropriate' aspects of the research to develop in their area. It was also proposed that there was a need to make a 'map' of the research going on in the IOE, "to weigh the importance of each; probably to choose priorities by the potential 'spill' of each into other areas" (IOE Centre for MCE, 1979a). At the same time, it was agreed that the Centre should not be attached to any one department, since "such identification might detract from its overall purposes" (IOE Centre for MCE, 1979a). The Centre should have its own physical space, "to exist in a well-defined physical location" and should be involved in teaching at all levels (IOE Centre for MCE, 1979a). Not least, it would also require additional staffing to be attached to the Centre, and an 'annual financial commitment' by the IOE for it to take its involvement in multicultural education seriously (IOE Centre for MCE, 1979b).

It appears from this archival evidence that the Centre was a high-level initiative in response to growing problems around the education of ethnic minority children in London. It began with clear and ambitious objectives to contribute to addressing this issue, and enlisted Gundara to lead the project. However, it was hampered by a departmental and disciplinary structure such as was characteristic of the modern research university. In the end it came to a compromise in which the Centre would be separate from the departments while sharing in the teaching and research. Meanwhile, it remained unclear how to gain staffing, finance, and physical resources that would allow it to make a strong contribution over the longer term.

Conclusions

Ten years later, the Centre reviewed its contribution with an academic plan, and agreed on two key measures for success. First would be "the extent to which the teaching and research of the Institute is now more relevant to the needs of a multicultural society than it was in 1979", and second would be "the national and international cooperation and network of contacts which the centre has been able to build" (IOE Centre for MCE, 1988). It could point to wide-ranging research and funding, contributions to courses, seminars and conferences, and work with teachers and others (IOE Centre for MCE, 1988). In terms of the measures for success proposed in 1998, it was likely to be more successful according to the second kind of measure rather than the first, although its 'relevance', or the nature of its contribution to improving the situation in the schools, was never tested. In the following years, while the title of the Centre was changed from 'multicultural' to 'intercultural', its annual report increasingly consisted of lists of published research by individual staff.

In 2022, the International Centre for Intercultural Studies (ICIS) was launched with the support of the IOE directorate and led by Professor Zhu Hua, aiming to promote "intellectually rigorous, practically relevant and interdisciplinary intercultural studies that advance understanding of the role of culture in society, education and communication and inform intercultural practices and policies" (ICIS, 2022). It was now part of the Department of Culture, Communication and Media in what continued to be a strongly departmental organisation. It emphasised its international links and dialogue with other networks rather than any direct contribution to 'anti-racism' in schools. Further research should help to develop in greater detail the historical contribution of centres of research on interculturality from around the world, like the one discussed in this chapter, in the light of their institutional constraints.

References

Abbott, A. (2002). The disciplines and the future. In S. Brint (Ed.), *The Future of the City of Intellect* (pp. 206–230). Stanford, CA: Stanford University Press.

Aldrich, R., & Woodin, T. (2021). *The UCL Institute of Education: From Training College to Global Institution* (2nd ed.). London: UCL Press.

Anderson, A., & Valente, J. (Eds.). (2002). *Disciplinarity at the Fin de Siecle*. Princeton, NJ: Princeton University Press.

Bash, L., & Coulby, D. (Eds.). (2016). *Establishing a Culture of Intercultural Education: Essays and Papers in Honour of Jagdish Gundara*. Newcastle: Cambridge Scholars Publishing.

Becher, T., & Parry, S. (2005). The endurance of the disciplines. In I. Bleiklie & M. Henkel (Eds.), *Governing Knowledge: A Study of Continuity and Change in Higher Education* (pp. 133–144). Dordrecht: Springer.

Bernstein, B. (1978). Letter to J. Gundara, 26 May (IOE archive, file IE/SFC/B/218).

Bourne, R. (2016). Jagdish Gundara obituary. *The Guardian*, 15 December 2016.

Burke, P. (2012). *The Social History of Knowledge, vol. II: From the Cyclopedie to Wikipedia*. Cambridge: Polity.

CCCS. (1971). *Sixth Annual Report*. Richard Johnson papers, Cadbury Research Library, University of Birmingham.

CCCS. (1981). *Unpopular Education*. London: Hutchinson.

DES. (1985). *Education for All: Education of Children from Ethnic Minority Groups*. London: HMSO.

Dorn, A., & Troyna, B. (1982). Multiracial education and the politics of decision-making. *Oxford Review of Education*, 8(2), 175–185.

Greaves, J., & Grant, W. (2010). Crossing the interdisciplinary divide: Political science and biological science. *Political Studies*, 58, 320–339.

Grosvenor, I. (1997). *Assimilating Identities: Racism and Educational Policy in Post-1945 Britain*. London: Lawrence and Wishart.

Gundara, J. (1978). Curriculum vitae (IOE archive, file IE/SFR/B/218).

Gundara, J. (2000). *Interculturalism, Education and Inclusion*. London: Sage.
ICIS. (2022). IOE website entry. https://www.ucl.ac.uk/ioe/departments-and-centres/centres/international-centre-intercultural-studies.
IOE Centre for MCE. (1979a). Steering committee, minutes of meeting, 15 January, minute 4c, Research (IOE archive, file IE/JGU/3/1/2).
IOE Centre for MCE. (1979b). Memorandum, 'Proposals' (IOE archive, file IE/STR/B/218).
IOE Centre for MCE. (1988). Memorandum, 'Action plan and five-year budget 1988–89 –1992–93' (IOE archive, file IE/JGU/3/1/2).
IOE Student Committee Against Racism in Schools. (1978). Memorandum, 'Proposals for the implementation of multicultural education and anti-racist practices in the University of London Institute of Education', 28 June (IOE archive, file IE/SGR/B/218).
IOE Working Party. (1978a). Report, 'Working party on multi-cultural education and the issue of racism in schools', n.d. [1978] (IOE archive, file IE/SGR/B/218).
IOE Working Party. (1978b). Report, staff weekend, 'Multicultural education: Its implications for the Institute', 13–14 October (IOE archive, file IE/SGR/B/218).
IOE Working Party. (1978c). Minutes of meeting, 19 October, minute 3b (IOE archive, file IE/SGR/B/218).
IOE Working Party. (1978d). Memorandum, 'MCE and problems of racism in schools' (IOE archive, file IE/SGR/B/218).
Jain, P., & Savvides, N. (Eds.). (2019). New perspectives on international, intercultural and global education. *Research Intelligence*, *140*, https://www.bera.ac.uk/publication/autumn-2019.
Jung, I., Nishimura, M., & Sabao, T. (Eds.). (2016). *Liberal Arts Education and Colleges in East Asia*. Dordrecht: Springer.
Klein, J. T. (1990). *Interdisciplinarity: History, Theory, and Practice*. Detroit: Wayne State University Press.
Koblik, S., & Graubard, S. (Eds.). (2017). *Distinctively American: The Residential Liberal Arts Colleges*. New York: Routledge.
Lawton, D. (1978). Memorandum, 'Multicultural education', June 1978 (IOE archive, file IE/SGR/B/218).
Lewin, R. (Ed.). (2009). *The Handbook of Practice and Research in Study Abroad: Higher Education and the Quest for Global Citizenship*. New York: Routledge.
McCulloch, G. (2014a). Birth of a field: George Baron, educational administration and the social sciences in England, 1946–1978. *Journal of Educational Administration and History*, *46*(3), 270–287.
McCulloch, G. (2014b). Interdisciplinarity in action: The centre for contemporary cultural studies, 1964–2002. *Journal of Educational Administration and History*, *46*(2), 160–173.
McCulloch, G., & Cowan, S. (2018). *A Social History of Educational Studies and Research*. London: Routledge.
Nishimura, M., & Sasao, T. (Eds.). (2019). *Doing Liberal Arts Education: The Global Case Studies*. Dordrecht: Springer.
Rapanta, C., & Trovao, S. (2021). Intercultural education for the twenty-first century: A comparative review of research. In F. Marine & M. Vrilki (Eds.), *Dialogue for Intercultural Understanding: Placing Cultural Literacy at the Heart of Learning* (pp. 9–26). Dordrecht: Springer.
Ruegg, W. (2003). *A History of the University in Europe, vol. 3, Universities in the 19th and early 20th Centuries, 1800–1945*. Cambridge: Cambridge University Press.

Sharma, N. (2022). Jagdish Gundara: Broadening the field of intercultural studies at the Institute of Education. *London Review of Education*, *20*(1), 17. https://doi.org/10.14324/LRE.20.1.17.

Tomlinson, S. (2019). *Education and Race from Empire to Brexit*. Bristol: Policy Press.

Weingart, P. (2010). A short history of knowledge formations. In R. Frodeman (Ed.), *Oxford Handbook of Interdisciplinarity* (pp. 3–14). Oxford: Oxford University Press.

Woodrow, D., Knerma, G., Rocha-Trindade, M. B., Campani, G., & Bagley, C. (Eds.). (1997). *Intercultural Education: Theories, Policies and Practices*. London: Routledge.

Part II
Change in the teaching of interculturality

7 Teaching interculturality

Changes in perspective (A story of change)

Robyn Moloney

Introduction

In line with this volume's commitment to portraying multiple perspectives on 'teaching interculturality', this chapter presents an account which is both professional and personal. It tracks my development as a teacher educator in my understanding of interculturality and its place in classrooms. The story features six changes in my pathways. These changes are not always historically discrete but overlapping and shifting. Change and development are essential to a dynamic and flexible approach to the notion of interculturality (Dervin, 2022). In this chapter, I will obliquely answer a number of the key questions asked in this volume, in relation to my context. Namely, how I understand interculturality; how my understanding may differ from, or resemble, the understandings of other scholars; and how I have changed in the way I teach about it.

I see interculturality as an individual and relational developmental process which must be navigated over time through critical reflection in the individual. I see it as core to both children's and teachers' development, and core to my teaching and writing. I see development of interculturality as constructed from 'the inside out' (Gorski, 2012). And yet, while the process may be an individual one, I strongly believe it must result in changed practice in schools and teachers. It must result in teachers with greater critical openness to a diverse classroom, to classroom languages, to tasks which encompass the practices of classroom families, to school cultures which actively embrace the language and cultures of their students (Moloney et al., 2022), to outcomes of greater equity and inclusion, of combatting racism, towards reconciliation, in the Australian context. As an Australian teacher of British settler descent, I recognise that Australia's colonial history is characterised by land dispossession, violence, and racism towards Aboriginal and Torres Strait Islander peoples. Reconciliation is both a personal and political responsibility to create initiatives which build respect and trust between the wider non-Indigenous community and Aboriginal and Torres Strait Islander peoples, in positive two-way relationships. Serious inequities continue to exist for Indigenous peoples in education, health, rates of incarceration, and many other areas.

I write here only of my own experience, I do not speak for all Australians. The development of my understanding of interculturality has been shaped by events in my professional and personal story, and through influential intersections with scholars and their writing. I began my career as a secondary school teacher of foreign languages, teaching French, German, and later Japanese. I was trained in an older pedagogic style, where culture was understood to be 'visible culture' (Lo Bianco & Crozet, 2003) only, such as food and festivals, commonly taught separately to linguistic content.

This split between language and culture, in fact reflected our national approach to multiculturalism in Australia. For many years, our public approach to multiculturalism focused exclusively on the cultures of immigrant groups, frequently excluding Indigenous peoples, and was often directed and voiced by White Australian (most commonly British settler origin) voices of the majority (Hage, 2012), such as myself. Its purpose was to observe and inclusively celebrate the visible culture of immigrant diaspora groups. While this had value in raising public knowledge and exposure, it failed to create any deeper effect. It did not engage the individual in self-reflection, nor result in any deeper critique of the observers' life or of the racism across Australian society. We may have acquired taste for Vietnamese (and many other) foods, but it certainly did not demand any personal adaptation or effort, such as learning the Vietnamese language. Crozet (2008) has commented that Australia's multicultural policies of the late 1970s and 1980s promoted 'difference' in abstract and distant terms at the macro level and failed to support any new patterns for relating across difference on equal terms.

Census data (ABS, 2021; Chik et al., 2018), however, tell us that nearly one in three residents speak a non-English language. In my state, New South Wales, we have annual data which shows the proportion of school students from a language background other than English (LBOTE). We know that the percentage of these multilingual students has grown steadily from 30.1% in 2011 to 37.2% in March 2021, an increase of 7.1 percentage points in ten years (CESE, 2022). The weekend schools, often parent-run, that children attend to learn their community/heritage languages are the single greatest site of language learning in Australia. They have almost no intersection however with school-based formal language teaching (Cruickshank et al., 2020).

I have been guilty of this language myopia myself. As part of the formal school-based language education system, I have myself, until recent years, known very little about either the vast community language field or the rapid growth of Indigenous languages programmes. Indeed, while there are exceptions, schools are overall not a productive environment for language learning. Of the 31% of children who enter the school system with a home language in addition to English, only 5% are studying their language by Year 12 (Cruickshank et al., 2020). There is weak support for formal language learning in schools. Australia ranks second from the bottom of Organization of Economic Development and Cooperation (OECD) countries in the provision and uptake of school language learning. Our poor performance in schools in learning non-English languages was dubbed a 'monolingual mindset' (Clyne, 2008; Hajek & Slaughter, 2014). Even today, it seems we are OK with 'multicultural' but not with 'multilingual'. Australian language teachers need a heroic optimism in this environment. But a new expression of what I understood to be the core meaning of language learning experience was about to change my life.

Change number 1

I was excited when scholars introduced to our syllabuses a new pedagogical approach called 'intercultural' (Liddicoat et al., 2003). This introduced a number of stimulating new ideas: that language and culture are inseparable (Kramsch, 1993, 1995), that culture is ordinary (Williams, 1958), and that language itself is a rich and always changing source of behaviour and curiosity. These were revelations which immediately resonated with me. It gave language teachers and learners a new scope of exciting intercultural enquiry. It supported my understanding that language learning with critical intercultural enquiry, (can) change Australian students' thinking, understanding, and lives. But this necessitated a shift in teacher perspective also to frame a new viewpoint, to ask searching questions which would elicit learner perspectives (Moloney & Harbon, 2010). For example, in a Spanish lesson focused on typical home dialogues around family practice, asking what do you notice here or what would your family do in this situation. Or, perhaps imagining, if e.g. someone called Huiling is coming to visit from Beijing, what things in your home will Huiling find strange. I participated in the initial writing of some sample units of language learning, which illustrated the Intercultural Language Teaching and Learning in Practice Project (now at https://iltlp.unisa.edu.au/). This represented for me a significant new opportunity, as a teacher, to challenge stereotypical thinking, to unseat the taken-for-granted, and to turn the 'culture mirror' on our own assumptions. My passion for this new pedagogy coincided with a personally challenging shift in perspective.

Change number 2

With a newly produced doctorate in intercultural research (Moloney, 2008) I had come to think that I knew a lot about interculturality. For this hubris, I was called to account. My younger daughter went to Western Australia (WA) as an anthropologist and married an Indigenous Australian. My husband and I travelled for the first time to WA to a very small remote town to meet his family. Coming from the northern suburbs of Sydney, we had met very few Indigenous people. In 'my own' country (but in fact on a particular Country which was not my own), I experienced culture shock equal or greater to that of any young exchange student going overseas. I didn't communicate or understand things well, I didn't know how to act, in the heat, and the red earth 'emptiness'. The only way to learn and adapt was to sit and listen to a yarn (a chat), to understand the slower pace and the life there. The extended family was patient with me. There were plenty of new things to learn about myself from that family's perceptions. I learnt I was an East-Coast Australian, White, relatively rich, with much higher expectations of public education, health and justice systems than those of Indigenous people. I met members of the Stolen Generations, the family connections to the real-life young girls in the *Rabbit Proof*

Fence book (Pilkington, 1996) and film (Noyce, 2002). The Stolen Generations are the Indigenous children removed forcibly from their families by the Australian federal and state government agencies and church missions, between 1910 and 1970. In some regions, up to 30% of Indigenous children were taken. My time in remote WA was a watershed experience in understanding my abject failure to have personally engaged with the Reconciliation movement in Australia, to actively recognise the injustice and inequities evident in almost all aspects of Indigenous life in Australia.

The privilege of this experience further sharpened my understanding of the absolute need for self-knowledge and reflection as part of intercultural discovery. Without it, there seemed to be no capacity for change. I was frustrated to find that many language teachers still clung to the old models. Teachers still pushed back against the involvement of the self and the local (teachers would ask me, "Why would I include Australia, when I am teaching about France?"). I was pleased that some school textbook publishers were producing new language textbooks with an explicit intercultural approach (for example Burrows et al., 2019). And yet some teachers continued to teach 'culture' as fixed stereotypes of the language's country, with the dead-end focus on 'difference' (Dervin, 2016) which reinforced stereotypes and prejudice. Was it fear of personal involvement, anxiety about handling classroom discussions, or too rigid understandings of professional responsibility?

Moving from the classroom to a tertiary position in language teacher education, I embarked on a ten-year research crusade 2009–2018 investigating intercultural learning in classroom learners, teachers, and preservice teachers (Moloney & Harbon, 2010; Moloney, 2013; Moloney & Oguro, 2015; Moloney et al., 2016; Moloney & Xu, 2016, 2018). I spoke at conferences and to teacher groups, and searched for models which would speak to the Australian context. Intercultural research was exploding, burgeoning with multiple definitions of intercultural competence, multiple studies globally all trying to follow what had been largely a European-dominated discourse. I struggled to apply and make meaning of the very worthy models to the Australian context. My development, like all good research and writing, stands on the shoulders of others. I engaged with wide reading and appreciated the diverse philosophical and political approaches. I owe a debt of gratitude to Dervin's (2016) writing, which brought a fresh critical perspective to the field. I related to Dervin's inclusion of the learning role of failure in intercultural experience, and an honesty in declaring a growing fatigue with terminology which was losing its meaning.

In the bigger picture however, a change was brewing. The potential of a critical intercultural approach was starting to be recognised as an educationally valuable activity across the curriculum, to build civic tolerance and anti-racism, in a country with a history of dispossession and frequent incidence of racism in schools (Forrest et al., 2016; Mansouri & Jenkins, 2010).

Change number 3

A new Australian Curriculum (ACARA, 2014) established the place of intercultural understanding (IU) as a general capability across the curriculum. This lifted intercultural out of the language education context and placed it in the school as a whole. It meant that all teachers need to engage with intercultural understanding as a general learning capability for all students in all learning areas: creative arts, English, geography, languages, mathematics, personal health, social studies, science. I understood that this placed 'intercultural' as part of a much bigger picture, a much bigger challenge. It positioned it as a concern of whole school culture. Called into question, for example, were the invisible everyday acts, rituals, exclusions, and taken-for-granted practice in schools.

The rationale for this curriculum shift was also mindful of the evidence of racism in Australian schools (Edgeworth & Santoro, 2015; Walton et al., 2013). It has been observed that school cultures can undermine teachers' confidence to manage cultural diversity even when they have the interest and desire to do so (Page et al., 2020). However, like the language teachers before them, it became evident quite quickly that many teachers had no idea how to implement the IU capability within their teaching. There has been an increasing number of calls for intercultural professional development for teachers to be recognised within Australia's broader movement towards reconciliation (Lowe et al., 2021).

To address school culture, we need an integrated holistic approach to interculturality which is reflective and courageous across a whole-school environment (Ohi et al., 2019). Research has shown that it is of limited value to train only a small number of teachers from a school. To achieve a longer-term effect, you have to capture the imagination of an entire staff, and set in motion a whole-school momentum of inclusion and embrace of student and staff languages and cultures, in the classroom, staffroom, and playground. I was excited by this much bigger challenge to impact teacher interculturality within the whole-school culture.

Change number 4

Leaving my language teacher educator identity, I embraced this new scenario, the need for whole-school professional development (PD) in the intercultural understanding capability of the curriculum. In 2018–2019, with colleagues, I designed and delivered a teacher PD course in five Sydney schools. We collected both quantitative and qualitative data relating to the teachers' response (for full details of the course, please see Moloney et al., 2022). We devised a process model for the PD of reflection, dialogue, scaffolding, creation, implementation, and follow-up reflection and dialogue.

We 'taught' teachers about interculturality by allowing them to access their own raw material of personal interculturality. I told a little of my own story, as a model, and then asked teachers to quietly reflect and optionally share their stories of small or large moments of intercultural learning. These are the experiences which we aim to create in small ways in classrooms. We need to create opportunities for asking 'what do you notice?', to stimulate small self-discoveries, in lessons, units, on the playground, at school assemblies, and so on. The process became a catalyst for creative thinking in pedagogy and in their critical vision of their school. But new pedagogy needs scaffolding and many examples of practice.

We offered the teachers many examples of new ways to represent the multilingualism of a school; to new ways of using the playground, surfaces, gardens, corridors. We offered teachers examples of simple ways to interculturalise units of work, to introduce multilingual projects, to play with the languages present in the school. We asked all teachers, in small groups, to design small projects for their class or the wider school. We went back after ten weeks to hear about the outcomes of the projects.

Even though the project was small in scope, we were pleased that this work appeared to produce significant teacher change and growth, through collaborative design of inclusive projects, involving students' diverse knowledges, languages, and families across the curriculum. The teachers showed surprise in their new critical awareness of building whole-school culture. Many of the teachers (but not all) got beyond a focus on difference and were able to dig deep in reappraising themselves and their school environment.

As an aside, in one of the five schools I was particularly impressed with something extra that appeared to be going on in relation to the languages within the school. As a school in the state of New South Wales, where only 23% of primary children are learning a non-English language (Chik, 2021), it was unusual. Every child in the school is involved in one or more options: to learn in a Korean immersion programme, to learn their community language, an additional foreign language, or to add English to their language repertoire. Regardless of whether staff were mono- or multilingual, every staff member was invested in the school's robust language education and had learnt to harness it as an active component of identity and learning in the school. Teachers told us that their attitudes and behaviour had been changed by the linguistic culture of the school. There seemed to exist an 'interculturality of language' (established long before our arrival), which seemed to act as catalyst for a very strong response to our PD programme (see Chapter 7 of Moloney et al., 2022). What was going on in this school?

Change number 5

At the same time as the five-school project I was also involved in collecting narratives for a book which investigated the relationship between language, religion, and spirituality (Moloney & Mansour, 2022). I was privileged to interview a number of teachers of Indigenous languages. These teachers had a very embodied, empowered perception of language within children's identity and education. These teachers' perceptions provided a new catalyst for thinking about interculturality, which intersected with the 'something special' which I had seen going on in the aforementioned language-aware school. Language diversity in these contexts was not about difference, but about affirmation and commonality, a catalyst for self-knowledge:

> Language is about what connects us, not what sets us apart.
> (Aunty Louise Campbell, Stolen Generation, 2022)

I reckon it's the best form of Reconciliation, sharing and learning about one another's languages. Learning that not everybody's language and culture are the same. ... helps them become a better human being.

(McNaboe, 2022)

I was particularly struck when Nathan Schreiber, an Indigenous teacher of Gunggay language at the Yarrabah State school, a small school north of Cairns, Queensland, told me:

I believe that learning language is building them from the inside out. ... the rest of the curriculum is building them from the outside in. But language is giving them identity and inner strength. I think the better they learn language, the better they can learn other things too.

(Schreiber, 2022)

These perceptions and interactions caused me to take a fresh look at language diversity and multilingualism as part of the bigger picture of interculturality in the Australian school context. I joined the dots between community languages, Indigenous languages, and school-taught languages to realise that there was an extraordinary fabric of extensive language knowledge across Australian schools. Could the interculturality shaped by linguistic diversity seen in the teachers of that Sydney school be more widely harnessed? I am with Dervin when he suggests that "we need to 're-think' Intercultural Competence frequently" (Dervin, 2020: 57).

In the aforementioned school research, I saw the impact on teachers of belonging to a school which was rich in languages education and multilingual identities. It seemed that critical and creative awareness of linguistic diversity may shape the identity and practice of all teachers and students within the school. If we could harness linguistic diversity, could this represent a catalyst in teacher interculturality in the Australian context? Could we raise critical language awareness in young teachers, towards impacting future leadership and staff in rural and urban Australian schools? This has brought me to my current change, the last one for this chapter.

Change number 6

I continue to want to explore interculturality as a developmental concept (from the inside out): a personal learning process which challenges the status quo in pedagogy and school culture, and which must act as a catalyst for wellbeing and critical learning abilities. I want to continue to challenge teachers' abilities to engage with the other, and the self, with empathy, respect, and curiosity, through challenging processes of perspective change. But I am currently asking, can this be done in Australia through greater engagement with linguistic diversity?

In the often monolingual-mindset, language-phobic Australian context, this direction may be risky. Language-anxious teachers and school principals may push back. Change is always risky! But I am encouraged that new perspectives will emerge. Dervin (2022: xi) has written: "As a complex 'chest of drawers', every time I open a new drawer of interculturality, new ones appear again and again ... Opening a new drawer, we must think and rethink interculturality all the time, making the notion really intercultural!"

In proposing to investigate interculturality within Australian schools' multilingualism, I have opened a new drawer, a new intercultural space in my educational context. I do not exactly know what I will find there or what it will contain. But I am setting out with colleagues to write a book about harnessing linguistic diversity in schools, as a fundamental intercultural educational resource and catalyst, towards supporting wellbeing and academic achievement in all students. To achieve this, we need to create language awareness in all teachers and students as part of an ongoing movement towards combatting racism, towards inclusion and reconciliation. In this context, teacher interculturality becomes not an option but a necessity (Alvarez Valdivia & González Montoto, 2018).

My story of progressive changes in understanding interculturality resonates with Dervin's perceptions when he notes his advice to students: "Accept and promote change and transformation. Consider every encounter as an opportunity to change" (Dervin, 2022: xii). It is a necessary element of my never-finished journey, not just to do new projects, but to be critically aware of direction and to examine change, as "doing, uttering and problematizing change together constitute interculturality" (Dervin, 2022: xiii).

References

Australian Bureau of Statistics. (2021). *2021 Census Quickstats*. Retrieved August 1, 2022, from https://www.abs.gov.au/census/find-census-data/quickstats/2021/AUS.

Australian Curriculum, Assessment and Reporting Authority (ACARA). (2014). *Intercultural Understanding* (Version 8.4). Retrieved August 2, 2022, from https://www.australiancurriculum.edu.au/f-10-curriculum/general-capabilities/intercultural-understanding/.

Álvarez Valdivia, I. M., & González Montoto, I. (2018). Teachers' intercultural competence: A requirement or an option in a culturally diverse classroom? *International Journal of Inclusive Education*, 22(5), 510–526.

Burrows, Y., Glynn, J., Nichols, J., Abe, N. F., Nishimura-Parke, Y., Bignell, J., & Perrin, J. (2019). *Ii tomo*. Melbourne: Pearson Australia.

Campbell, L. (2022). Language is about what connects us, not what sets us apart. In R. Moloney & S. Mansour (Eds.), *Language and Spirit: Exploring Languages, Religion and Spirituality in Australia Today*. London: Palgrave Macmillan.

CESE (Centre for Education Statistics and Evaluation). (2022). *Linguistic Diversity in Schools 2021*. Retrieved May 29, 2022, from https://education.nsw.gov.au/about-us/educational-data/cese/publications/statistics/language-diversity-bulletin.

Chik, A. (2021). Conference paper: Societal multilingualism in Sydney: The implications for individual. Conference: The Value of Languages in a Multicultural World 13–15 December, 2021 (online). https://www.multilingualsydney.org/conference-2021.

Chik, A., Benson, P., & Moloney, R. (Eds.). (2018). *Multilingual Sydney*. Abingdon: Routledge.

Clyne, M. (2008). The monolingual mindset as an impediment to the development of plurilingual potential in Australia. *Sociolinguistic Studies, 2*(3), 347–366.

Crozet, C. (2008). Australia's linguistic culture and its impact on languages education. *Babel, 42*(3), 19–24.

Cruickshank, K., Jung, Y. M., & Li, E. B. (2020). *Parallel Lines: Community Languages Schools and Their Role in Growing Languages and Building Communities*. Report, Sydney University.

Dervin, F. (2016). *Interculturality in Education: A Theoretical and Methodological Toolbox*. London: Palgrave Macmillan.

Dervin, F. (2020). Creating and combining models of intercultural competence for teacher education/training: On the need to rethink IC frequently. In F. Dervin, R. Moloney, & A. Simpson (Eds.), *Intercultural Competence in the Work of Teachers: Confronting Ideologies and Practices* (pp. 57–72). Abingdon: Routledge.

Dervin, F. (2022). Foreword. In R. Moloney, M. Lobytsyna, & J. DeNobile (Eds.), *Interculturality in Schools: Practice and Research* (pp. x–xv). Abingdon: Routledge.

Edgeworth, K., & Santoro, N. (2015). A pedagogy of belonging: Troubling encounters with ethnic and religious difference. *Cambridge Journal of Education, 45*(4), 415–426.

Forrest, J., Lean, G., & Dunn, K. (2016). Challenging racism through schools: Teacher attitudes to cultural diversity and multicultural education in Sydney, Australia. *Race, Ethnicity and Education, 19*(3), 618–638.

Gorski, P. (2012). Equity and social justice from the inside-out: Ten commitments for intercultural educators. In N. Palaiologou & G. Dietz (Eds.), *Mapping the Broad Field of Multicultural and Intercultural Education Worldwide: Towards the Development of a New Citizen* (pp. 388–401). Newcastle: Cambridge Scholars Publishing.

Hage, G. (2012). *White Nation: Fantasies of White Supremacy in a Multicultural Society*. Abingdon: Routledge.

Hajek, J., & Slaughter, Y. (Eds.). (2014). *Challenging the Monolingual Mindset*. Clevedon: Multilingual Matters.

Kramsch, C. (1993). *Context and Culture in Language Teaching*. Oxford: Oxford University Press.

Kramsch, C. (1995). The cultural component of language teaching. *Language, Culture and Curriculum, 8*(2), 83–92.

Liddicoat, A. J., Papademetre, L., Scarino, A., & Kohler, M. (2003). *Report on Intercultural Language Learning*. Canberra: Commonwealth of Australia.

Lo Bianco, J., & Crozet, C. (2003). *Teaching Invisible Culture: Classroom Practice and Theory*. Melbourne: Language Australia.

Lowe, K., Skrebneva, I., Burgess, C., Harrison, N., & Vass, G. (2021). Towards an Australian model of culturally nourishing schooling. *Journal of Curriculum Studies, 53*(4), 467–481.

Mansouri, F., & Jenkins, L. (2010). Schools as sites of race relations and intercultural tension. *Australian Journal of Teacher Education (Online), 35*(7), 93–108.

McNaboe, D. (2022). Narrative. In R. Moloney & S. Mansour (Eds.), *Language and Spirit: Exploring Languages, Religion and Spirituality in Australia Today*. London: Palgrave Macmillan.

Moloney, R. (2008). *Young Language Learners and Their Intercultural Competence: An Immersion Classroom Case Study*. Chisinau: VDM Verlag Dr. Müller.

Moloney, R., & Harbon, L. (2010). Student performance of intercultural language learning. *Electronic Journal of Foreign Language Teaching, 7*(2), 177–192.

Moloney, R., Harbon, L., & Fielding, R. (2016). An interactive, co-constructed approach to the development of intercultural understanding in pre-service language teachers. In F. Dervin & Z. Gross (Eds.), *Intercultural Competence in Education: Alternative Approaches for Different Times* (pp. 185–213). London: Palgrave Macmillan.

Moloney, R., Lobytsyna, M., & De Nobile, J. (2022). *Interculturality in Schools: Practice and Research*. London: Routledge.

Moloney, R., & Mansour, S. (Eds.). (2022). *Language and Spirit: Exploring Languages, Religions and Spirituality in Australia Today*. London: Palgrave Macmillan.

Moloney, R., & Oguro, S. (2015). The effect of intercultural narrative reflection in shaping pre-service teachers' future practice. *Reflective Practice*, *16*(1), 96–108.

Moloney, R., & Xu, H. L. (Eds.). (2016). *Exploring Innovative Pedagogy in the Teaching and Learning of Chinese as a Foreign Language*. London: Springer.

Moloney, R., & Xu, H. L. (2018). *Teaching and Learning Chinese in Schools: Case Studies in Quality Language Education*. London: Springer.

Moloney, R. A. (2013). Providing a bridge to intercultural pedagogy for native speaker teachers of Chinese in Australia. *Language, Culture and Curriculum*, *26*(3), 213–228.

Noyce, P. (2002). *Rabbit Proof Fence* (film).

Ohi, S., O'Mara, J., Arber, R., Hartung, C., Shaw, G., & Halse, C. (2019). Interrogating the promise of a whole-school approach to intercultural education: An Australian investigation. *European Educational Research Journal EERJ*, *18*(2), 234–247.

Page, S., Holt, L., & Thorpe, K. (2020). Fostering Indigenous intercultural ability during and beyond initial teacher education. In F. Dervin, R. Moloney, & A. Simpson (Eds.), *Intercultural Competence in the Work of Teachers: Confronting Ideologies and Practices* (pp. 237–254). Abingdon: Routledge.

Pilkington, D. G. (1996). *Follow the Rabbit Proof Fence*. St Lucia: University of Queensland Press.

Schreiber, N. (2022). In R. Moloney & S. Mansour (Eds.), *Language and Spirit: Exploring Languages, Religion and Spirituality in Australia Today*. London: Palgrave Macmillan.

Walton, J. Priest, N., & Paradies, Y. (2013). Identifying and developing effective approaches to foster intercultural understanding in schools. *Intercultural Education*, *24*(3), 181–194.

Williams, R. (1958). *Culture is Ordinary*. Reprinted in A. Gray & J. McGuigan (Eds.), *Studying Culture* (pp. 5–14). London: Edward Arnold.

8 Is there any communication that isn't intercultural?

Etta Kralovec

I'd like to start by confessing to being an interloper in conversations about interculturality. I am a teacher educator, and my field does not typically use the term. My perspective comes from my 50-year career as an educator and I root my analysis in the classroom, where, I would argue, every communication is an intercultural communication. I began my career as an educator in the early 1970s in Laguna Beach, a wealthy beach community in Southern California (USA). At the time, the field of teacher education was dominated by the ideas of multicultural education, and I considered myself a multiculturalist, someone who saw the need for a curriculum beyond the literary and historical canon that existed at the time. I taught Minority Voices, a class that introduced the literary works of Latinos, Blacks, and Native Americans.

When I went to Columbia University to earn a doctorate in philosophy, I was in classes with students from all over the world. In a Hegel class, a student from Haiti took Hegel to task for his misunderstanding of Voodoo. For me, that was the first time I heard an unsanctioned reading of Hegel, a questioning of his world view. For me, this was the first time that knowledge beyond the West was displayed in a classroom. I came to see that the Western philosophical canon, like the literary canon, was limited and narrow. There I studied with Foucault and Derrida and learned that truth wasn't truth after all, but historically contingent.

A Fulbright scholarship in Zimbabwe helped me to understand the post-colonial experience of young Africans who were preparing to be teachers. My students and I coauthored a book, *Identity in Metamorphosis* (Kralovec & Chitiyo, 2009), in which the students shared the tensions that exist between traditional culture and Western culture, the relationship of language to culture, and their hopes for the future. It was there that the dean said to me, "University students are the same around the world; some work hard, some party hard, some cheat, some excel." He also said to me that I couldn't meet a study group at 1:00 pm, because that was lunch time in 'his traditional culture'. It was then that I became confused; my students talked about traditional culture before colonisation, and here the dean was talking about traditional culture as the British culture.

Now certainly, this was an intercultural experience, but had I not done the deep dive with the students that writing a book entailed. I would have probably been like other visiting scholars, intent on bringing my knowledge to the

DOI: 10.4324/9781003345275-10

students, yet failing to understand who my students were. When I returned, I studied post-colonial theory to try to understand the experience I had had in Zimbabwe, *looking through the lens of Said (1978), who asks who is the other; Spivak (1994), who asks if the subaltern can speak; and Bhabha (1994), who asks where the location of culture is.* From engaging with this work, I now saw the dean's call for me to respect the 'traditional culture' as an instance of what Bhabha calls mimicry. For Bhabha, mimicry appears when members of a colonised society imitate and take on the culture of the colonisers. Bhabha is notorious for his use of new concepts and language, he wants us to see that "the meaning and symbols of culture have no primordial unity or fixity" (1994: 29). I was drawn to this work because it brought my work in Zimbabwe into a different focus, but most importantly it frees culture from its frozen state. Being a student of post-colonial studies has reshaped my understandings of intercultural. When I taught Minority Voices, I thought of cultures as fixed, rooted in history, ethnicity, race, and geography. I now understand that intercultural is that space where cultures meet and reshape themselves in the process, that Third Space that Bhabha defines.

I moved on to teach at the University of Arizona; my campus is five miles from the Mexican border and sits next to a major military installation. I came to see my challenge as, first, understanding the cultures that my students represented, and being on the border, that meant for me learning about Mexican culture. Being next to a military base meant we had many veterans in our teach preparation programme. I gradually came to see that the simple categorising of students by 'cultures' wasn't easy. My students sat at the intersection of many cultures: *military culture, Mexican culture, gay culture, border culture, student culture, Mormon culture.*

As I said, in my field, teacher education, we don't typically use the term interculturality. But as someone trained in philosophy, I must question what interculturality and culture itself mean in this phrasing. In philosophy we use the term *intersubjectivity* and focus on its role in creating meaning. I get that. But interculturality adds a messiness: What culture do I manifest? What is the relationship of the individual to their culture? Can we pick our culture? What is culture if not fixed? In the context of Zimbabwe, interculturality was clear to me, yet the 'culture' of my students in Zimbabwe was not evident. Some embraced Western cultural forms, as did their parents. They were as British as any students studying for international exams. Yet the traditional culture they referred to had been suppressed and, in some cases, erased.

As for the problem of 'interculturalising the intercultural' proposed by Fred Dervin (see, e.g., Dervin & Jacobsson, 2022; Dervin, 2022) and making space for a more inclusive understanding of the intercultural, we have to confront the hegemony of the Western intellectual traditions, starting with metaphysics. For Derrida (1982: 216):

> Metaphysics – the white mythology which resembles and reflects the culture of the West: the white man takes his own mythology, Indo-European

Is there any communication that isn't intercultural? 113

mythology, his own logos, that is the mythos of his idiom, for the universal form of that he must still wish to call Reason.

Why does Derrida insert race into this definition? And why does Derrida call metaphysics, the branch of philosophy born in ancient Greece, a white mythology? Thinking back to the Haitian student in my Hegel class, her questions were really challenging the very definition of reason that Hegel was after and I now know – so do post-colonialists. Does this definition of metaphysics help us understand why the idea of 'interculturalising intercultural' faces enormous challenges? We are forced to confront the power relations that exist between cultures. Can we, in the 21st century, still think that the very definition of reason belongs to one culture alone?

Our history is not filled with examples of intercultural understandings but rather of the colonial repression of one culture by another. But do we have examples of interculturalising interculturality? Do we have spaces where the historic repressions of cultures give way to a forum for the creation of meaning, the negotiation of power, a space where the subaltern can speak a truth that goes against the white mythology that dominates contemporary academic thought? As Fanon (2004) reminds us, power is never given up without a fight. And in the US, our culture wars wage around whose history will be taught; the battles around critical race theory in my country should alert us to the fight that ensues when there are calls for a reinterpretation of our history.

All that said, the 21st century presents different challenges we face when we try to enter the world as interculturalists. For one, we live in a media-saturated world, that bombards us with global 'imaginaries' about nations, cultures, and religions. As intercultural teachers, we must first interrogate the imaginaries that we bring into our classrooms.

I have come to think that we don't teach *about* interculturality, *we perform interculturality*. By that I mean that interculturality is something we *do*; it is a practice, not a curriculum. Sure, we can have our students read diverse authors about their lived experience, show our students films about different cultures; we can teach language and provide international exchange programmes, and present alternative interpretations of history that broaden our students thinking about the world. *But doing interculturality requires something different.*

Doing interculturality begins with an interrogation of identity that a teacher must engage in. As teachers, we need to know who we are, what privileges we bring into the classroom, and what assumptions we have about who our students are. Any exploration of identity is difficult, requiring self-reflection and honesty about how we benefit from the power structures in our society. We have to confront how our authority as 'teachers' shapes our students' ability to open up to us in authentic ways and to learn from us.

Doing interculturality means we need to understand who our students are, how they interpret and give meaning to their lived experience. For me, it means we need to create an intersubjective space where we come to know each other. The book project in Zimbabwe was such a space. We all had a common goal; the student editors were free to challenge ideas and move the book in new directions. There were no grades, no right or wrong, just a book to get out. But our classrooms are places where power is embedded in the teacher. Doing interculturality means we have to know and understand our students' cultures.

This brings us to the question of the problems related to teaching interculturality that need to be solved. For me, this raises the prior question of the purposes of education. Education has been seen as a way for a society to bring the young into becoming functioning members of the society, which includes inculcation of the 'national culture'. This idea that schools are an instrument of the state and serves state interests is generally agreed upon, at least in the US, where we salute the flag at the start of each school day and where state legislators are responsible for making decisions about school curriculum and select school textbooks. It is why American exceptionalism is taught in schools and why we are currently fighting culture wars over critical race theory. It is why transgender youth are banned from sports teams and why Florida is trying to ban the use of the term 'gay' in schools. In my country, the teacher must uphold the 'national narrative' or face losing their job. At its root, this is the fight in Tucson (Arizona) over ethnic studies, an interdisciplinary study of difference and power. In Tucson, high school ethnic studies programmes are credited with providing Latino students with their own history and explorations of their own cultural identity. The programme was outlawed by the governor and has been tied up in courts for over ten years. This may be an extreme example of a problem related to the teaching of interculturality, but it highlights just what teachers are up against when their classrooms become a site for intercultural exploration.

I would like to pose a few provocative questions: If intercultural is something we *do* rather than teach, is there any teaching that isn't intercultural? And for fun, could we say, is there any interaction that isn't intercultural? And what about the very term *culture*? Whose interests are served in the calls for cultural purity? 'France for the French.' What social order are those calls holding up? Has the very term culture been called into question with its deep roots in our colonial past and the racism that helped spawn the field of anthropology? And what about TikTok/Douyin and Twitter? Are those cultures? If so, how do they challenge our ideas of culture? The use of social media is one place where parents and their children collide, and I suspect this transcends cultures. It may have more to do with our intuitions that our children are entering a different world than ours.

And when I think about what I want my students to learn I think, 'What do students need to learn *at this moment in time*?' And this is no ordinary moment in time. The last time there was a worldwide pandemic, WWI was ending. We have flipped that and now we have the COVID-19 pandemic and WWIII might begin. And as we academics tweak our syllabi and fight with students over course assignments, the world burns. And what about our burning earth? Environmental destruction defies our boundaries of borders, cultures, language, and religion. There are no cultural differences when we are fleeing from a wildfire or trying to outrun a storm. The very term *interculture* compels us to look for difference. I suspect history will eventually have us focused on our similarities rather than differences as we try to solve the profound problems we face as a planet.

I don't want to end on this very depressing thought, so let's go back to the problems of the intercultural. In the US, the intercultural is often code for racial differences. We are a country with a violent history of slavery, with a racist past and present. In the 1950s and '60s when the US was rocked with race wars, and our society seemed to be coming apart at the seams, the compelling question being asked was, How do we solve the race problem in America with its roots in slavery? Robert Hutchins, president of the University of Chicago, one of the most prestigious institutions in the US, and a vocal public intellectual, had this to offer: "The race problem in America will be solved in the bedroom." Aside from being provocative, which he was well-known for, Hutchins was alluding to that intersubjective space where we negotiate meaning beyond our cultural imaginaries and confront another human being who we are reaching out to for connection. I would argue that should be our practice in *all* our communications, whether we are in the bedroom or the classroom.

References

Bhabha, H. (1994). *The Location of Culture*. New York: Routledge.
Derrida, J. (1982). *White Mythology: Metaphor in the Text of Philosophy*. Sussex: Harvester Press.
Dervin, F. (2022). *Fragments in Interculturality: A Reflexive Approach*. Singapore: Springer.
Dervin, F., & Jacobsson, A. (2022). *Intercultural Communication Education: Broken Realities and Rebellious Realities*. Singapore: Springer.
Fanon, F. (2004). *The Wretched of the Earth*. New York: Grove Press.
Kralovec, E., & Chitiyo, M. (2009). *Identity in Metamorphosis: An Anthology of Writings from Zimbabwe Students*. New York: Nova Science Publishers.
Said, E. (1978). *Orientalism*. New York: Pantheon Books.
Spivak, C. (1994). *Can the Subaltern Speak?* New York: Routledge.

9 Interculturality-as-altering

Observality as a method for 'silent' reflexivity and criticality

Ning Chen and Fred Dervin

On the need to observe interculturality

This chapter recommends preparing students for observing interculturality as an object of research and education. We problematise observing under the neologism of *observality* for 'silent' reflexivity and criticality. Observality refers to the complex chain of observations that goes hand in hand with interculturality: from the position of the observed to that of the observer and back. Our discussion of observality is aimed at educators but also scholars and students in higher education who wish to complement and enrich their take on interculturality from a more personal perspective, urging them to let their 'eyes laugh' (as the Chinese idiom has it: 眉开眼笑, méi kāi yǎn xiào, brows raised in delight, meaning 'beaming with joy'), to take pleasure in the polysemy and complexities of interculturality and move away from one-sided conceptualisations. Surprisingly today's literature is somehow 'quiet' about the importance of observation in relation to interculturality. There have been exceptions in the past, especially in relation to the use of ethnography for (language and) interculturality in education (e.g. Byram & Fleming, 1998; Roberts et al., 2000; Dervin & Fracchiolla, 2012; see Hua, 2015). However, observing was problematised in somewhat crude ways and it seemed to serve the purpose of confirming certain (dominating) ideologies of interculturality, e.g. around the problematic concept of 'culture', rather than leading learners to reflect deeply on the real complexities of the notion. The work of Adrian Holliday (e.g. 2022), where narrative and observation take centre stage, could be an exception here, although his take on interculturality is clearly positioned within Western non-essentialism – thus orienting observation towards specific ideologemes, training the eyes of the observer to 'see' in prefabricated ways.

Our chapter starts from the argument that we all face, experience, and practice the different facets of observality on a daily basis – we repeat: *all of us*! We observe the other, ourselves, and other (non-)living things, as well as the complex intersections between all these elements. We argue that the ways we have been made to consider, think about, and believe in the notion, do influence our take on observing interculturality, and, sometimes, prevent us from seeing beyond these 'veils'.

DOI: 10.4324/9781003345275-11

In the chapter we discuss the power of practising observality for 'silent' reflexivity and criticality for interculturality. We argue that observation allows us to slow down and to take a break from the 'known', the 'taken-for-granted' of interculturality; to test things for ourselves; *to think, unthink, rethink, do, undo and redo*; to look at ourselves, those around us, our worlds, and the ideologies that we are being fed with, from a distance, while always remaining in close proximity – all these happening in a never-ending process. In a world of overcommunication where we are forced/force ourselves to produce words and pictures, and consume them, moments of pause are important to reflect and be critical of both the results of our reflections and of our criticality. The chapter does not propose a practical guide for observing interculturality. Neither do we intend to 'lecture' our readers about what interculturality is (not). We simply suggest taking time regularly for ourselves, based on observality to do what Canetti (1989: 61) recommends: "Think a lot. Read a lot. Write a lot. Speak your mind about everything, but silently." *Silently* here refers to *'silencing' the current noise* about interculturality around us; to reconsider what we hear, see and experience about it, the multiple and yet singular ideologies, the sense of stability and logic that we have created around it – soaking in new sounds, colours, flavours ... and as we shall see, mostly importantly, *to change*.

Interculturality-as-altering in research and education

In what follows we explore the idea of *interculturality-as-altering* as a proposal to deal with interculturality as a fluid object of research and education that could be the focus of observality. The idea of interculturality-as-altering is a multiple tautology, i.e. it repeats the same idea several times, and this idea is that of *change*. This tautology is deemed necessary here to both indicate the centrality of change and the specific position that we take on interculturality here (see also Moloney, Chapter 7, this volume, about change). In the very word interculturality, change is contained in each component of the word: *inter-* (co-constructing in-between people, experiencing clashes, fusions, (polite) rebuttals), *culture* (understood here through its 'former' Chinese equivalent as change happening between us when we interact; see Fang, 2019), and *-ality* (a never-ending process of change). Altering represents another layer of the change tautology. We chose specifically the verb *to alter* based on its etymology. From Latin *alter* (the other of the two) and based on the Proto-Indo European root *al-* for beyond and the comparative suffix *-ter*, 'to alter' refers to becoming otherwise, to make different in some way. Its etymology also makes a reference to a central character in interculturality: *the other*.

Interculturality is both alive and fertile. Although we might speak about it as if it were a mere object, it is clear that we will never be able to grab, grasp, and capture the notion. We might have the illusion that we have been able to tame it by using certain ideological constructs or educational objectives and models, however, as soon as we observe what is happening in interaction with others, interculturality escapes us. Change is multifaceted in the thousands of ways of understanding and engaging with interculturality around the world and this is why we argue against solidifying the notion, closing it down in one single definition.

Let us review several aspects of the centrality of *change*. When we experience, consider, and analyse interculturality, what we have been taught, made to believe in; the views and beliefs that we hide *backstage* (which we may not voice in front of others); what we experience and co-construct with others; all the inconsistencies, discontinuities, intersections, and contradictions that this can all trigger necessarily lead us to alter the way we see and talk about the notion *again and again* – even when we resist change. One of the main ways of engaging with interculturality as scholars and educators is to speak/write about the notion. Jumping from one language to another (including *within* one's language, with different interlocutors and in different contexts) urges us to (re)negotiate interculturality, to do, undo, and redo it constantly, im- and explicitly. Through the use of language, which always involves the (in)direct presence of others, we can never set interculturality in stone like a museum piece – we try, but, again, it escapes us as soon as we try to voice it.

Using three Chinese words/phrases related to change, we might find clues as to how change occurs when we engage with interculturality as an object of research and education:

- 化 can translate as 'turn, melt, transform, expend, and change into'. It indicates gradual and subtle change.
- 变 means 'change, become, transform, and vary', pointing at manifest and obvious change.
- 潜移默化 can be translated as 'silent transformations, unknowingly changing'. This idiom from a Confucian scholar reminds us that we go through quiet and unconscious transformations when we experience new things (see Dervin, 2022).

We might also want to add that change can be *underground/silenced*; *faked, used as a way of protecting our face*; *misused and abused*.

With interculturality-as-altering, we propose to prepare students to learn to shift their perspective from viewing interculturality as a 'solid' object of research and education, whereby one adopts a single (imposed) ideological perspective (e.g. (non)essentialism, democratic culture, transcultural), to reconsidering the notion through the principles of *criticality of one's own criticality* (e.g. bearing in mind that non-essentialism is an ideal, accepting and acting upon one's ideological biases), *interculturalising interculturality* (e.g. listening to silenced voices in the field), and *placing the influence of the economic–political* at the centre of one's analyses of interculturality.

Observality for 'silent' reflexivity and criticality

We are natural-born observers. We spend most of our time observing (un)consciously the world around us. Doing observation as part of, e.g., our formal learning experience can be experienced as a daunting experience. We present observality here as a way of liberating ourselves from this fear of a very 'natural' phenomenon. We are not aiming at preparing/training 'ethnographers' here but 'simple' observers working for themselves, in silent dialogues with themselves – a process that we find necessary against the *noisy lack of dialogue around interculturality* today. Since our focus is interculturality-as-altering, we wish to remind readers that the task is in itself idealistic in a sense. *To attempt to catch change is like putting one's hand under a tap to grab hold of water.* Observality is meant to help us 'catch' *snapshots of snapshots of snapshots ...* of change with a view to build up our self-reflection and sense of criticality towards what we do and say; how we understand, explain, and interpret things by being confronted with what we perceive in how interculturality is being discussed and 'done'. Noting change in self and others is central in the process. Observality is not to be considered as a miraculous recipe that will, e.g., make us better at 'doing' interculturality and/or teach us the intricacies of interculturality. This, as many authors in this volume argue, is impossible. As much as one will never be a 'perfect human', one will never be an 'impeccable' interculturalist ... especially in research and education.

This chapter suggests a solitary approach to observation that is personal, for ourselves as individuals who engage with interculturality, so that we can work on our own reflections and critiques 'silently'. There is no other reason than being with oneself here; *it is just a gratuitous activity*. Observality is based on the idea of interculturality-as-altering and is meant to make us aware of and liberate us from some of the ideologies of interculturality that we have been fed with and that we have passed onto others *and* to open up our own eyes and ears to the complex world of interculturality. Nietzsche's (2017: 107) figure of *the wanderer* corresponds somehow to what we suggest here:

> He who has attained the freedom of reason to any extent cannot, for a long time, regard himself otherwise than as a wanderer on the face of the earth – and not even as a traveller towards a final goal, for there is no such thing. But he certainly wants to observe and keep his eyes open to whatever actually happens in the world; therefore he cannot attach his heart too firmly to anything individual; he must have in himself something wandering that takes pleasure in change and transitoriness.

The philosopher uses important keywords that comfort the idea of interculturality-as-altering and the support that observality can provide: *keeping one's eyes open*; *avoiding attaching one's heart too firmly to anything individual*; *taking pleasure in change and transitoriness*. These require having doubts and asking questions as well as surveying/studying ourselves in the processes of observation. Since our senses are guided by previous experiences, habits, and ideological orders that have been passed onto us, we also need to observe these elements. All in all, we argue that observality can help us feel more at ease with multifaceted change in us and others in relation to interculturality.

It is important to clarify again that observality refers to the multiple cases of observation that we face in everyday situations, which lead to observation always being embedded in participation (see, e.g., Behar, 1997, who maintains that the idea of participation observation is an oxymoron since observation cannot do away with participation). As a complex social phenomenon, which cannot be separated from other social aspects, observality forces us to reflect on the complex chain of positions of observation in which we are placed: (re)observer, (re)observed, *observerd* (portmanteau word based on observer + observed).

All in all, we suggest adopting both a poetic and an artistic attitude to observality. This is well summarised in what Gibran (2011: 43) proposes: "Observe the wonders as they occur around you. Don't claim them. Feel the artistry moving through and be silent." This is close to the idea of being *neither too detached, nor too attached*. Gibran's silence is also an important aspect of our approach.

Working principles for observality

How to 'do' observality then? How to prepare students for it – and as a reminder: all for *themselves*?

Let us reflect on the very phrase *to observe*. Based on Latin *observare* (to watch over, note, heed, look to, attend to, guard but also comply with), the word is composed of *ob-* for 'in front of' and 'before'; and *servare* for 'to watch, keep safe'. *To observe* is then etymologically to watch and keep safe in front of something or someone. When one searches for synonyms for *to observe* one finds a wide range of words in English: *behold, look, perceive, regard, see, view, gape, gaze, glare, look on, peer, stare, guard, study, monitor, spy, peek, peep* (amongst others). The importance of the eye, to see is noted in most of these words. However, the way we problematise observation here goes beyond mere 'seeing' and includes, e.g., the five senses as much as possible. As much as *to listen to* someone is not just *to hear them* (see Dervin, 2022), we argue that *to observe* is not just *to see*.

In Chinese many characters refer to the idea of observing too:

- Like the English word, 睹 contains the subcharacter 目 for 'eye, too look at, to see'.
- 观 (guān) translates as 'to observe, to watch, to survey, to examine' (amongst others) and has an ideographic of 'to see' (见) 'again' (又). This character is found in words referring to notion, thought, ideology (观念 guān niàn); spectators, audience, visitors to an exhibition (观众 guān zhòng) but also objective and impartial (客观 kè guān).
- Finally, 察 (chá) translates as 'to examine, to inquire, to observe, to inspect' (but also 'clearly evident') and is formed by means of 宀 for 'roof' and 'house' as well as 祭 for 'to sacrifice to, to worship'. This character, unlike the two previous ones, does not indicate directly the use of eyes to observe and seems to hint at an origin related to (religious?) worship.

Of interest here and as an important reminder, the last character is contained in the idiom 明察秋毫 from Confucius, which means 'hear what he says and observe what he does'. This underlines the importance to observe the potential differences between what one says and asserts and what one does – a core element in observability.

This leads us to the dichotomy of subjectivity and objectivity. Since what we propose is for solitary usage, we can push aside the controversial idea of objectivity. Often, discussions of observation and ethnography are embedded in the idea of keeping a distance from what one observes and of silencing the self, in a sense. We suggest that you let (inter)subjectivities emerge and confront and even relish in them, while accepting your own vulnerability: you can't/don't know everything about interculturality (since you have been 'formatted' to think about it in limited ways); you cannot be in control of everything. Chalmers (2013) reminds us rightly that we cannot separate our knowledge, experiences, beliefs, and expectations from our observations and interpretations of these observations. Observality in interculturality requires confronting naïve empiricism (*reality is not there to be 'caught'*). As such we can only observe what others let us see and hear, and what we let them see and hear. Feel free to observe what you like, how you like, and for the reasons you like, as long as these observations (which you might want to write down, see later) allow you to confront yourself with yourself about interculturality first and foremost. Observality here is not about finding and/or describing a truth but to observe how in the complex forms of observality that we experience and trigger, we (co-)construct realities of interculturality. This means, obviously, that autobiographical considerations have to be taken into account. We observe, we are observed, we observe how we are being observed, we are *observerds* and thus our complex selves are always there, being (re)shaped. In fact, one could say that observation is the basis of change and that *it is change by itself. When I observe and reflect on my observations, changes take place in me as far as interculturality is concerned. I note how the way I see interculturality influences me in observing how interculturality is 'done' and I change. My goal is to explore these changes while surveying myself.* This also requires observing silences in what you and the other say and do, together and/or separately.

To finish on the issue of subjectivity: There is only one thing that we might have certitudes about – what *we, as individuals,* feel, think, experience (in unstable changing ways). But we can never be sure that what we are observing in the other is 'right' and that it corresponds to what is happening 'inside' of them. This is why observing interculturally is not about confirming our 'knowledge' of the other, of their 'culture', 'identity', 'community', 'language', but about questioning how we perceive these elements, how much influence we might have on them, what ideologies they might reveal of ourselves and (maybe) of the other. It is first and foremost about reflecting on ourselves. *The mirror of the observerd.*

Our next point concerns the very 'essence' of observality. Although the etymologies of the verb *to observe* in Chinese and English reveal an emphasis on seeing, we insist here on exploring other senses such as listening to (versus hearing), smelling, and possibly tasting and touching. Today's focus on seeing disregards these other senses in observing. We also need to bear in mind that the ways that we have been guided to listen, smell, see, taste in disapproving or appreciative ways also have to do with ideological orders. *A colour, a simple word, vibrations, and a smell* can trigger certain perceptions, feelings, and reactions in us because of specific economic–political positions that have had a big influence on us. In a course that we gave on intercultural communication education one of our students wrote the following entry in their learning diary, which summarises in a somewhat direct, controversial but telling way the issue that we are discussing here:

> Regarding the sense of smell, I thought of a classmate of mine in high school who did well academically. In the summer, his body always smelled of sweat. However, few people laughed at her for that. Because the smell of sweat meant she was busy. Busy with the problems she was struggling with, she forgot to take a shower, and sometimes she forgot to eat, so she was also very thin. Of course, part of this is what my eyes tell me. Based purely on smell, I would hate her because the smell of sweat on her body was very unbearable to me. But if you add hearing and sight, I understand why she doesn't take a bath. I had a lot admiration for her.

We need to observe our senses too, to explore them beyond the usual and to hold off this usual for a while – not to censor it but to reflect on why it is that we see this and not that, feel this and not that, the reason why we are sensitive to a particular smell or not, and the specific positions that we attach to them. In Chinese Traditional Medicine, it is interesting to note that the character wén (聞 or 闻) can be used for both 'smelling' and 'listening'. Based on the senses, observing interculturality focuses on changes in people (ourselves included, and our reactions to others' behaviours, thoughts, feelings, word and non-word languages) as well as things-with-people and places-with-people (which cannot be separated): *How, who, and what, when, and why change is taking place? How, who, and what, when, and why change is resisted, silenced, and/or apparently faked? How, who, and what, when, and why change is changed? What does multifaceted change in your observations tell you about your own change as an observerd? What is the role of the five senses in your observality and analyses of/derived from it?*[1] All of this should occur with modesty, uncertainty, reflexivity, and criticality of our own criticality (amongst others).

The last point to raise here about observality has to do with time. As aforementioned, observation is an activity that we engage in all the time, (sub)consciously. It can be short term and/or long term, once/on many occasions. For example, when one looks at a work of art (let's say a painting), the observation period is usually much shorter than when, e.g., we listen to music, which requires listening to the entire piece to be able to make sense of it and to appreciate it. Observation navigates somehow between these two 'models' of engagement with art and music. It is important to note that any moment of observation is always an unfinished 'interaction', a piece of a jigsaw that has no end and to whose entirety we may not always have access. This has an influence on how we might analyse the observation and the conclusions we might draw from it. If we have access to long-term observation, we might be able to reflect deeper on (our own) change – but not necessarily. If we go back to the three types of change from the Chinese that we discussed earlier, short-term observation can trigger enough interesting 'silent' and 'solitary' reflexivity and criticality in us. As said earlier, the main issue we face with focusing on change is that we have to satisfy ourselves with *snapshots of snapshots of snapshots of* ... change since we cannot have access to change as a full-length phenomenon. This means that we always need to 'freeze' it in time (and space) through words that do not necessarily allow us to describe and engage with its complexity. Considering time, we need to adopt an open–closed perspective on observality of and for interculturality. In any case, we need to avoid what Genette (1980: 40) calls *prolepsis*: representing a future act or development as if it were already accomplished or existing – a trend in interculturality whereby one tends to decide beforehand what is occurring in interactions through specific ideological positions such as *non-essentialism, decolonialism* – deciding on the outcome become observing. We need to let our observality talk for itself through ourselves. We need to let irregularities, variations, instabilities, uncertainties guide our senses short and/or long term.

Observing *our* observality

In what follows, to make our proposal more concrete for educators, we share three observations made in relation to our experiences of China. We do not (wish to) analyse these observations in this chapter since they are based on 'silent' and personal acts of observality, which only concern us. What we provide instead is a list of questions for you to consider these observations *for yourselves*. Although these are personal notes that can only be used for ourselves since we know how they were embedded in our lives, the specific contexts where they occurred, our own (changing) feelings and especially the multifaceted changes that they presented and triggered in us, we want you to try to consider them from the perspective of interculturality-as-altering: *What might they have done to us according to the three categories of change that we have discussed earlier (i.e. gradual and subtle change, manifest and obvious change, and silent change)? How might we have used our five senses in rendering and examining our observations? How would you fare yourself in our position? Have you experienced something similar and/ or had similar thoughts about what is discussed in the observations? How did you change?*

Observing as a way of reflecting on one's discomfort

Reminders

The words *civilisation* and *civilised* are omnipresent in Chinese cities. As such, most street posters include a Chinese word related to the idea of civilisation. The word shares the same root as *culture* in Chinese. Civilised is polysemic in the language and it is often used on posters and signs as a synonym for being polite, well-behaved, respectful of others (and, e.g., of the environment). Often, he[2] feels that the word is used as a substitute for something that would be too blunt for the one seeing or listening to it in China. The signs do not say *do not smoke*, *do not drink and drive*, *do not pollute*, but, instead, *be civilised* or *a civilised person is...*! Interestingly the oft-available English translations do include the word *civilised* too. He has started using the Chinese word for civilisation, *wenming,* when he speaks English with his friends to refer to politeness (e.g. "Remember to be wenming" when someone forgets to say thank you). He thinks that in the West the very word is avoided except maybe in museums (e.g. Mesopotamian civilisation) and in the phrase *the clash of civilisations*. As a final note, someone wrote a puzzling sentence in English on Chinese social media one day: "Culture is freer than civilization". He wonders if this was a direct translation from the Chinese. He finds it hard to understand the content of the quote.

Questions:

- Why would the use of the word *civilisation* (*wenming* in Chinese) make someone from outside China feel uncomfortable? How would you determine the kind of 'clash' that might be happening here?
- The observer refers to the West; what might this mean concretely to him (and to you)? What do you know about the use of the word *civilisation* in the 'West' and/or in your own context(s)? Is that a word you often use? When was the last time you used it and for what purpose(s)?
- What could the evaluation of the use of the word *civilisation* in this observation reveal about the one who wrote this paragraph? How might he feel when he reads again what he has written?
- What omnipresent words or phrases related to interculturality do you hear and/or see in your own context(s)? Who uses them and for what purposes? Why do you think they are 'preferred'?
- What does "Culture is freer than civilization" mean to you and what could it reveal about the person who posted it in English on Chinese social media? Why might it be that the one who wrote the paragraph does not understand this sentence?
- When you try to make sense of the sentence "Culture is freer than civilization", what ideologies (i.e. 'orders') cross your mind? What do they tell you about the way you have been made to think about this idea?
- What do the previous questions reveal of the positions we are taking towards our own observality?

Observing things to shake the senses

This section is based on two non-living things. As an important reminder, non-living things are also constitutive of interculturality; they take part in and often mediate our interactions with others although they tend to be 'ignored'. Some of these objects have to do with labelling things interculturally. While reading these observations, pay special attention to:

Interculturality-as-altering 125

- How we talk about the objects and the values that we attach to them.
- How we construct the different ways they are labelled in Chinese-English and other languages.
- Any sign of change/altering in the way the objects are discussed and perceived either for ourselves or others.
- Ideological constructs that reveal what these objects mean to us and how we imagine them to be for others (here mostly: the Chinese as a broad category).
- What might these things tell us about ideologies shared by the Chinese.
- What senses seem to be put into use to observe the things.

Coca Cola

Coca Cola is omnipresent in China. In Chinese: 可口可乐 (Kěkǒukělè); 可口 = 'tasty'; 可乐 = 'cola', with 乐 for 'happy'. The red label helps – red being a powerful colour for the Chinese. Often the word *Coca Cola* is written in Chinese on the labels and if one does not pay attention, one does not always notice that it is a Coca Cola bottle. Coca Cola is referred to as the 'happy drink' in China and it is used in celebrations such as weddings, graduations, birthdays. He has seen newlyweds at 'traditional' Chinese weddings drinking Coca Cola – bottles of Coca Cola everywhere on the tables, accompanied by piles of real banknotes (the red 100 RMB ones with Chairman Mao on them). The Coca Cola company releases a special traditional Chinese New Year gift box every year. In some parts of the world, Coca Cola is disliked and even rejected because it symbolises 'bad' globalisation and the Americanisation of the world. The Chinese do not seem disturbed by this and have adopted it as a 'happy (and tasty?) drink'.

Hometown

The word *hometown* (家乡, Jiāxiāng, with the first character referring to 'family') is often used by the Chinese to refer to the place where they were born or where their family comes from. It might be used for a village, town, and city, but also to mention a region or even a country in some cases. When some Chinese use its English equivalent, the word sounds interesting. One day someone referred to his hometown as being 'Paris', which was interesting because the word did not seem to correspond to his representation of what a hometown is – for him a hometown refers to the place where he lives and to which he might have moved. The flavours appear to be different. In Chinese *hometown* has to do with family *not where one lives*. At least three generations having lived in the same place can call the place a *hometown*.

Conclusion

This chapter has introduced several elements and arguments for working on the complex notion of interculturality. It was aimed at scholars, students, and educators who have an interest in enriching and challenging their own take on this somewhat controversial notion *silently* – above and beyond the current noise of interculturality, which is limiting the way we are made to conceptualise and problematise the notion.

We started by claiming that observation is constant in relation to encounters with the other. We problematise the idea of observality through the figure of the *observerd* – this continuum of a figure between the observer and the observed. *The observed becoming an observer, the observer becoming observed, the observed self-observing, the observer self-observing, the observer/the observed observing observing, the observer/the observed observing becoming observed.*

Our focus was on how to revise and enrich our take on interculturality by benefiting from observality that confronts, e.g., (others' and our) ideologies, positions, feelings, biases. For those of us involved in problematising interculturality in research and education, this is more vital than trying to 'analyse', 'interpret', but also 'prepare' and, eventually 'judge', those involved in 'doing' interculturality in everyday life – providing them with illusionary miraculous recipes for 'meeting the other'. Since so many of us have very different ideological positions on what interculturality is and should entail (e.g. democratic culture, non-essentialism, intercultural competence), it is increasingly problematic to do so without indoctrinating students. As scholars and educators of interculturality, we have a responsibility to not indoctrinate or judge people for what they do based on our own ideologies and economic–political views (often hidden under *the scientific*) but to try to understand why they 'do' interculturality in certain ways, how they explain 'doing' it, by taking into account the potential resulting clashes of ideologies between others and them. We say *to try* since one can never be sure that anyone can be successful at 'doing' these things. At the same time, we have a responsibility to look at oneself in 'the' mirror of what they say and 'do' to reflect on and be critical (of our own criticality). This modest position is central in the observality method that we propose.

In the chapter we suggest focusing on *interculturality-as-altering* in order to sharpen our eyes, ears, and other senses. Change is omnipresent in interculturality, and it becomes an important indicator of inconsistencies, contradictions, fluidity – or, in one word, *complexities* – which are fundamental characteristics of interculturality. The presence of others always turns interculturality into constant changing fields of practice and theory. Observality is thus not about generalising about the other and/or self – although it will but that is something we must try to address and resist temporarily through 'silent' reflexivity and criticality. Observality can help us look at oneself as 'producers', 'consumers', and promoters of selected knowledge of interculturality.

China invented so-called *Chinese magic mirrors*, which are made of bronze. We would like to suggest that these mirrors are a great metaphor to explain what observality for 'silent' reflexivity and criticality can do for interculturality. On the back of the mirror there is a design in relief (e.g. Chinese signs of the zodiac). The front of the mirror is smooth and polished, and works as a mirror. If one shines a light onto the front surface of the mirror, then project the reflected light onto a blank surface, one will see the image of the back design on the surface.

Observality is about using this mirror with the light onto the front surface so we can see ourselves and what lies behind (e.g. others' takes on interculturality), critiquing and reflecting on them simultaneously.

Notes

1 Bearing in mind *gradual and subtle change, manifest and obvious change*, and *silent change* (see our discussion of these Chinese ideas in a previous section).
2 'He' refers to either of the authors in the examples.

References

Behar, R. (1997). *The Vulnerable Observer: Anthropology That Breaks Your Heart*. New York: Beacon Press.
Byram, M., & Fleming, M. (1998). *Language Learning in Intercultural Perspective: Approaches Through Drama and Ethnography*. Cambridge: Cambridge University Press.
Canetti, E. (1989). *The Secret Heart of the Clock*. New York: Farrar, Straus, Giroux.
Chalmers, A. (2013). *What is this Thing Called Science?* London: Open University Press. https://www.chinesethought.cn/EN/.
Dervin, F. (2022). *Interculturality in Fragments: A Reflexive Approach*. Singapore: Springer.
Dervin, F., & Fracchiolla, B. (2012). *Anthropology, Interculturality and Language Learning-teaching: Are They Compatible?* Bern: Peter Lang.
Fang, W. (2019). *Modern Notions of Culture and Civilisation in China*. London: Palgrave Macmillan.
Genette, G. (1980). *Narrative Discourse: An Essay in Method*. Ithaca, NY: Cornell University Press.
Gibran, K. (2011). *The Treasured Writings of Kahlil Gibran*. New York: Philosophical Library.
Holliday, A. (2022). *Contesting Grand Narratives of the Intercultural*. London: Routledge.
Hua, Z. (2015). *Research Methods in Intercultural Communication: A Practical Guide*. London: Wiley.
Nietzsche, F. (2017). *Writings of Nietzsche, Volume III*. Woodstock, ON: Devoted Publishing.
Roberts, C., Byram, M., Barro, A., Jordan, S., & Street, B. (2000). *Language Learners as Ethnographers*. Clevedon: Multilingual Matters.

10 Interculturality holding hands with education for emergencies

Heidi Layne and Abitha Chakrapani

Introduction

Interculturality in Finnish education is commonly understood through the lens of educating students from diverse backgrounds and considering their varied needs in terms of language and culture. This has been the prevailing ideology in Finnish policies since intercultural education became a part of education research in Finnish universities in the 1990s. Finnish education policies have a history of promoting internationalisation, global and sustainable education, and the Universal Declaration of Human Rights (1948). In the five-million inhabitant Nordic country, internationalisation initiatives are applied to every level of education. As such, the Ministry of Education and Culture in Finland (OKM) has developed specific policies for the internationalisation of higher education to facilitate the integration of English medium education programmes and to attract international students to study in Finnish higher education institutions (HEIs). Furthermore, these policies suggest that students graduating from Finnish HEIs should adopt a willingness to be involved in international and intercultural environments (OKM, 2017: 3).

Amid the COVID-19 pandemic, followed by the increased uncertainty that the war in Ukraine is causing in Finland, not to mention the climate crisis being nowhere near solved, we propose that interculturality in education continues to have an important role. Yet, there may be alternative paradigms and lenses that are needed to be added to the discussion. As such, education for emergencies represents an exciting perspective to support future teachers and policymakers in being prepared to consider how intercultural education can be more sustainable in terms of understanding the unequal structures that may hinder the development of intercultural environments that promote fair and safe spaces for all students regardless of their backgrounds.

By education for emergencies, we refer to short- and long-term crises and events occurring around the world. Longer-term issues are currently targeted by the UNESCO Sustainable Development Goals 4 (SDG4 hereafter), such as unequal access and structures in education, racism, wars, and famine, as well as shorter-term issues, including pandemics, conflicts, and natural disasters caused by the climate crisis. It is not always easy to draw clear lines between short-term and longer-term emergencies. However, these might have an impact on education and also on how young people view and plan their future. Pandemics and wars have also led to an increase in racism, specifically shifting the target of racism towards groups that are somehow identified as being responsible for specific events, e.g. the Chinese for the COVID-19 pandemic and Russians for the war in Ukraine.

The war in Ukraine has led to a dangerous political shift in Europe where policies are changed to accommodate so-called White European refugees. At the same time, asylum seekers from other parts of the world are not as warmly welcomed. For example, programmes have been developed in Finnish universities to accommodate easy access for students fleeing the war in Ukraine, while other asylum seekers are asking on social media why their lives do not matter equally.

Considering all these tragedies, we argue that interculturality needs to be rethought in relation to the political, the historical, and the sociocultural. Our chapter thus aims to reflect on interculturality within the framework of education for emergencies which we consider useful for, e.g., future teacher educators and policymakers. The chapter first explores interdisciplinary lenses in interculturality in education and further links it with what is known about the effects of current emergencies in education. We then discuss a small survey on recent emergencies conducted with students registered at Finnish universities and draw (temporary) conclusions about what it could mean for 'teaching interculturality otherwise'.

A different lens for interculturality: Towards education for emergencies?

One aim of this chapter is to unpack the role of interculturality in education in terms of dealing with emergencies. Boix-Mansilla et al. (2000) emphasise the importance of interdisciplinarity in curricula and how different lenses can and should be incorporated to provide a more in-depth view for students to analyse particular phenomena. For Boix-Mansilla et al., interdisciplinarity means that the students are provided with different lenses such as scientific and historical (sociological) perspectives on how, e.g., the Holocaust was possible and how events that led to it can be explained in multiple ways. They introduced the importance of questioning students about what happened and how all the injustices linked to the Holocaust were possible. In their study, students were asked, through different epistemologies, about the obedience of Germans towards Hitler's orders; whether science was correct in terms of, e.g., 'racial categorisation'; and to what extent students were able to link propaganda and false representation of knowledge (Boix-Mansilla et al., 2000). This interdisciplinary understanding is essential when dealing with both short- and long-term emergencies and when thinking about the role of education, specifically in relation to interculturality.

In the European context, plurilingual and intercultural education is a concept developed by the Council of Europe's Language Policy Unit in the late 1990s as the basis for education in and through cultural and linguistic diversity in societies marked by increasing mobility, plurality, and complexity. The *Guide for the Development and Implementation of Curricula for Plurilingual and Intercultural*

Education (2016) shows that plurilingual and intercultural education has two aims. First, it facilitates the acquisition of linguistic and intercultural abilities, which involve adding to the linguistic and cultural resources that make up individual repertoires, using the available means efficiently. Second, it covers teaching all languages: languages of schooling, foreign languages, regional or minority languages, and classical languages (e.g. Latin). Aims differ according to learners' needs, languages, and contexts (Beacco et al., 2016). In Finland, the type of lens guiding interculturality in education policies is, however, insufficient for dealing with interdisciplinarity, inequalities, and breaking down norms. In their study on language hierarchies and parents' perceptions of plurilingualism in several countries, including Finland, Daryai-Hansen, Layne, and Lefever (2018) concluded that European mainstream languages are yet very much favoured in language learning and language policies, and that less attention is paid to minority languages and languages that are not officially taught as foreign languages in schools.

Another important aspect is that culture (a central concept in inter*cultur*ality) can take on diverse forms to determine what interculturality is about in education. Within the discipline of intercultural communication, culture is understood as a toolbox of communicative resources and ways to behave and interact when meeting others (e.g. Hofstede, 2001). Applied linguistics, e.g. Adrian Holliday's work (2018), divides the analysis of culture into *small* and *big cultures*, bringing more interdisciplinary and intersectional studies to the field. Throughout his career, Dervin (e.g. 2011, 2016) has brought an in-depth linguistic (and beyond) lens to enrich understandings of interculturality 'beyond' and even 'without' culture. For Dervin (2016), the prefix *inter-* refers to the importance to take into account other identity markers such as gender, class, race, ethnicity, and interest, but also knowledge in our understanding and observation of interculturality. The post-colonial lens also calls for a more interdisciplinary sociological approach to structural injustices and the role of power, questioning the dominating voices represented in intercultural education (e.g. R'boul, 2021). Both analysing intersectionally and decolonising interculturality are increasingly needed. By the decolonial approach, we refer to the analysis of knowledge and lenses that currently dominate curricula and curriculum development. When teaching and applying interculturality in education, we can encourage our students to view the scientific roots and knowledge systems that we use in our teaching and, simultaneously, challenge students' thinking by investigating why they think or know the way they do.

Lastly, education has created 'ideals' for supporting learners to become self-reflective and critical thinkers without offering clear definitions of what, e.g., criticality can look like. Interdisciplinarity should focus on having the potential of redressing the neglect of social problems, particularly the consequences of racial inequalities and the exclusion of, for example, indigenous and minority knowledge and languages in the classroom. Interdisciplinarity in education can be analysed as a didactic approach used in teaching intercultural competence-focused individualistic strategies. It can also be embedded in critical pedagogy, integrating the understanding of the social implications of oppression and discrimination or power relations in a given society (Ruiz & Sánchez, 2011). We shall apply

Interculturality holding hands with education for emergencies 131

the idea of *lenses* later in the chapter when we examine and discuss discourses on emergencies and guidelines to deal with them. Teachers have a central role to play in providing support through education and creating a safe space to reflect on ongoing world events through intercultural lenses. In what follows, we discuss different types of emergencies, short-term and long-term ones, and how, at times, it is difficult to determine the difference between them. In addition, we show how emergencies often result in increasing inequalities. Lastly, we report on a survey conducted with university students in Finland to understand their experiences of (recent) emergencies.

Definitions of long-term and short-term emergencies

> [Abitha's experience as a teacher during the lockdown in India] I worked as a teacher in the Northern Part of Karnataka State in India, and we, as a group of teachers, put in efforts to interact with our students. We explored and experimented with many methods and modes to engage children, looking for the most suitable one. We surveyed the number of students who have a smartphone with internet connectivity. We found that nearly 60% of our children did not have a smartphone in their family, and more than 20% did not have a mobile phone. Looking at the compromises in emotional connection with the children, the quality of engagement with them, and the equity to teach every child irrespective of any socioeconomic condition, we felt that the online mode was a poor substitute for face-to-face interaction with children. Hence, we sorted to do village visits, such as home visits, and meet the children there. We continued that practice for months, which also came with shortcomings due to increased COVID cases.

Humanity has faced diverse emergencies in the past and can presume to expect many more in the future. Across the plethora of events having taken place over generations, some can be considered *emergencies* while others are *crises*. As the words suggest, an emergency is a sudden and short-term intrusion, while a crisis refers to prolonged disruptions (Al-Dahash et al., 2016). An emergency could lead to a crisis over time, thus becoming a long-term emergency. The distinction between *short-term* and *long-term emergencies* can be problematic since the impact caused by any emergency varies among different communities across time and space – for instance, some groups are disproportionately affected by the COVID-19 pandemic. The inequalities created by these emergencies could also be perceived differently depending on the observer.

In this chapter, the term 'emergency' encompasses 'crisis' to discuss the effect of education, e.g. natural disasters, the spread of disease, and political conflicts. Shifting to post-COVID-19 in education, the war in Ukraine started. Finland shares 1,300 kilometres of border with Russia and has recently decided to join NATO. In the Nordic country, youngsters are often prone to living circumstances that adults and the economic–political system impose on them. An example of this is the neglect to recognise how the war in Ukraine has marginalised people from other war zones, and favouritism towards White European refugees may have a long-term impact on other refugees and asylum seekers living in Finland and beyond. In addition, people are demonised in the popular media and affected by politics based on quick-fix solutions to emergencies. After the 9/11 incident in New York, Giroux (2003) wrote about the 'abandoned generation' and the danger of creating a culture of fear. He thus proposed 'civic engagement', 'public intelligence', and conditions for making the government accountable for its actions (Giroux, 2003: 20). Similarly, Butler (2002) pointed out that fatuous moralism cannot replace responsibility over one's actions in the world. This relates to many emergencies taking place today. While we are dealing with these emergencies, we might discriminate against others. This motivated us to create a survey for the students to reflect on their experiences and share their perspectives on current emergencies.

Different inequalities caused by emergencies

Conjoining interculturality and education for emergencies means giving space to interdisciplinary understanding and sociocultural contextualisation in the way the notion is used in education. In the Indian landscape, lockdown revealed multiple facets of 'othering' enacted by citizens based on differences across religion, language, and geographical origin of people (Chakrapani & Nithya, 2020). While all countries or regions are vulnerable to any emergency, some are prone to a greater extent than others. For example, frequent natural disasters in Nepal can cause more significant disruption to the education sector than in other parts of the world. Furthermore, the spread of certain communicable diseases across the African continent can increase disparity in education among children in some African regions when compared to the rest of the world (Tarricone et al., 2021).

On the other hand, political conflicts such as the ongoing Ukraine war, the Syrian civil war, the Kivu conflict, the war in Afghanistan, and many more have withdrawn the right to education for many children. These conflicts reduce access to education immensely by causing damage to the physical infrastructure of schools or by preventing children and teachers from attending school. The local atmosphere of these conflict areas then becomes very unsafe (Tarricone et al., 2021).

Another effect of emergencies is population displacement, which creates a type of emergency that lasts longer than the initial conflicts. Population displacement creates refugees who are forced to leave their home country due to active conflicts in a given area. When people flee one region, their adaptation to another is prevented in many ways (Tarricone et al., 2021). As a consequence, children's access to education is reduced. In countries such as Sierra Leone, during violent conflicts and civilian wars, women suffer directly and experience more forms of abuse than men. Many girls and women are abducted and forced into slave labour; many others are inflicted with physical and sexual assault creating fear in addition to the conflict at hand (Maclure & Denov, 2009). Due to many such incidents, girls' enrolment in schools is poor, affecting generations of learners.

The inequalities caused by emergencies can differ depending on gender and other social categories, aggravating the existing disparities in a given society. For instance, long-term emergencies can result from a fixed social stratification (Nash, 1990), such as the caste system in India, where upward social mobility through, e.g., education is impossible. Besides, not all people have equal access to participate in education, nor is the education of the same quality for all. Given the complex intersectionality of different social divisions in India, inequality continues to exist in various forms across the country. Moreover, experiences of schooling affect trends of intergenerational occupational stability in India. Society is stratified, and the structure is maintained by the dominant groups who successfully impose their ideologies on other subordinate groups leading to inequality. As such, a child of a lower-class society does not have a choice on which school to attend. A child may have access to a high-budget school only if their parents are financially able to afford it; therefore, the economics of a family hinders any child's choice of school. Having this as a basis for school, the curriculum and pedagogy in these (private and government) schools differ vastly and can provide only specific access to improve children's abilities. Therefore, the availability of resources for teachers and students to develop their potential varies. A child from a government school does not have the same access as a child from a private school. After schooling, students might lack skills to cope in society and thus have to continue working in their parents' professional fields. This cycle continues generation after generation. In times of emergency, the capacity to grow and learn is further hindered by these forms of inequality, causing long-term emergencies.

Preparedness for developing an intercultural lens in education in times of emergency can come in various ways. *Planning*, *response*, and *recovery* are critical factors in building a resilient education system that can withstand even the times of the worst emergencies and enhance intercultural understanding (Tarricone et al., 2021). Thinking about interculturality beyond the teaching of language and culture, interculturality for education in emergencies involves:

- Planning the process to ensure students have access to education which acknowledges their diverse backgrounds in terms of, e.g., race, ethnicity, socioeconomic background, knowledge systems, geopolitical dispositions.
- Supporting students with required infrastructure also makes distance education possible and provides equal access to all.
- Creating a curriculum that enhances students' resilience and recognition of diverse sociopolitical dispositions in the context of emergency.
- Monitoring the learning progress of each student, as there is a greater risk of learning disruption as not all students may be in the immediate observation of their teacher and lack the guidance required for learning in times of emergency. Advice needs to be relevant and tailored based on the students' background.
- Assessing learning and wellbeing is required to plan and respond to the recovery plan and ensure that enough support is available

Understanding the effects of war and emergencies on university students for problematising interculturality in relation to education for emergencies

The 2020 pandemic has changed the way we think about education. At the same time, during the past years, people have experienced uncertainties that might have changed how they think about their future. However, in teaching, we do not always have ways to consider students' uncertainties and diverse life experiences. This has a direct impact on how we think about interculturality in education during times of emergencies. In this section we focus on what we call *renegotiated lenses for teaching interculturality*, adding the diversity of student voices and dispositions to curricula and teaching. In their study, Machado et al. (2020) pointed out how crucial it is for the voices of young people to be heard through dialogues on their life stories, beliefs, and critical values, as well as in relation to how they deal with differences and conflicts. We also agree that universities should move away from a universal knowledge system and, for example, a universal understanding of intercultural competencies. In our work, we aim to move beyond cultural and language competencies in teaching interculturality towards developing ways to include diverse knowledge systems and life experiences into (but not limited to) higher education. This is why we designed a survey in May 2022, which we distributed to colleagues based in different universities in Finland. The survey covered questions about how students have experienced ongoing emergencies and their experiences of how they have been discussed in Finnish universities. The survey further allowed students to provide ideas and solutions on how emergencies could be addressed taking into account students' diversity.

By the time of writing this book chapter, we had received 23 responses from 4 different universities and of many different nationalities: Finnish (5); Chinese (3); United States of America (3); Greek (2); and Indian, Namibian, Russian-Finnish, Mexican-German, Spanish, British, USA-Finnish, Mexican-German, Finnish-Greek-German, and Italian (1 each). One respondent did not indicate their nationality. We are aware that the number of responses is minimal, however, our intention is not to offer generalisable knowledge but to provide interdisciplinary lenses and understanding through the students' experiences.

Here we reflect on how these answers may add value to teaching and guiding students from two perspectives: (1) their *intersubjective, bodily experiences*; and (2) viewing the emergencies on a *global macro level*. We argue that both perspectives are important in renegotiating interculturality in education. Barbara Hill Collins (2009) has used the term *bodily experience* to refer to how the personal experiences of, e.g., discrimination, poverty, and racism, shape one's own understanding of the world. Although how interculturality could be taught beyond a cultural and language understanding has been questioned, we propose to provide a safe environment for sharing these bodily experiences. In the survey responses to the question on how the current emergencies were impacting students' lives, we noted concrete bodily experiences from some respondents. In the first excerpt, the war has a direct impact on the student's own country or family. The same student of Russian nationality, responding to another survey question, also expressed his concern of being discriminated against based on nationality. The second excerpt reflects on a specific emergency that has touched this student, besides the global ones, expanding the understanding of the experiences of the student.

Excerpt 1

The war is concretely affecting I am scared for my family's safety both in Russia and in Ukraine. I haven't seen my grandparents in many years due to the pandemic and now the war. I feel helpless and anxious, but I am very grateful to my classmates, teachers, and colleagues at the university for their emotional support and empathy.

Excerpt 2

Too much to handle! Literally. I would never expect to have experienced already in my thirties, the economic crisis of my country, a pandemic and a war. I would expect that the policies of international bodies and institutions would have prevented, or at least control more successfully, tragic incidents like the aforementioned.

In some cases, the emergencies represent a concern but observed from a distance:

Excerpt 3

Slightly. I have experienced random bouts of anxiety when thinking about certain emergencies, for example, if war comes to Finland and I am conscripted, what will happen to my family, etc. Also, the food shortage that is expected to come next year and the increasing gas prices are all causing anxiety.

In the survey, students were also asked about their potential experience of being discriminated against during emergencies, which might relate to bodily experiences. Only two students reported discrimination: one based on a student's sexual orientation, which is tied to belonging of the minority group, and another has to do with the experience of being denied entry to an event because of non-EU COVID-19 vaccine certification.

The following excerpts reflect on examples of experiencing emergencies from a *global macro-level perspective*, looking at the emergencies from an 'outsider-insider' position (by this, we mean how the students reflected on global emergencies and their opportunities to act against them):

Excerpt 4

> Pandemic, war, climate crisis, political polarisation, growing human rights issues in powerful countries and other issues in combination with their influence over the economy and politics in Europe and globally are all adding to

anxiety. The anxiety stems mainly from the feeling that the world is going to an alarming direction, and there's very little one can do but watch it happen and prepare for the worst.

Interestingly, some students reported differently about their opportunities to play an active role and to be able to make a difference. We argue that this is a very relevant topic for discussing interculturality and education during emergencies.

Excerpt 5

The war has a smaller effect than climate change and the pandemic. Climate change is a more global issue that affects many of my daily decisions (recycling, public transport etc.). The pandemic has immensely affected my mental health and made me very lonely. It's the lack of interaction that stresses me and not the pandemic itself at this point.

To learn more about how the emergencies should be dealt with in education, we also asked students about their experiences of how things were and are being discussed at the time of the survey: *What kind of conversations have taken place? Who were they initiated by? What are your feelings about how the war situation is discussed and handled at university, in public, and in the media?* Regarding interculturality, it is of utmost importance to be aware of the multiple layers of geopolitics and power imbalances that take place in such conversations. The interdisciplinary idea of interculturality can guide students to think about why some emergencies occur, what made them possible, while reflecting on and (re)negotiating their own experiences. In the students' answers, the extent to which the emergencies were dealt with varied, as well as the need for reflection, as, for some students, talking might cause anxiety as much as not talking to other students. The suggested interdisciplinary perspective for handling emergencies is essential when it comes to media and propaganda. The students read different media in different languages and therefore received diverse media perspectives based on what they read and their sources of information. In what follows, we provide some examples of students' responses:

Excerpt 6

The war has not been really addressed at the university or if it has, the comments have been quite subtle. In a way this is good, because also talking constantly about the war may increase anxiety. It is good to concentrate also on other things.

Excerpt 7

I have received numerous messages from some of my classmates, teachers, and colleagues at the university expressing support. I have myself sent personal messages to the classmates who I know have been affected. I find such personal messages helpful and comforting, at least to some extent. I prefer not to bring the topic up myself at any public sessions or events, as they make me feel too emotional. I appreciate emails and announcements calling for anti-discrimination towards Ukrainian- and Russian-speaking individuals.

Excerpt 8

A lot of times, the war has been alluded to in different places. On the first days of war, we discussed the war quite a lot with peers in informal settings. One of us is from Russia and she was really upset and anxious over the war, wondering what it meant to be Russian in the middle of all this, and I almost felt as if she was feeling guilty for it, so we tried to make sure that she would feel safe with us. The university has made some official announcements about the war in emails etc. and I think they have offered the possibility to go and talk to someone about anxiety etc. I don't think they could have done anything more about informing etc, but I feel that the university could have organised ways to help Ukraine that all the student and staff could have taken part in.

Excerpt 9

The conversation was about our feelings and perception of the situation. It was initiated by the professor and continued in breakout rooms with peers. One of the aspects that scare me the most is that the media are not always reliable, fake news are very common, and it is not always easy to tell what is real from what is it. This adds to the general feeling of uncertainty.

Conclusions and discussions

De Santos (2017) believes that while we are fighting the climate crisis and various conflicts, we might not solve them by going back to the 'past' that has led us to these emergencies. Similarly, we might have to change the way we think about diversity when interculturality ties hands together with education for emergencies.

This chapter aimed to reflect on the meaning of interculturality in education during times of emergencies. Emergencies can be understood as long or short term. They are not easy to categorise as, e.g., inequalities, wars, famine, climate change, political conflicts, and pandemics can all shift from short term to long term. Interculturality is indeed polysemic (Dervin, 2011). As a notion, it does not represent or contain *one* truth, but it is embedded in the experiences and narratives of *diverse* people (here: university students in Finland). As such there is neither a universal form of intercultural competence nor a single story about emergencies. One aim of interculturality in education could be to support analysing multifaceted emergencies and personal experiences through different theoretical lenses. Since students reported isolation and a lack of contacts during the pandemic, universities should provide safe spaces for having conversations about these elements. This is how we see the role of interculturality in education; *this is what interculturality can teach us* – rather than us teaching it.

As we are writing the conclusions for this book chapter, the only Finnish national newspaper, *Helsingin Sanomat* (*HS* 28 July 2022), reported about deeply rooted racism and discrimination in the country. It is important to note that racism relates mainly to race, skin colour, immigrant status, and religion in Finland. According to the article, numerous surveys and studies report the same results about the Nordic country (for example a report by the European Union in 2018 and a study conducted by the Finnish Institute for Health and Welfare). This is an emergency in itself, and a sign that, e.g., interculturality in education needs a shift to include the voices of people being discriminated against or fearing discrimination. Analytical tools to bring in various theoretical lenses and knowledge systems are needed. Interdisciplinary dialogue should allow diverse knowledge systems and experiences to be included.

To finish this chapter, we would like to share with our readers the words of one of our survey respondents who (in)directly calls for the kind of interculturality in education that we suggest:

> Thank you for giving me the opportunity to share my thoughts. I found the questions to be respectful. Crisis is affecting each person in their own way. For me, the pandemic and then the war affected my whole family, causing fear for their safety, increased fear of the unknown, and uncertainty for the future. A friendly and loving university community is what keeps my spirit up. Regarding the question about who I can talk to about these issues, I believe there are people with whom I can talk about my feelings, yet I feel that there are unfortunately too many things which cannot be resolved by me talking about them, instead requiring actions that are out of my control. (…) As a Russian-Finnish individual, I am worried about myself or my loved ones facing nationality-based discrimination as my home countries strive further apart. The more time passes, the more I struggle to be proud of my identity and nationality. I hold on to the hope that people will differentiate culture and nationalities from politics.

References

Al-Dahash, H., Thayaparan, M., & Kulatunga, U. (2016). Understanding the terminologies: Disaster, crisis and emergency. In P. W. Chan & C. J. Nielson (Eds.), *Proceedings of the 32nd Annual ARCOM Conference, ARCOM 2016*, 5–7 September, Manchester, UK, Association of Researchers in Construction Management (pp. 1191–1200).

Beacco, J. C., Byram, M., Cavalli, M., Coste, D., Cuenat, M. E., Goullier, F., & Panthier, J. (2016). *Guide for the Development and Implementation of Curricula for Plurilingual and Intercultural Education*. Strasbourg: Council of Europe.

Boix Mansilla, V., Miller, W. C., & Gardner, H. (2000). On disciplinary lenses and interdisciplinary work. In S. Wineburg & P. Grossman (Eds.), *Interdisciplinary*

Curriculum: Challenges of Implementation (pp. 17–38). New York: Teachers College Press.

Butler, J. (2002). Explanation and exoneration, or what we can hear. *Grey Room*, 7, 56–67.

Chakrapani, A., & Nithya, R. (2020, May 1). How lockdown measures have disproportionately affected migrant workers. *Deccan Herald*. https://www.deccanherald.com/opinion/how-lockdown-measures-have-disproportionately-affected-migrant-workers-832157.html.

Collins, P. H. (2009). *Black Feminist Thought*. New York: Routledge.

Daryai-Hansen, P., Layne, H. J., & Lefever, S. (2018). Language hierarchisations and hehierarchisations: Nordic parents' views towards language. *International Journal of Bias, Identity and Diversities in Education*, 3(2), 60–76.

de Sousa Santos, B. (2017). Uncertainty, between fear and hope. *The CLR James Journal*, 23(1), 5–11. https://doi.org/10.5840/clrjames2017121951.

Dervin, F. (2011). Cultural identity, representation and othering. In J. Jackson (Ed.), *The Routledge Handbook of Language and Intercultural Communication* (pp. 195–208). London: Routledge.

Dervin, F. (2016). *Interculturality in Education*. London: Palgrave Macmillan.

Giroux, H. A. (2003). *The Abandoned Generation: Democracy Beyond the Culture of Fear*. New York: Palgrave Macmillan.

Hofstede, G. (2001). *Culture's Consequences: Comparing Values, Behaviors, Institutions and Organizations Across Nations*. Thousand Oaks, CA: Sage Publications.

Holliday, A. (2018). *Understanding Intercultural Communication: Negotiating a Grammar of Culture*. London: Routledge.

Machado, E. B., Freire, I. P., Caetano, A. P., Vassalo, S., & Bicho, L. (2020). The voice of young people – Contribution for their involvement in the school. *Intercultural Education*, 31(3), 300–313.

Maclure, R. & Denov, M. (2009). Reconstruction versus transformation: Post-war education and the struggle for gender equity in Sierra Leone. *International Journal of Educational Development*, 29(6), 612–620.

Nash, R. (1990). Bourdieu on education and social and cultural reproduction. *British Journal of Sociology of Education*, 11(4), 431–447.

OKM. (2017). *Better Together for a Better World. Policies to Promote Internationalisation in Finnish Higher Education and Research 2017–2025*. Helsinki: Publications of the Ministry of Education.

Ortega Ruiz, P., & Romero Sánchez, E. (2011). Intercultural education and migration: Educational proposals. *Education Research International*, 2011, 1–7. https://doi.org/10.1155/2011/434079.

R'boul, H. (2021). North/South imbalances in intercultural communication education. *Language and Intercultural Communication*, 21(2), 144–157.

Tarricone, P., Mestan, K., & Teo, I. (2021). *Building Resilient Education Systems: A Rapid Review of the Education in Emergencies Literature*. Melbourne: Australian Council for Educational Research.

Part III
Insights into interculturalising interculturality

11 Teaching interculturality 'beyond' culture

Challenges and future possibilities

Giuliana Ferri

Interculturality 'beyond' culture

This chapter presents the reader with a question: Is it possible to teach interculturality 'beyond' culture? I begin by contextualising this question in existing conceptualisations of interculturality that interrogate culture as a problematic analytical category (see Dervin, 2014, 2016; Dervin et al., 2020; Ferri, 2014, 2018) and that highlight the role of intersectionality as more apt to capture the contingent, tentative, power-laden, and contested meanings that are embedded in interaction (see Dervin, 2020; Ferri, 2020, 2022). Despite these examples, culture remains a central construct in interculturality. Thus, in this chapter, I use the phrase *'beyond' culture* to take distance from essentialist notions of culture seen as static entities employed to assign fixed sets of traits to characterise people and in particular those seen as 'other' from us. To this end, I clarify that interculturality is not a neutral term and that it is always ideological and political (Dervin et al., 2013; Dervin & Chen, 2020; Dervin & Jacobsson, 2020; Dervin & Simpson, 2021). In particular, referring to Dervin and Simpson's (2021) argument, I highlight here the need to make clear my own stance, including the context in which I operate, in order to illustrate how writing about interculturality is always embedded in wider political influences as well as in the reflexivity of the author.

The chapter begins with an overview of the ideological assumptions that underpin the dominance of Western-centric constructs of intercultural competence in the field of interculturality, including intercultural awareness and intercultural adaptation. I then contextualise interculturality within current movements to decolonise knowledge. However, I am aware of the dangers implicit in 'false generosity' towards peripheral voices (Dervin & Chen, 2020; Dervin & Simpson, 2021), of the double bind (Spivak, 1988) implicit in critiquing a field from the inside, and of the need to exercise critical vigilance when talking about interculturality from a critical perspective (Ferri, 2018). Therefore, I do not intend to suggest a linear and unproblematic narrative of emancipation from Western-centric constructs to an opening towards 'global' perspectives. As I have argued at length elsewhere (Ferri, 2020, 2022), individual intercultural becomings are entangled in narratives of power, displacement, misunderstandings, resistance, translations, negotiation, and emotional work. This personal, autobiographical

DOI: 10.4324/9781003345275-14

144 *Giuliana Ferri*

dimension of interculturality made of everyday interactions in the context of small cultures (Holliday, 2016) that create hybridity, third spaces (Bhabha, 1994), and unique intercultural translations (Ferri, 2022), interacts with the grand narratives of national culture and essentialist 'us–them' narratives (Amadasi & Holliday, 2018). My main aim in this chapter is to highlight complexity and the ideological struggles over conflicting definitions of culture, in particular the ways in which this complexity is applied to education with reference to my own context of teacher education in England.

Starting from my context in England, and London more specifically, the chapter will outline the educational philosophy that underpins the introduction of intersectional and intercultural approaches to the curriculum in a teacher education course and how this project sits in direct confrontation with current ideological debates or 'culture wars' in the UK around colonial heritage and the legacy of empire, and an anti-immigrant, nationalistic agenda that has exacerbated and become even more polarised after the Brexit referendum in 2016. I will suggest possible approaches to teach interculturality 'beyond' culture, presenting some of the challenges that emerge when leaving the comfort zone of cultural difference and intercultural competence. The chapter aims to highlight the need to introduce critical, decolonial, intersectional, and reflexive practices that equip pre-service teachers to become agents of change in their own contexts. My argument is that ultimately every critical pedagogical project needs to take into account the wider political and ideological forces that are brought to bear in the micro-context of the classroom.

Self, other, and cultural essentialism

An important constant presence in intercultural communication and other subfields of knowledge is the concept of competence. A generally accepted understanding of competence is underpinned by the need to bridge cultural differences through knowledge of the other and the understanding of different communicative styles and behaviours in the context of differing cultural expectations and values. This is applied to disparate fields such as business, diplomatic relations, education including language education, health settings, and multicultural workplaces. Examples of current competence frameworks in education foreground democracy and dialogue in diverse societies, for instance the Reference Framework of Competences for Democratic Culture (Council of Europe, 2018), The Common European Framework of Reference for Languages (Council of Europe, 2020), and the UNESCO Guidelines on Intercultural Education (2006). Despite the focus on dialogue and the acceptance of diversity, the concept of competence is problematic on a number of levels, which I summarise according to two main themes. First, the claim that the acquisition of specific skills, knowledge, and competencies can assist in achieving transparency in communication originates from a reductionistic understanding of culture as a set of fixed traits that can be used to categorise groups of people, and as a result the processual, tentative, and at times conflictual dynamic of interaction is undertheorised in these frameworks. Second, competence presumes a separation between self and other. This separation stems from a tendency to assign cultural traits as the defining characteristics of the 'cultural other', seen as the essentialised bearer of culture (Ferri, 2014, 2018; see also Sercu, 2010). In other words, the discourse underpinning these frameworks glosses over the social interrelationships between speakers (Dervin, 2011, 2016; Simpson & Dervin, 2019) and culture as "a site of discursive struggle between competing groups" (Dasli, 2019: 227). This brief overview of the concept of competence brings to the fore the complex semantic web of the word culture and the issue of determinism.

Culture, determinism, and agency

The word *culture* is one of the most complex words in the English language (Eagleton, 2000), denoting a concept that derives etymologically from the Latin *colere*, meaning 'to tend, to cultivate the land'. In this sense, as Eagleton (2000: 3) writes, "nature produces culture which changes nature", meaning that there is a dialectical aspect in this relationship between nature and culture, and that we are not only the product of nature but that we also refashion nature through human activity. This dialectic raises the issue of agency, or of freedom and determinism, in understanding ourselves as self-reflexive beings who claim a place in a world in which nature is fashioned by human activity but within the limits set by nature itself. Another related meaning of culture is attached to the concept of civilisation, of particular importance in this context is the 19th century movement of European Romantic nationalism, and the idea of culture as expression of the unique identity of a group of people connected by the same language, customs, and tradition (Müller-Funk, 2012). Referring to the birth of European national identities, Anderson (1983) described nations as imagined communities because they are imagined by people who perceive themselves as part of a distinct group. This dynamic can be observed in the methodological nationalism (Willem & Schiller, 2002) adopted in the social sciences that assumes culture as bounded by the limits of the nation state.

From a different perspective, the critical cultural theorist Stuart Hall (2018) relates the word culture to hegemony and the distinction between popular and elite culture, highlighting how cultural relations are embedded in structures of dominance, conflict, and struggle. In this sense, culture represents a conflicting terrain in which ideological struggles are played out between differing groups with the top-down imposition of dominant discourses interacting with the dynamic complex of forces that reproduce and transform them. On a similar note, Street (1993) presents culture as a verb, denoting culture as a discursive construction built in interaction. This indeterminacy of cultural meanings is visible in written texts as well as in verbal interactions (Kramsch, 1998), and the role of our social identities is crucial in this meaning-making activity. To summarise, the two main issues that arise when we look at culture from the perspective of hegemony are the agency of individuals in fashioning their own meanings and the contested narratives of competing groups and their right to claim a separate identity.

Although the field of intercultural communication has traditionally oversimplified the concept of culture according to the parameters set by romantic nationalism, or imagined communities, many have engaged with the polysemic nature of the word and presented a view of culture as dynamic, processual, and fluid (see, for example, the notion of *liquid culture* in Dervin, 2011; *small culture* in Holliday, 2011, 2013; *the transculturing self* in Monceri, 2003, 2009; *the double swing model* in Yoshikawa, 1987). Piller (2011) emphasises the sociolinguistic dimension of interculturality, arguing that the role of culture in misunderstanding and conflict in intercultural interaction is inflated. Furthermore, Piller describes how intercultural communication is marketised in the globalised circulation of cultural symbols and languages, for example with the use of ethno-cultural stereotypes in advertising. Despite their critical stance, these models (with the exception of Yoshikawa) are still operating within a Western-centric paradigm and the notion of culture in particular reflects this limited worldview. In attempting to establish a counternarrative to this dominance, Asiancentricity (Miike, 2007), Afrocentricity (Asante, 2013), and Minzu education (Dervin & Yuan, 2021) reclaim agency in creating knowledge from a non-Western standpoint, shifting the hegemony of European colonial domination towards different epistemological perspectives.

In my vision of interculturality, the recognition of this macro historical context determined by colonialism is crucial in order to contextualise interpersonal and intercultural relations within a wider perspective that accounts for power and epistemic inequality. In her book *Can the Subaltern Speak?* Spivak (1988) describes epistemic silencing in a colonial context as a process of erasure of other types of knowing that are outside of the dominant group. The process of epistemic silencing is increasingly coming to the fore in critical readings of the field of interculturality (see Phipps, 2014; Phipps & Sitholé, 2022; Aman, 2014; Ferri, 2022), and R'boul (2022a, 2022b) in particular reflects on the dominance of English-speaking scholars, bringing forward an argument in favour of interepistemic dialogue between southern scholars and the advancement of decolonial approaches that relativise and syncretise different epistemologies.

Nelson's Ship in a Bottle

The contested nature of the word culture and its connections with hegemony and epistemic silencing is visible in the artwork of British-Nigerian artist Yinka Shonibare. In his *Nelson's Ship in a Bottle* (2009), Yoshibare creates a visual representation of the legacy of colonialism and of its ramifications in contemporary formulations of cultural identity and belonging.[1] This replica of the *HMS Victory*, the British Royal Navy flagship captained by Lord Nelson in 1805 during the Battle of Trafalgar, deviates from the original model with the addition of 37 sails that are printed with patterns that are normally associated with West African identity (Shirey, 2019). The artwork is on permanent display at the National Maritime Museum in Greenwich Park in London, after being installed as a temporary fourth plinth between 2010 and 2012 in Trafalgar Square where Lord Nelson's statue is displayed to commemorate this significant victory that symbolises British naval supremacy. Shonibare's replica represents a powerful metaphor of the complex global web of influences and hegemonic relations that characterise the process of cultural identification in post-colonial contexts. The choice of Dutch textiles of Indonesian origin, now associated with West Africa through trade and colonial relations, challenges the national narrative of British colonial power and naval dominance focusing on the multiplicity of possible identifications that result from living in a post-colonial global metropolis such as London. One important intercultural lesson that we can learn from analysing this artwork is that the process of questioning a familiar cultural symbol such as the *HMS Victory* and observing it from a different perspective adds a number of interpretative layers to accepted understandings of national identity and cultural belonging. Lau (2019: 130) describes this process as a *come-and-go* dynamic "between moments of familiarity and strangeness, of identification and differentiation, of recognition and distanciation, of affirmation and negation". In other words, the process of interrogation of familiar cultural symbols attests to the dynamic and reciprocal relation between individuals and their cultural environments. This is described by Lau as acquiring a *cultural flesh* understood as a lived, embodied experience of interculturality. However, this relation is never devoid of power in particular through the silencing of 'other' voices (Spivak, 1988) that are excluded from group narratives of belonging and cultural identification. This issue becomes salient in the context of the 'curriculum wars' currently taking place in my context in England between those who advocate the return of a traditional curriculum based on facts, rote learning, and a cohesive narrative of national identity, and those who are working to decolonise the curriculum in response to the Black Lives Matter movement, reclaiming a multifaceted, multicultural view of modern Britain.

Teacher education in England

The project of educational restoration towards a regressive traditionalism (Ball, 1993) across the English-speaking world started in the late 1980s and early 1990s with the Thatcher and Reagan governments in the UK and USA, respectively. In the context of the UK, this regressive traditionalism translated into a form of distrust towards multiculturalism and progressive ideas of education, leading to the introduction of the National Curriculum under the Conservative government headed by Prime Minister Margaret Thatcher in 1989, which gave unprecedent powers to the Secretary of State for Education to control the content and orientation of the curriculum. This alignment between a conservative political agenda and schools as sites of reproduction of dominant ideology (Apple, 2000; Bourdieu & Passeron, 1970) is still visible in current 'culture wars' over the curriculum in the UK. On the one side, and since 2010 in particular, successive Conservative Secretaries of State for Education have insisted on ensuring that curriculum content actively promotes a narrow vision of national identity and a nostalgic vision of Empire as force for good (Peterson, 2016; Watson, 2020, Nelson-Addy, 2021). On the other, following the Black Lives Matter movement and the Windrush scandal,[2] there is a growing debate in the UK around the legacy of colonialism and the need to enlarge the definition of Britishness to reflect diversity and multiculturalism. This debate has also been underpinned by a controversial policy that was first introduced in 2011 (Gov.UK, 2014) requiring all education institutions to actively promote a set of 'fundamental British values', namely democracy, the rule of law, individual liberty, mutual respect, and tolerance. The introduction of this policy is rooted in the Islamophobia that followed the terror attacks in the USA on 11 September 2001 and London in July 2005, when politicians across the political spectrum declared the failure of multiculturalism and the need to encourage social cohesion through the reformulation of a common definition of Britishness that would lead to a renewed sense of national identity. It is important to note that the introduction of 'fundamental British values' sits alongside the antiterrorist policy Prevent[3] requiring teachers and other education professionals to detect possible signs of radicalisation in students and their communities and to report any suspicious activities to the police. The fundamental Islamophobic and exclusionary character of the notion of 'fundamental British values' and of the Prevent policy is not the main focus of this chapter (see Richardson, 2015, and Habib, 2017. for a discussion of these policies), however they signal a strong reactionary response to ideas of hybridity, multiculturality, and diversity in British life.

The tension between a conservative and exclusionary vision of Britishness and the reality of multicultural life in the UK underpins post-2010 Conservative reforms in the English education system with their focus on discipline, conservatism, and standards (Cushing, 2021), as well as advocating a return to rote learning, factual knowledge, basic literacy, and numeracy (Brundrett, 2015), with an emphasis on fundamental British values. The push towards a simplified and narrow curriculum based on factual knowledge, and a return to a more traditional focus on discipline and behaviour management in the classroom has entailed a reform of teacher education. Since 2011 the government in England has attempted to remove teacher education from universities, promoting school-based training as more effective in preparing teachers for the profession (Mutton et al., 2017). This process culminated with the introduction of the Core Content Framework in 2019 (DfE, 2019), a mandatory curriculum for all teacher training institutions based on cognitive science, with little acknowledgement of the cultural and social factors that influence learning. This turn in education policy towards a regressive and limiting view of the purpose of education and of the role of teachers translates in a number of dilemmas for both practising teachers, pre-service teachers, and teacher educators committed to interculturality, social justice, diversity, and inclusion. However, I argue that this turn also demonstrates the urgency of revising what it means to practise interculturality and what it means to be an interculturalist.

The London context

London is a multicultural city with a population of about nine million people, of which about 37% are immigrants from many parts of the world, and more that 300 languages are spoken in schools (London Datastore, 2021). From my vantage point as an educator in the context of a global metropolis like London, I place regressive national policy drivers in contrast with the conviviality (Gilroy, 2004) of lived intercultural reality in a post-colonial city. From this perspective interculturality becomes a modus operandi, a practice of teaching interculturally that is embedded in all aspects of classroom life as a form of resistance to dominant narratives of a unified national culture and a uniform standard language. This ethos informs my practice as an intercultural educator working in a diverse, multicultural, multilingual context. I do not subscribe to the idea of competence, and I focus on encouraging student teachers to think critically about culture and how interaction is a complex and dynamic process constituted by many layers including power differentials, the historical heritage of colonial relations, and the many intersecting facets of identity in a post-colonial global space such as a London classroom. Teaching interculturally for me is a critical endeavour that develops along two intersecting axes, one based on a critical understanding of the contested ideology underpinning the National Curriculum in England and the other based on self-reflexivity. The two are brought together through a reflective understanding of the ways in which our own positionalities underpin our practice as educators according to the vision of the critical pedagogy of Freire (1970) and hooks (1994).

Teaching interculturality/teaching interculturally

An important part of the master's-level course I am involved in entails preparing pre-service teachers to teach the humanities. Reflecting on the contested nature of knowledge and the ways in which its translation in a school curriculum is ideologically inflected (Apple, 2019), pre-service teachers are introduced to the notion of the hidden curriculum and how hegemony works in the transmission of dominant values. In this regard, Apple (2019: 161) writes:

> Through the definition, incorporation, and selection of what is considered legitimate or 'real' knowledge, through positing a false consensus on what are appropriate facts, skills, hopes, and fears (and the way we all should evaluate them), the economic and cultural apparatus are dialectically linked. Here knowledge is power, but primarily in the hands of those who have it already, who already control cultural capital as well as economic capital.

This hegemonic appropriation and transmission of knowledge through the school curriculum is obvious in the humanities and particularly in the subjects of history and geography (see Gov.uk, n.d., for an overview of the English national school curriculum at both primary and secondary levels). Much of recent debates on the curriculum in England revolve on the lack of diversity in the humanities and the promotion of an outdated image of the country that erases diversity and promotes a homogeneous ideal of British identity. In this context, Wemyss (2009) uses the image of the Invisible Empire to describe this hegemonic discourse of Britishness, and important initiatives like the Black Curriculum Report (Arday, 2020) and Runnymede Perspectives (2015) highlight the systematic omission from the national curriculum of the contribution of Black and ethnic minority groups in the creation of modern Britain. In order to counteract this hegemonic narrative, pre-service teachers are encouraged to challenge these tacit assumptions relating to British values and Britishness. We reflect on our own overlapping identities and critically evaluate a number of sources that depict life in multiethnic, multilingual, diverse Britain, and consider how this diversity is often glossed over in everyday life, in the media, in textbooks, and in the curriculum. This is an important step in working with pre-service teachers to develop their critical understanding of the ideological discourses that underpin the creation of the school curriculum, in particular the silences and the invisibilities that are made operational in the mandate to promote British exceptionalism, as exemplified by the compulsory teaching of fundamental British values and the policing of language use based on a monolingual ideal of Standard English (Cushing, 2021). It is significant that in the decentralised school systems in the UK the teaching of languages is an undervalued aspect, particularly in England, and despite various government initiatives (see House of Commons Briefing Paper, 2020), there has been very little progress made to improve the provision of foreign language teaching in schools, which it could be argued is a direct reflection of the aforementioned policy drivers that promote British exceptionalism.

The ability to reflect critically on one's own practice with the aim to transform the lives of students is one of the main tenets of critical pedagogy (Door, 2014). Critical pedagogical practice is underpinned by an understanding of the ways in which knowledge is used to consolidate hegemonic narratives (Giroux, 2020) and by reflexivity intended as the process of thought–reflection–action (Frizelle, 2020; Holmes & Peña Dix, 2022). One aspect of critical pedagogy that is discussed in the master of arts (MA) course is Freire's (1970) notion of banking education. In Freire's words (1970: 56), banking education assumes "a dichotomy between human beings and the world: a person is merely in the world, not with the world or with others: the individual is spectator, not re-creator". Students become passive minds who receive "deposits of reality from the world outside", and they are thus deprived of agency and of the ability to change the world in which they live. This issue is particularly relevant for pre-service teachers who are entering a profession in which teachers' and students' agency is severely restricted, and reflexivity is constrained by multiple competing pressures aimed at raising standards and imparting decontextualised skills to young children and young people. Despite the many restrictions imposed on teacher educators and on pre-service teachers by this culture of performativity, self-reflexivity aligns theory with practice and places transformative action at the centre of education. hooks (1994: 44) writes about the importance of recognising that education is never politically neutral, embracing multicultural reality as a source of strength:

> Multiculturalism compels educators to recognise the narrow boundaries that have shaped the way knowledge is shared in the classroom. It forces us all to recognise our complicity in accepting and perpetuating biases of any kind.

Practising interculturality in this context means to attune pre-service teachers to the complexity of the multicultural classroom and to appreciate individual differences, cultures, languages, and needs. In other words, interculturality is enacted through education by embedding difference as a positive value in everyday practice.

Conclusion: What does it mean to 'interculturalise interculturality'?

Following Dervin and Jacobsson (2021, 2022), this volume proposes to 'interculturalise interculturality'. To me this means to assume difference as a starting point for the creation of a more just and equal world through education. Thinking about epistemic violence, one problem that has occupied me is the ways in which we think about the self and the other but in particular how we use our bodies in intercultural communication. A lot of attention is paid to language and interaction through language, and fixing communication through linguistic competence, but the question of the ways in which we behave interculturally with our bodies when we interact is still underexplored. Linked to this issue, I am interested in how some bodies are seen as 'other', as different, and how this connects to wider intersectional inequalities. For example, the area of queer intercultural communication (Yep, Lescure, & Russo, 2019) highlights the crucial role of sexuality and gender in the practices of cultural identity opening to non-Western epistemological frameworks (Eguchi & Asante, 2016; Asante, 2018). There is also an emerging field of feminist intercultural communication, looking at, for example, rape and sexual assault and how this is institutionalised in different cultural contexts (Zenovich & Cooks, 2018), or at the construction and performance of gender from a decolonial perspective (Lengel et al., 2020). I believe these interventions bring important new perspectives to interculturality, opening a dialogue with intersectional, queer, and feminist studies. In closing, I see interculturality moving forward in regarding culture beyond the methodological nationalism of grand narratives to investigate the dialectic between *small cultures* and *big cultures* (Holliday, 2011), or in other words how culture in interaction is embedded in and influenced by wider geopolitical issues.

Notes

1 Yinka Shonibare, *Nelson's Ship in a Bottle*. The artwork can be viewed at the National Maritime Museum website (rmg.co.uk, 2022): https://www.rmg.co.uk/national-maritime-museum/attractions/nelsons-ship-bottle.
2 The 'Windrush' generation are those who arrived in the UK from Caribbean countries between 1948 and 1973. Many took up jobs in the nascent National Health Service and other sectors affected by Britain's post-war labour shortage. The name 'Windrush' derives from the *HMT Empire Windrush* ship which brought one of the first large groups of Caribbean people to the UK in 1948. As the Caribbean was, at the time, a part of the British Commonwealth, those who arrived were automatically British subjects and free to permanently live and work in the UK.

The Windrush scandal began to surface in 2017 after it emerged that hundreds of Commonwealth citizens, many of whom were from the Windrush generation, had been wrongly detained, deported, and denied legal rights (The Joint Council for the Welfare of Immigrants, n.d.).
3 *The Counter Terrorism Security Act* (Gov.UK, 2015).

References

Amadasi, S., & Holliday, A. (2018). 'I already have a culture': Negotiating competing grand and personal narratives in interview conversations with new study abroad arrivals. *Language and Intercultural Communication, 18*(2), 241–256.

Aman, R. (2014). *Impossible Interculturality? Education and the Colonial Difference in a Multicultural World*. Linköping: Linköping University, Department of Behavioural Sciences and Learning.

Anderson, B. (1983). *Imagined Communities: Reflections on the Origin and Spread of Nationalism*. London: Verso.

Apple, M. W. (2019). *Ideology and Curriculum*. New York: Routledge.

Apple, M. W. (2000). *Official Knowledge: Democratic Education in a Conservative Age*. New York: Routledge.

Arday, J. (2020). *The Black Curriculum: Black British History in National Curriculum Report 2020*. Retrieved 2 July 2022, from https://diversityuk.org/wp-content/uploads/2020/06/The-Black-Curriculum-Report-2020.pdf.

Asante, M. K. (2013). Afrocentricity: Toward a new understanding of African thought in the world. In M. K. Asante, Y. Miike, & J. Yin (Eds.), *The Global Intercultural Communication Reader* (pp. 101–110). New York: Routledge.

Asante, G. (2018). "Where is home?" Negotiating comm(unity) and un/belonging among queer African migrants on Facebook. *Borderlands, 17*(1), 1–22.

Ball, S. J. (1993). Education, majorism and 'the curriculum of the dead'. *Curriculum Studies, 1*(2), 195–214.

Bhabha, H. K. (1994). *The Location of Culture*. London: Routledge.

Bourdieu, P., & Passeron, J. C. (1970). *Reproduction in Education, Society and Culture*. London: Sage.

Brundrett, M. (2015). Policy on the primary curriculum since 2010: The demise of the expert view. *London Review of Education, 13*(2), 49–58.

Council of Europe. (2018). *Reference Framework of Competences for Democratic Culture*. Retrieved 10 June 2022, from https://www.coe.int/en/web/education/competences-for-democratic-culture.

Council of Europe. (2020). *Common European Framework of Reference for Languages: Learning, Teaching, Assessment. Companion Volume*. Strasbourg: Council of Europe. Retrieved 10 June 2022, from https://rm.coe.int/common-european-framework-of-reference-for-languages-learning-teaching/16809ea0d4.

Cushing, I. (2021). Policy mechanisms of the standard language ideology in England's education system. *Journal of Language, Identity & Education*. https://doi.org/10.1080/15348458.2021.1877542.

Dasli, M. (2019). UNESCO guidelines on intercultural education: A deconstructive reading. *Pedagogy, Culture & Society, 27*(2), 215–232.

Dervin, F. (2011). A plea for change in research on intercultural discourses: A "liquid" approach to the study of the acculturation of Chinese students. *Journal of Multicultural Discourses, 6*(1), 37–52.

Dervin, F. (2014). Exploring 'new' interculturality online. *Language and Intercultural Communication*, *14*(2), 191–206.

Dervin, F. (2016). *Interculturality in Education: A Theoretical and Methodological Toolbox*. London: Palgrave Pilot.

Dervin, F. (2020). Creating and combining models of intercultural competence for teacher education/training: On the need to rethink IC frequently. In F. Dervin, R. Moloney, & A. Simpson (Eds.), *Intercultural Competence in the Work of Teachers: Confronting Ideologies and Practices* (pp. 57–72). London: Routledge.

Dervin, F., & Chen, N. (2020). Intercultural research must be political. In K. Trimmer, D. Hoven, & P. Keskitalo (Eds.), *Indigenous Postgraduate Education: Intercultural Perspectives* (pp. 299–304). Charlotte, NC: Information Age Publishing.

Dervin, F., Gajardo, A., & Lavanchy, A. (2013). *Politics of Interculturality*. Newcastle: Cambridge Scholars.

Dervin, F., Härkönen, A., Yuan, M., Chen, N., & Zhang, W. (2020). "I want to feel that I live in China": Imaginaries and hospitality in international students' (mis-)encounters at a top Chinese university. *Frontiers of Education in China*, *5*(4), 588–620.

Dervin, F., & Jacobsson, A. (2020). *Teacher Education for Critical and Reflexive Interculturality*. London: Palgrave Macmillan.

Dervin, F., & Jacobsson, A. (2021). *Interculturaliser l'interculturel*. Paris: L'Harmattan.

Dervin, F., & Jacobsson, A. (2022). *Intercultural Communication Education: Broken Realities and Rebellious Dreams*. London: Springer.

Dervin, F., & Simpson, A. (2021). *Interculturality and the Political Within Education*. London: Routledge.

Dervin, F., & Yuan, M. (2021). *Revitalising Interculturality in Education: Chinese Minzu as a Companion*. London: Routledge.

DfE. (2019). *ITT Core Content Framework*. Retrieved 23 June 2022, from https://www.gov.uk/government/publications/initial-teacher-training-itt-core-content-framework.

Door, V. M. (2014). Critical pedagogy and reflexivity: The issue of ethical consistency. *The International Journal of Critical Pedagogy*, *5*(2), 88–99.

Eagleton, T. (2000). *The Idea of Culture*. Oxford: Blackwell.

Eguchi, S., & Asante, G. (2016). Disidentifications revisited: Queer(y)ing intercultural communication theory. *Communication Theory*, *26*(2), 171–189.

Ferri, G. (2014). The development of ethical communication and intercultural responsibility: A philosophical perspective. *Language and Intercultural Communication*, *14*(1), 7–23.

Ferri, G. (2018). *Intercultural Communication: Critical Approaches and Future Challenges*. Basingstoke: Palgrave Macmillan.

Ferri, G. (2020). Difference, becoming and rhizomatic subjectivities beyond 'otherness': A posthuman framework for intercultural communication. *Language and Intercultural Communication*, *20*(5), 408–418.

Ferri, G. (2022). The master's tools will never dismantle the master's house: Decolonising intercultural communication. *Language and Intercultural Communication*, *22*(3), 381–390.

Freire, P. (1970). *Pedagogy of the Oppressed*. London: Penguin.

Frizelle, K. L. (2020). The personal is pedagogical (?): Personal narratives and embodiment as teaching strategies in higher education. *South African Journal of Higher Education*, *34*(2), 17–35.

Gilroy, P. (2004). *After Empire: Melancholia or Convivial Culture?* London: Routledge.

Giroux, H. A. (2020). *On Critical Pedagogy* (2nd ed.). London: Bloomsbury.

Gov.UK. (n.d.). *The National Curriculum*. Retrieved 27 June 2022, from https://www.gov.uk/national-curriculum.

Gov.UK. (2014). *Guidance on Promoting British Values in Schools Published*. Retrieved 1 August 2022, from https://www.gov.uk/government/news/guidance-on-promoting-british-values-in-schools-published#:~:text=All%20have%20a%20duty%20to,'Prevent'%20strategy%20in%202011.

Gov.UK. (2015). *Prevent Duty Guidance*. Retrieved 27 July 2022, from https://www.gov.uk/government/publications/prevent-duty-guidance.

Habib, S. (2017). *Learning and Teaching British Values: Policies and Perspectives on British Identities*. London: Palgrave Macmillan.

Hall, S. (2018). Popular culture, politics and history. *Cultural Studies*, *32*(6), 929–952.

Holliday, A. (2011). *Intercultural Communication and Ideology*. London: Sage.

Holliday, A. (2013). *Understanding Intercultural Communication: Negotiating a Grammar of Culture*. London and New York: Routledge.

Holliday, A. (2016). Revisiting intercultural competence: Small culture formation on the go through threads of experience. *International Journal of Bias, Identity and Diversities in Education (IJBIDE)*, *1*(2), 1–13.

Holliday, A. (2020). Culture, communication, context and power. In J. Jackson (Ed.), *Routledge Handbook of Language and Intercultural Communication* (2nd ed., pp. 39–52). London: Routledge.

Holmes, P., & Peña Dix, B. (2022). A research trajectory for difficult times: Decentring language and intercultural communication. *Language and Intercultural Communication*, *22*(3), 337–353.

hooks, b. (1994). *Teaching to Transgress: Education as the Practice of Freedom*. New York: Taylor & Francis.

House of Commons Briefing Paper. (2020). *Language Teaching in Schools (England)*. Retrieved 7 July 2022, from https://researchbriefings.files.parliament.uk/documents/CBP-7388/CBP-7388.pdf.

Kramsch, K. (1998). *Language and Culture*. Oxford: Oxford University Press.

Lau, K. (2019). Whither intercultural philosophy? Responses to comments and questions on phenomenology and intercultural understanding: Toward a new cultural flesh. *Dao: A Journal of Comparative Philosophy*, *18*(1), 127–136. https://doi.org/10.1007/s11712-018-9647-1.

Lengel, L., Atay, A., & Kluch, Y. (2020). Decolonizing gender and intercultural communication in transnational contexts. In G. Rings & S. Rasinger (Eds.), *The Cambridge Handbook of Intercultural Communication* (pp. 205–226). Cambridge: Cambridge University Press.

London Datastore. (2021). Retrieved 24 June 2022, from https://data.london.gov.uk/dataset/londons-population.

Miike, Y. (2007). An Asiacentric reflection on Eurocentric bias in communication theory. *Communication Monographs*, *2*(74), 272–278.

Monceri, S. (2003). The transculturing self: A philosophical approach. *Language and Intercultural Communication*, *3*(2), 108–114.

Monceri, S. (2009). The transculturing self II. Constructing identity through identification. *Language and Intercultural Communication*, *9*(1), 43–53.

Müller-Funk, W. (2012). *The Architecture of Modern Culture: Towards a Narrative Cultural Theory*. Berlin and Boston, MA: De Gruyter.

Mutton, T., Burn, K., & Menter, I. (2017). Deconstructing the Carter review: Competing conceptions of quality in England's 'school-led' system of initial teacher education. *Journal of Education Policy*, *32*(1), 14–33.

Nelson-Addy, L. (2021). The Newbolt report: Discussing empire, race and racism in the classroom. In A. Green (Ed.), *The New Newbolt Report: One Hundred Years of Teaching English in England* (pp. 149–166). London: Routledge.

Peterson, A. (2016). Different battlegrounds, similar concerns? The 'history wars' and the teaching of history in Australia and England. *Compare: A Journal of Comparative and International Education*, 46(6), 861–881.

Phipps, A. (2014). 'They are bombing now': 'Intercultural dialogue' in times of conflict. *Language and Intercultural Communication*, 14(1), 108–124.

Phipps, A., & Sitholé, T. (2022). Interrupting the cognitive empire: Keynote drama as cultural justice. *Language and Intercultural Communication*, 22(3), 391–411.

Piller, I. (2011). *Intercultural Communication: A Critical Introduction*. Edinburgh: Edinburgh University Press.

R'boul, H. (2022a). Postcolonial interventions in intercultural communication knowledge: Meta-intercultural ontologies, decolonial knowledges and epistemological polylogue. *Journal of International and Intercultural Communication*, 15(1), 75–93.

R'boul, H. (2022b). Epistemological plurality in intercultural communication knowledge. *Journal of Multicultural Discourses*. https://doi.org/10.1080/17447143.2022.2069784.

Richardson, R. (2015). British values and British identity: Muddles, mixtures, and ways ahead. *London Review of Education*, 13(2), 37–48.

Runnymede Perspectives. (2015). *History Lessons: Teaching Diversity in and through the History National Curriculum*. Retrieved 2 July 2022, from https://assets.website-files.com/61488f992b58e687f1108c7c/61c32c93a3ed66996d0a850e_History%20Lessons%20-%20Teaching%20Diversity%20In%20and%20Through%20the%20History%20National%20Curriculum.pdf.

Sercu, L. (2010). Assessing intercultural competence: More questions than answers. In A. Paran & S. Sercu (Eds.), *Testing the Untestable in Language Education* (pp. 17–34). Clevedon: Multilingual Matters.

Shirey, H. (2019). Engaging black European spaces and postcolonial dialogues through public art: Yinka Shonibare's *Nelson's Ship in a Bottle*. *Open Cultural Studies*, 3, 362–372.

Simpson, A., & Dervin, F. (2019). The Council of Europe reference framework of competences for democratic culture: Ideological refractions, othering and obedient politics. *Intercultural Communication Education*, 2(3), 102–119.

Spivak, G. C. (1988). *Can the Subaltern Speak?* Basingstoke: Macmillan.

Street, B. (1993). Culture is a verb. In D. Graddol, L. Thompson, & M. Byram (Eds.), *Language and Culture* (pp. 23–43). Clevedon: BAAL and Multilingual Matters.

The Joint Council for the Welfare of Immigrants. (n.d.). Retrieved 30 July 2022, from https://www.jcwi.org.uk/windrush-scandal-explained.

UNESCO. (2006). *UNESCO Guidelines on Intercultural Education*. Retrieved 23 June 2022, from https://www.jcwi.org.uk/windrush-scandal-explained.

Watson, M. (2020). Michael Gove's war on professional historical expertise: Conservative curriculum reform, extreme whig history and the place of imperial heroes in modern multicultural Britain. *British Politics*, 15, 271–290.

Wemyss, G. (2009). *The Invisible Empire: White Discourse, Tolerance and Belonging*. Aldershot: Ashgate.

Wimmer, A., & Schiller, G. N. (2002). Methodological nationalism and beyond: Nation–state building, migration and the social sciences. *Global Networks*, 2(4), 301–334.

Yep, G., Lescure, R., & Russo, S. (2019). Queer Intercultural Communication. *Oxford Research Encyclopedia of Communication*. Retrieved 11 October 2022, from https://

oxfordre.com/communication/view/10.1093/acrefore/9780190228613.001.0001/acrefore-9780190228613-e-170.

Yoshikawa, M. (1987). "The double swing" model of intercultural communication between the East and West. In D. L. Kincaid (Ed.), *Communication Theory: Eastern and Western Perspectives* (pp. 319–329). San Diego, CA: Academic Press.

Zenovich, J. A., & Cooks, L. (2018). A feminist postsocialist approach to the intercultural communication of rape at the ICTY. *Communication Studies, 69*(4), 404–420.

12 Interculturalising the teaching of interculturality in Swedish higher education

Andreas Jacobsson

Setting the stage

In a fairly similar way to other higher education contexts around the world, *interculturality* has been a prominent keyword in Swedish higher education for the last three to four decades. Interculturality is today integrated as a perspective in different academic subjects, amongst them business studies, education, health care, languages, linguistics, literary studies, religious studies, sociology, and social work. However, it is only recently that 'intercultural studies' have been acknowledged as a free-standing academic subject with entitlement to award qualification at one Swedish university.[1]

Interculturality has been regarded as pivotal in discourses on internationalisation in higher education – primarily regarded as a specific quality in the form of *intercultural competence* that students can acquire by (merely) taking part in, e.g., study abroad exchange programmes where they will experience cultural and linguistic differences, or from so-called internationalisation at home in the form of globalised study materials. Intercultural competence has also been activated as a functionalist response to demographic changes that gradually but swiftly has turned Sweden into a highly multicultural society – a process that started with work migration in the 1960s and continued with different waves of immigrants, refugees, and exiles since the 1980s, and is still ongoing. This explication clarifies that interculturality in Sweden covers two very different areas of cultural encounters: (1) international relations and (2) the local multicultural demography. To cover such a wide area of interest is the concept's strength and weakness at the same time. Wide-scoped and overarching notions open for scholars to develop interdisciplinary and creative theoretical syntheses. But there is also a risk that, instead, one ends up with blurred theoretical boundaries and all too simple solutions to complex issues. Unfortunately, it is to a large extent the latter outcome that has come to haunt interculturality in Swedish higher education.

A closer look at interculturality from a historical perspective in Sweden shows that it primarily has been promoted as *intercultural communication*. It is also this version of the notion that is still dominating academic discourses in Sweden. The focus on communication and/or dialogue connects Swedish interculturality to a traditional strand of teaching and researching interculturality – stating that when

DOI: 10.4324/9781003345275-15

158 *Andreas Jacobsson*

people with different cultural backgrounds and different languages are communicating it often leads to misunderstandings, miscommunication, or communication breakdown (e.g. Gudykunst, 2003; Hofstede, 2010; Ting-Toomey, 1999). According to textbooks, the recipe to avoid these communication problems is to develop so-called intercultural competence – a specific skill set developed for mastering communication with cultural and linguistic Others (e.g. Stier, 2019). Interculturality in Sweden can thus be characterised as primarily functionalist and practice-oriented. The theories and methods used for developing intercultural competence are influenced by documents promoting guidelines for education by supranational organisations such as UNESCO and the Council of Europe.

Regarding this brief introduction, it is possible to state that in Sweden interculturality is used as a cross-disciplinary notion with relevance for a variety of academic subjects. However, the widespread cross-disciplinarity of interculturality has also restricted the potential for a more developed and reflexive theoretical dialogue that is commonly found in academic disciplines with lively and ongoing critical meta-reflections. Critical discussions on interculturality are scarce in Sweden, even if exceptions do exist and slowly are becoming more visible (e.g. Aman, 2014; Dahlén, 1997; Hill, 2020). Many of the Swedish scholars and teachers who are using interculturality in their research and teaching (in different academic subjects) seem to take the notion for granted as reasonably transparent and concise enough not to find it necessary to problematise further.

My take on interculturality: A personal reflection

I have been teaching interculturality for more than a decade, and my personal take on the notion has varied over time. Initially, I was interested in identifying, discussing, and analysing cultural differences. The diversity and complexity of the world around us genuinely intrigued me – and it still does. In multicultural classes with exchange students from many parts of the world, I have engaged in stimulating and exciting dialogues on everything from cultural difference to philosophical ideas on values, (cultural) relativism, perspectivism, politics, stereotypes, aesthetics, history, food, nationalism, and globalisation. I have learned a lot from these classes – and I sincerely hope the students have done that too. What I am less sure of is if what we learned always has had something to do with interculturality. As time passed and the more classes that I have taught on interculturality – and the more experienced I have become – the less sure I am of what interculturality is and what it can potentially be. Ever since I started in intercultural studies, I have struggled with being part of an academic discipline that is frequently focused on a 'negative' interpretation of interculturality, in the sense that problems with differences in social interaction are highlighted as the main object of study – for example, the already mentioned failure to communicate – and that a functionalist interpretation of intercultural competence is seen as the best way to handle said problems.

Gradually I have also come to realise that the intercultural theory that is promoted in popular textbooks of intercultural communication (e.g. Holliday, 2018;

Jackson, 2019; Jandt, 2020; Liu et al., 2018) is not very helpful in providing answers to questions arising when interacting with students in class and trying to make sense of the ambivalent, complex, messy, and 'glocal' reality that appears in our discussions. There is simply too much emphasis on the highly polysemic concept of *culture* as a catch-all explanation for pretty much everything (e.g. Breidenbach & Nyíri, 2015), and not enough emphasis on problematising the Eurocentric and Western-centred epistemology that is permeating textbooks on interculturality so clearly. To be perfectly honest it is a liberating sensation for a teacher to free oneself from the limitations that textbooks bring to a course. Instead of spending your valuable teaching hours on the tedious task of contradicting prefabricated 'truths' that are impossible to agree with, you can choose a selection of teaching materials in the form of research articles that provide different approaches, ideas, methods, and perspectives – from different parts of the world and from different academic contexts.

Coming from an academic background in the arts and humanities (film and media studies), I have also found it rather difficult to reconcile with the reductionist interpretation of the concept of culture that implicitly or explicitly are (still) used in most of the disciplines that are applying the notion of interculturality in Swedish higher education. I am more comfortable with using hermeneutically inspired (research) methods, focusing on the interpretation and analysis of empirical cases rather than developing practical methods for social interaction based on the idea of culture as a determining framework for group behaviour.

To come to terms with my own theoretical and methodological problems with interculturality, at the same time as I am adhering to the explicit disciplinarity in the field, I have been propagating for taking inspiration from the arts and humanities to approach interculturality as something that is necessary to analyse and *think with*, rather than learn how to master with a pre-established skill set (Jacobsson, 2017). And even more importantly, for a long time, I have been inspired by the more explicitly political tradition of cultural studies (e.g. Shohat and Stam, 1994/2014; Hall & Du Gay, 1996; Shohat, 2006; Grossberg, 2010). The presumed neutral (scientific) aspiration of interculturality in Sweden did not match well with my focus on critique of ideology and post-colonial perspectives.

The feeling of ambivalence was still vividly present during the next phase in the development of my understanding of interculturality. I gladly sided with the bourgeoning critical turn that finally started to scrutinise many of the outdated ideas that had been repeatedly reproduced. Fred Dervin (2011) criticised culturalist interpretations of the Other in intercultural communication education and pleaded for a more open and 'liquid' conceptualisation of culture. Dervin has expanded his critique over the years and has considered completely disregarding the concept of culture – due to its very low relevance for explaining interculturality (2015) – and thoroughly problematised the field of intercultural education (2016). Dervin has consistently proposed that it is necessary to take different ideologies into consideration when approaching interculturality. There are a few other researchers who have highlighted ideology as a key concept for clarifying aspects of intercultural communication (e.g. Holliday, 2010; O'Regan, 2014). These critical perspectives made perfect sense in relation to my personal view of interculturality as far from neutral. They also helped me to come to terms with a 'scientism' that I often see as taken for granted in studies on interculturality.

Ingrid Piller is another scholar who has had an impact on my teaching. Piller (2010/2017) problematised simplistic usages of culture and clarified that even if languages are highlighted as vital for interculturality, other aspects are regularly treated as more important for understanding intercultural communication – as for example norms and values, stereotypes, and nonverbal communication. According to my experience, this relative invisibility of languages and linguistics can be explained by (1) the fact that many researchers in the field only (are able to) communicate in English, (2) the opinion that 'Global English' or 'English as lingua franca' is the primary form of communication for intercultural communication overshadows other opinions, and (3) there is a strong perception that learning a new language automatically leads to 'learning' a new culture (e.g. Dervin & Jacobsson, 2021a).

Influenced by the critical scholars, I formulated (for myself) a tentative definition of interculturality as *cultural encounters developing simultaneously as social, communicative, and political processes*. From my perspective it seemed necessary to create an open-ended definition that includes as wide an area as possible regarding potential cultural encounters. A keyword for my definition is *movement*, as a foundational concept of contemporary times (e.g. Nail, 2015, 2018). People, things, ideas, mediations, and representations are constantly on the move in different directions for different reasons, and meetings and encounters are taking place everywhere, resulting in new expressions – or not. To engage with interculturality is to look at things from different perspectives, and to be able to shift perspectives. This shifting is required to take the prefix *inter-* as in-between seriously, and to problematise geopolitical and epistemological precedence. I borrowed the term 'polycentric' from Shohat and Stam (1994/2014) to highlight that this approach to interculturality departs from the basic logic that the world has not one but several centres (Jacobsson, 2017). According to my understanding, teaching and researching interculturality strives for breaking down any form of centre-periphery hierarchies and promoting epistemological equality.

With this very open (and politically oriented) definition, the object of study when using interculturality becomes elusive and hard to pinpoint. Rather, I am using interculturality as an umbrella term, capturing a general interest in issues connected to movement and meetings over so-called cultural boundaries – in practically unlimited forms and shapes. It seems to be quite pointless to pursue a consensus with other scholars, either locally or globally, who are propagating for more restricted and nuanced definitions of the notion. Scrutinising the terminological debates and discourses on interculturality, it becomes apparent that scholarly positioning and nuanced interpretations overshadow productive academic dialogues (e.g. Meer et al., 2016; Dietz, 2018).

The challenges of decolonising interculturality

An important aspect of the critical turn in intercultural communication studies is that the strong Western bias in the field has started to be scrutinised and problematised. Inspired by an influential article by Paul Gorski (2008), and recent publications in anthropology, sociology, and cultural studies, several scholars have started to apply the notion of *decolonisation* in their teaching and research (e.g. Andreotti, 2011; Martin-Pirbhai-Illich, 2016; Aman, 2018; Guilherme, 2019; Pineda et al., 2020; R'boul, 2021). For my own understanding of interculturality, decolonisation is a term that I am well acquainted with in relation to my background in film and media studies. To problematise the effects that colonial structures have had on the world has been a priority in my teaching for a long time, both in film studies and in intercultural studies.

A Swedish scholar who has reinvigorated the thinking on decolonisation in intercultural education is Robert Aman. Aman (2014, 2018) has critically problematised dominant Western epistemologies and characterised intercultural education as mostly a unidirectional learning from and about the Other. By introducing the term 'inter-epistemic' as an additional aspect of interculturality, taking colonial structures and different knowledge systems into consideration, Aman allows for an ideologically conscious stance on comparative intercultural education. Aman clarifies the importance of acknowledging the polysemy of interculturality by contrasting the notion with the Spanish term *interculturalidad*. Aman (2015) argues that it is wrong to treat these terms as equivalents. In parts of Latin America interculturalidad is interpreted as indigenous group identities connected to specific rights. This interpretation is quite far from Western fluid ideas of culture as anti-essentialist. Comparing the notions by looking closer at how they are used in different contexts and are affected by colonial structures and political systems will be helpful for detecting how interculturality is interpreted in different knowledge systems. To clarify and problematise different epistemologies paves the way for a potential dialogue between different ways of knowing – hence the notion of *inter-epistemology* (Aman, 2018).

In intercultural communication education, a fair amount of research papers includes 'decolonising' either as a keyword or as part of the main argument. However, there are still questions remaining to what extent and how education, classrooms, and curricula are *colonised* today. We also have to ask questions about *who* is supposed to decolonise education and for what purpose. The general impression is that the term decolonising is either too broad, and generally stating that education should be aware of global inequalities or to narrow focusing on minor aspects of national educational systems.

Two scholars who often are used as theoretical support for the argument to decolonise intercultural education are the Portuguese sociologist and law scholar Boaventura de Sousa Santos (2014, 2018) and Argentinian literary scholar Walter Mignolo (2007, 2011), who both work in the Western academic system. If one reads these scholars carefully, they seem to be way more radical, anti-Eurocentric, and activistic in their writings than what is transferred to the critical turn in intercultural communication education. It is not an easy task to decolonise – whatever we mean by the term – an interculturality that is promoting (communicative) consensus and is dominated by functionalist ideas, as in Swedish higher education. A question that arises is to what extent is it possible to combine interculturality with the idea of 'decoloniality' and 'delinking' as theorised by Mignolo (2007) – as a geopolitical, economic as well as an epistemological breaking free from Western Eurocentric structures (by the Global South) – a process that, according to Mignolo, is pluralistic (see Aman, 2015). In a recent collection of his articles, Mignolo (2021: xi) elaborates on the terminology:

> The prefix 'de-' takes the field, breaking up Western universality and totality into multiple temporalities, knowledges, and praxes of living. (…) The de- prefix means that you disobey and delink from a belief in unipolarity and universality; you take what you need to restitute that which has been destituted and that is relevant to the arising *multipolarity* in the interstate relations and *pluriversality*.

These ideas seem to be in conflict – or even incompatible? – with Western academic ideals of interculturality. If we agree with Mignolo that delinking is a radical break with modernity and Eurocentric structures, why bother with 'decolonising' curricula at Western universities? It will only end up in a discourse of strictly Western interest. I have formulated this question with the intention to be deliberately provocative for two different reasons: (1) it is a very positive thing that scholars in intercultural communication education are becoming critically inclined, (2) but at the same time it is highly important to carefully rethink the notions and concepts that are used not to run the risk of conflating incompatible issues and/or activating what one thinks is critical concepts but in reality is just a continuous reproduction of academic truisms (Dabashi, 2019).

Interculturalising interculturality

It remains to be seen how radical the critical and decolonial turn will be in the future. To effectuate many of the critical ideas on interculturality that have been addressed recently, based on Fred Dervin's (2021) proposal to interculturalise interculturality, we have developed the idea in our joint publications (Dervin & Jacobsson, 2021b, 2022). To interculturalise interculturality is to open and expand interculturality for a polyvocal symphony of interpretations, ideas, and perspectives from different geopolitical contexts. It is about including diverging ideas from voices (such as teachers and researchers) from outside the dominating structures and discourses. It is about breaking down Eurocentric and Western dominance regarding the production of intercultural knowledge. It is about acknowledging the importance of ideology for different interpretations of interculturality. It is about accepting and encouraging the use of different languages and to regard linguistic differences as a challenging source for digging deeper into the complexity of interculturality. It is about being against, e.g., the simplistic idea of intercultural competence as a solution to 'problems' of diversity. Interculturality is not and can never be an ideologically neutral 'scientistic' notion, therefore it is about constantly rethinking, updating, and reinventing the notion. And finally, it is about envisioning a proper 'dissensual' scholarly dialogue where disagreement and conflicting ideas are regarded as potential ways to move forward in conversations and in publications. No one has precedence regarding interculturality (Dervin & Jacobsson, 2022).

In short interculturalising interculturality is about practising what we have (all) talked about doing! To develop frameworks and nuanced interpretations of notions and concepts is one thing, to give meaning to ideas of decentring, polycentrism, decolonising, non-/anti-essentialism, etc., we also must act accordingly. This is a demanding task that requires extensive reading and research and the courage to question your own positions and prior knowledge. It entails being open for *investigating* historical, geopolitical, and ideological perspectives rather than promoting a specific idea. And finally, it encourages comparisons in different languages (Dervin & Yuan, 2021; Dervin & Jacobsson, 2021a). We are all linguistically restricted in the sense that we only can speak and/or read a certain number of languages. However, this does not entail that we are unable to interact cross-linguistically. We will get a long way by expanding our linguistic competence as much as we can possibly master, by speaking to colleagues who are linguistically versatile, and by consulting literature and dictionaries. To comply with English as an academic lingua franca will never help us to interculturalise interculturality.

To work with interculturalising interculturality in class is a challenging task. I regularly encourage my students to investigate the course material, as for example, the literature that they are reading, the films that they are watching, and the course outline that I have provided. As a teacher, to engage in this kind of dialogue is an efficient way to encourage students to develop so-called critical thinking. In Swedish higher education, critical thinking is regarded as the main norm of education. However, it is still unclear how critical thinking should be interpreted. A pedagogical 'trick' that I have tried out together with my colleague Olle Sjögren – when we introduced world cinema to our film studies courses two decades ago – was to change the common-sense ordering of film history. Instead of following the content of Western textbooks in film history (e.g. Thomson & Bordwell, 1994; Nowell-Smith, 1997) – where European national cinemas and the Hollywood production systems are treated as a foundational base for the history of moving images – we reversed the 'normal' structure and started the course by introducing different world cinema film cultures and followed up by problematising how to unthink the notion of Eurocentrism that was (and partly still is) permeating Western film studies (e.g. Shohat & Stam, 2014/1994). When I started teaching intercultural studies, I brought this idea with me to my new courses, and it soon became glaringly apparent that to unthink Eurocentrism was as relevant in my new subject as it had been in my old. To twist and turn on the students' expectations is as I see it an important aspect of teaching interculturality. I would also emphasise that this can be regarded as part of the process to interculturalise interculturality, since it destabilises both preconceived notions about interculturality and the students' ideas on what knowledge should be.

Interculturalising interculturality with the support of world cinema

Watching and analysing film from different parts of the world, so-called *world cinema*, has been a vital source of inspiration in my strive for interculturalising my teaching of interculturality. The way that I have used world cinema is as audiovisual empirical material from film cultures outside of your own vantage point. Depending on your geographical, cultural, and/or political position, what is considered as world cinema is relative and shifting. From a Swedish/European perspective, film cultures outside of Europe/the West will constitute world cinema. From an African, Asian, or Latin American perspective, European cinema will instead be regarded as a part of world cinema. The next step is to problematise the actual categorisation of the world into different geopolitical contexts and contemplate on the relevance of national and regional distinctions – thereby adding another layer of complexity to the discussion. This line of thinking counteracts a common hierarchisation of centre and periphery that is often present in the study of film as well as of interculturality. According to this interpretation of world cinema, the world does not have one but multiple centres, and by watching films from different parts of the world this multiplicity can be clarified for the students.

One basic but important aspect of interculturalising interculturality is to open for and include new ideas and different perspectives from a variety of geopolitical contexts in teaching and researching interculturality. For this purpose, world cinema can be used as highly accessible empirical material for audiovisual intercultural experiences. I have previously argued that the act of watching a film can be considered as audiovisual intercultural encounters (Jacobsson, 2017). Watching a fiction film or a documentary activates cognition and emotion in a more direct way than other forms of artistic representation, such as literature or theatre (Grodal, 2009). The audiovisuality of filmic depictions carries a potential to introduce the spectator to environments and contexts from different parts of world and different historical times. However, to make sense of this potential it is necessary for the teacher to develop a methodological framework for the interpretation and analysis of film. I have previously proposed that to analyse film from an intercultural perspective (Jacobsson, 2017), students as well as researchers must include the following four intersecting aspects into their analysis: (1) themes and motives; (2) aesthetics – style and form; (3) potential viewer positions; and (4) film as a philosophically motivated source of knowledge – to *think* and create ideas about interculturality with the support of film. The first three aspects are straightforward and lucid but require a systematic approach. It is necessary to get accustomed with different aesthetic traditions and conventions of style and form to be able to fully make use of film for this purpose. The fourth aspect is more abstract and complex and could be described as something to strive for to achieve. The inspiration for treating film as special sources of knowledge to think *with* about interculturality is taken from French philosopher Gilles Deleuze (1986, 1989) and his two books on cinema. Deleuze propagated for using film as something else than mere representation or illustration of actuality – for him film could fill the function of audiovisual material that instigates new ideas (and in this case about interculturality) that eventually could be developed into philosophical concepts.

In my teaching I have used world cinema as a companion for thinking about interculturality. Starting my academic research career as a film scholar with a keen interest in world cinema in general and in Latin American and African cinema in particular, two specific ideas have guided my teaching and my research. Both of these ideas are, as I see it, equally important for teaching and researching interculturality: (1) unthinking of Eurocentrism (e.g. Shohat & Stam, 1994/2014) and (2) shifting perspectives as *intercultural viewer positions*.

To expand on these two ideas, I will here provide an example of a film that I have used in my teaching on many occasions in different courses. I find this film particularly efficient for stimulating student discussions about different perspectives, film cultures, aesthetic traditions, and epistemologies. *Island of Flowers* (*Ilha das Flores*, 1988) is a short, inventive, and playful Brazilian 'documentary' directed by Jorge Furtado. The film is a rapidly edited stream of images, telling a story about the circuit of life of a tomato in an interconnected chain of events – from being cultivated to harvested, sold, or refined, or being redeemed as garbage and ending up on the ironically named 'Island of flowers' that is used as landfill. On the island the waste is offered to the pigs as food. The waste that the pigs reject is finally offered to very poor 'human beings' (children and women) without means to support themselves because 'they have no money', or owner – as the pigs have. From this perspective the film is telling the story of a globalised economy, inequity, and inequality. The sardonic narrator states that human beings are distinguished by being free, however freedom is 'what no one can explain, or fail to understand'.

There are several layers of complexity to both the story and the film's form and style. When I use the film in my teaching, the following questions are provided to the students for group discussions:

1. What is the message communicated by *Ilha das Flores*? To what degree do you feel that more contextual information is needed for you to fully understand the film?
2. Discuss the importance of style and form in relation to message. Make use of the concepts of *mixing* and *hybridity*.[2]
3. Identify different viewer positions and the consequences they may have for different potential interpretations of the film.
4. What do you think the filmmaker wishes to say with the literal and metaphorical use of 'waste' in the film?

The audiovisual narration is a *collage* of moving pictures, pictures, and animations. A voice-over guides the viewer through the imagery, sometimes providing very detailed information (humans are repeatedly defined as someone with "highly developed telencephalon and opposable thumbs"), sometimes ironic commentaries, and intermittently very precise (educational) information. The film is supposedly "a letter to a Martian who knows nothing of the earth and its social systems" (Stam, 2003: 44). In the collage of images, the filmmaker is ironically playing with ethnic stereotypes, nuclear family, capitalism, poverty, and finally what knowledge is. To focus on the issue of knowledge, the images in the film are predominantly 'Western', depicting world historical events of Western relevance, for example, the leaning tower of Pisa, scientific diagrams, the Tower of Babylon, the explosion of the atom bomb, Jesus Christ, and Jews in Nazi concentration camps. In one sequence the narrator asks the question of what history is. The answer provided is a factual history test presenting history as progressing in a linear timeline, visualised in the form of a schoolgirl's answer on a piece of paper found in the garbage piles on the Island of flowers. The natural question that arises from watching these images is why is this Brazilian documentary depicting a Western conceptualisation of world history.

To provide an answer to this question it is first necessary to first take a closer look at Brazilian modernist avantgarde aesthetic traditions. Robert Stam connects *Island of Flowers* to the Brazilian tradition of 'garbage aesthetics' – a filmic underground movement with roots in 1970s underground counterculture ('udigrudi') depicting different forms of garbage to problematise social inequality in relation to transnational capitalism. From this perspective, Brazil is presented as a wasteland "being obliged to recycle the materials of the dominant culture" (Stam, 2003: 42). However, this is only one of several Brazilian aesthetic traditions that is possible to trace in the film. In the cinematic new wave (*cinema novo*) of the 1960s an important trope was anthropophagy. Filmmakers were frequently posing the question to the audience about who the real cannibals are: those who are consuming human flesh or the colonial oppressors (e.g. Jacobsson, 2013).[3] The cinema novo filmmakers were in turn getting their inspiration from the poet Oswald de Andrade's *Cannibal Manifesto* (*Manifesto antrópofago*) published in 1928. Garcia has in a recent study (2020) characterised the relevance of regarding Andrade as a major source for Brazilian decoloniality: "As a decolonial thinker *avant la lettre*, the Brazilian philosopher articulates thus a political project aiming at a long-run unity among the colonized subjects so that a new possibility of being can emerge" (p. 138). De Andrade was promoting an aesthetic idea where the images of the colonial powers were digested by artists, mixed in their stomachs, and finally spewed out, forming collages where the colonial images were reversed depicting decolonial counter-images. We have now run full circle and can make sense of the Western imagery in *Island of Flowers* as a metaphorical decolonial cannibal collage. This contextual information can aid students to answer all four of the discussion questions. The genius of this short film which makes it so rewarding to use for interculturalising interculturality is that it is perfectly possible to watch and understand from different perspectives: (1) as an educational critique of globalisation and capitalism from a global (read Western) perspective; (2) as an ecological critique of waste management; and (3) as an anthropophagic decolonial aesthetic, turning Western cultural dominance on its head.

Early teacher education: Changes from below

The next example of teaching interculturality is from the field of early childhood teacher education. I have been involved in teacher education since 2003, but regularly teaching interculturality in early childhood teacher education since 2015. Early childhood teacher education in Sweden is particularly interesting and challenging at the same time for teaching interculturality and even more so for interculturalising interculturality. Teacher students strongly identify themselves as Swedish pre-service preschool teachers, who will work in educational contexts that are firmly connected to the Swedish educational system. However, they are also aware of the multicultural demography of Sweden, and they frequently request more knowledge (in Swedish) to be prepared for teaching in multicultural and multilingual preschools.

Most publications on interculturality in Swedish are targeting education and are produced either by educational scholars or by practitioners with experience in school teaching, writing handbooks filled with practical tips. The functionalist approach to interculturality has been and still is prominent in different teacher education programmes and in research in educational sciences in Sweden (e.g. Lahdenperä, 2004; Lorentz & Bergstedt, 2016; Lorenz, 2018; Stier & Sandström, 2021). However, there are voices promoting critical perspectives, not the least in early childhood education research (e.g. Björk-Willén et al., 2013; Rosén & Wedin, 2018; Garvis & Lunneblad, 2019). Developing a teaching methodology for more efficient teaching of multicultural and multilingual student bodies has been the main prerogative for activating interculturality in teacher education. This line of thinking is saturated with a good-willed tolerance of difference and diversity, but on the other hand constantly risks tipping over into processes of otherisation and culturalisation of the perceived Other. This tension makes interculturality in education highly interesting to critically discuss further.

The ambition of my teaching in teacher education has therefore been to motivate the students to question preconceived notions of the Other and to move into other directions more open for complexity. This entails questioning the formulations in the national curriculum for preschool (Lpfö 18), that on the one hand is promoting equal opportunities for all children and on the other hand cultural identity as (a relatively fixed notion, and) important for the development of the individual child. Björk-Willén et al. (2013) have accordingly discussed the multicultural Swedish preschool as a context characterised by contradictory demands and as an arena for integration. To problematise the curricula is particularly challenging since it is to a high extent regarded as a document with strong 'truth value' for preschool teacher students and practising preschool teachers – according to my own experience from discussing these issues many times in class and in the field.

One approach that I have used in class is to critically scrutinise the 'banal nationalism' (Billig, 1995) of everyday routines, materials, and pedagogical activities. If the students have encountered materials signalling cultural and linguistic difference in the form of, e.g., flags, maps, pictures, and books, they will get the task to 'demystify' these objects by discussing the meaning of the material and placing material and activities in different perspectives. The students can also be asked to investigate and compare what the symbol of a flag might mean for people from different contexts. Flags are commonly used in Swedish preschools, often with good intentions of acknowledging diversity. To follow up on their investigation, the students speculate on how different children may experience the feeling of being connected to a specific flag, and thereby also being identified as the Other. This exercise is planned as a way for the students to activate their critical thinking regarding the necessity to shift perspectives in discussions of interculturality. I use similar exercises with other teaching materials in focus, such as problematising the geopolitical perspectives in different versions of world maps by analysing the overarching content of imagery in the educational setting, by investigating the content of books and other storytelling materials that the teachers and children are reading.

A complex issue that is hard to solve is the resistance among teacher students toward reading texts in other languages than Swedish. Regardless of why the students prefer to read in Swedish, it is a problem for interculturalising interculturality in Swedish teacher education, especially since very little is published in Swedish critiquing the functionalist understanding of interculturality. Critical scholars in Sweden, as in many other academic contexts, are mainly publishing in English. This is a structural problem with deep roots in the educational system in Sweden. A major conundrum for teachers on all levels is the struggle to motivate children and students to read longer and more demanding texts. In addition to this problem, the students' interest in foreign language education (as well as the structures for language education) is gradually being reduced in Swedish higher education institutions – except for English, which is regarded as the main language for international communication. To interculturalise interculturality together with early childhood education teacher students in relation to these structural circumstances is hard but not impossible. In my teaching I highlight these issues and discuss them reflexively with my students with the sole aim of raising their awareness.

Even if I as a teacher have limited means to change structures, the students show a keen interest in learning more about interculturality and they respond positively to the demand of developing critical thinking and being open to different and new perspectives.

Concluding remarks

To regularly reflect on one's own teaching of interculturality is rewarding while being a daunting task. As a researcher I constantly twist and turn on what I already know and what I need to find out to be able to produce (new) ideas and knowledge. My teaching is running the risk of being fossilised to a much higher degree. It is time-consuming to reinvent lectures and seminars. The teaching hours are always too few and valuable, and there is an alluring efficiency in reusing material time and time again. This description of my guilty teaching conscience does not rhyme well with the ambition of interculturalising interculturality. To work as a teacher in line with these ideas requires being open for extensively reading and discussing international research. But it is also vital to highlight the importance of teaching in higher education. Teaching is frequently regarded as less 'important' in comparison to research. Even if several steps have been taken in Swedish higher education to raise the status of teaching, there is much more to be done.

If there is one thing that I would like to change about my teaching, it is to be as critical of my teaching as of my research, and to rethink and update my teaching and teaching material more regularly than I do today, and in dialogue with other teachers in different academic contexts. This includes integrating linguistic diversity in my teaching so that my students can make sense of my efforts and regard languages as an important aspect of their education to bring into their practice as teachers.

Notes

1 At Karlstad University since 2020. I had a position in intercultural studies at Karlstad University between 2010 and 2022.
2 The notions of mixing and hybridity are included here as main ideas in research on world cinema and intercultural film. Film is an "impure" medium (Nagib & Jerslev, 2013). Aesthetics, themes, and motifs have continuously been used as inspirational sources between different film cultures over so-called cultural borders of national cinemas. To investigate mixing in a film is an important analytical aspect of approaching world cinema, and to interpret if something qualitatively new has been developed (hybridity) is equally important for analyzing intercultural film (Jacobsson, 2017).
3 This question who the real barbarians are is also the main question in the frequently referenced essay "On the Cannibals" (1580) by French philosopher and essayist Michel de Montaigne.

References

Aman, R. (2014). *Impossible Interculturality? Education and the Colonial Difference in a Multicultural World.* Linköping: Linköping University.
Aman, R. (2015). Why interculturalidad is not interculturality: Colonial remains and paradoxes in translation between indigenous social movements and supranational bodies. *Cultural Studies, 29*(2), 205–228.
Aman, R. (2018). *Decolonising Intercultural Education: Colonial Differences, the Geopolitics of Knowledge, and Inter-Epistemic Dialogue.* London: Routledge.
Andrade, O. (1928/1991). Cannibalist manifesto. *Latin American Literary Review, 19*(38), 38–47.
Andreotti, V. (2011). (Towards) decoloniality and diversality in global citizenship education. *Globalisation, Societies and Education, 9*(3–4), 381–397.
Billig, M. (1995). *Banal Nationalism.* London: Sage.
Björk-Willén, P., Gruber, S., & Puskas, T. (2013). *Nationell förskola med mångkulturellt uppdrag.* Malmö: Gleerups.
Breidenbach, J., & Nyíri, P. (2015). *Seeing Culture Everywhere: From Genocide to Consumer Habits.* Seattle and London: University of Washington Press.

Dabashi, H. (2019). *Europe and Its Shadows: Coloniality after Empire*. London: Pluto Press.
Dahlén, T. (1997). *Among the Interculturalists: An Emergent Profession and its Packaging of Knowledge*. Stockholm: Stockholm Studies in Social Anthropology.
Deleuze, G. (1986). *Cinema 1: The Movement Image*. London: Athlone.
Deleuze, G. (1989). *Cinema 2: The Time Image*. London: Athlone.
Dervin, F. (2011). A plea for change in research on intercultural discourses: A liquid approach to the study of the acculturation of Chinese students. *Journal of Multicultural Discourses*, 6(1), 37–52.
Dervin, F. (2015). Towards post-intercultural teacher education: Analysing 'extreme' intercultural dialogue to reconstruct interculturality. *European Journal of Teacher Education*, 38(1), 71–86.
Dervin, F. (2016). *Intercultural Education: A Theoretical and Methodological Toolbox*. London: Palgrave Macmillan.
Dervin, F. (2021). *Critical and Reflexive Languaging in the Construction of Interculturality as an Object of Research and Practice* (19 April 2021). Digital series of talks on plurilingualism and interculturality, University of Copenhagen.
Dervin, F., & Jacobsson, A. (2021a). *Teacher Education for Critical and Reflexive Interculturality*. London: Palgrave Macmillan.
Dervin, F., & Jacobsson, A. (2021b). *Interculturaliser l'interculturel*. Paris: L'harmattan.
Dervin, F., & Jacobsson, A. (2022). *Intercultural Communication Education: Broken Realities and Rebellious Dreams*. Singapore: Springer.
Dervin, F., & Yuan, M. (2021). *Revitalizing Interculturality in Education: Chinese Minzu as a Companion*. London: Routledge.
Dietz, G. (2018). Interculturality. In H. Callan (Ed.), *The International Encyclopedia of Anthropology*. Hoboken, NJ: John Wiley & Sons.
Garcia, L. F. (2020). Only anthropophagy unites us – Oswald De Andrade's decolonial project. *Cultural Studies*, 34(1), 122–142.
Garvis, S., & Lunneblad, J. (2019). Understanding culturally specific pedagogy and practices within Swedish early childhood education and care. In S. Faas, D. Kasüschke, N. Nitecki, M. Urban, & H. Wasmuth (Eds.), *Globalization, Transformation, and Cultures in Early Childhood Education and Care* (pp. 105–117). Cham: Springer.
Gorski, P. C. (2008). Good intentions are not enough: A decolonizing intercultural education. *Intercultural Education*, 19(6), 515–525.
Grodal, T. (2009). *Embodied Visions: Evolution, Emotion, Culture and Film*. New York: Oxford University Press.
Grossberg, L. (2010). *Cultural Studies in the Future Tense*. Durham, NC, and London: Duke University Press.
Gudykunst, W. (2003). *Bridging Differences: Effective Intergroup Communication*. London: Sage.
Guilherme, M. (2019). The critical and decolonial quest for intercultural epistemologies and discourses. *Journal of Multicultural Discourses*, 14(1), 1–13.
Hall, S., & Du Gay, P. (Eds.). (1996). *Questions of Cultural Identity*. London: Sage.
Hill, H. (Ed.). (2020). *Perspektiv på interkulturalitet*. Huddinge: Södertörns Högskola.
Hofstede, G., Hofstede, G. J., & Minkov, M. (2010). *Cultures and Organizations: Software of the Mind* (3rd ed.). Montreal, QC: McGraw-Hill.
Holliday, A. (2010). *Intercultural Communication and Ideology*. London: Sage.
Holliday, A. (2018). *Understanding Intercultural Communication: Negotiating a Grammar of Culture*. Abingdon, Oxon: Routledge.

Jackson, J. (2019). *Introducing Language and Intercultural Communication.* London: Routledge.
Jacobsson, A. (2013). Kannibalism som modernitetskritik: Antropofagi i global filmmodernism. In D. Brodén & K. Noheden (Eds.), *I gränslandet: Nya perspektiv på film och modernism* (pp. 47–65). Stockholm: Gidlunds.
Jacobsson, A. (2017). Intercultural film: Fiction film as audio-visual documents of interculturality. *Journal of Intercultural Studies, 38*(1), 54–69.
Jandt, F. (2020). *An Introduction to Intercultural Communication: Identities in a Global Community.* London: Sage.
Lahdenperä, P. (2004). *Interkulturell pedagogik i teori och praktik.* Lund: Studentlitteratur.
Liu, S., Volcic, Z., & Gallois, C. (2018). *Introducing Intercultural Communication: Global Cultures and Contexts.* New York: Sage.
Lorentz, H., & Bergstedt, B. (2016). *Interkulturella perspektiv: Pedagogik i mångkulturella lärandemiljöer.* Lund: Studentlitteratur.
Lorenz, H. (2018). *Interkulturell pedagogisk kompetens: Integration i dagens skola.* Lund: Studentlitteratur.
Martin, F., & Pirbhai-Illich, F. (2016). Towards decolonising teacher education: Criticality, relationality and intercultural understanding. *Journal of Intercultural Studies, 37*(4), 335–372.
Meer, N., Modood, T., & Zapata-Barrero, R. (2016). *Multiculturalism and Interculturalism: Debating the Dividing Lines.* Edinburgh: Edinburgh University Press.
Mignolo, W. (2007). Delinking: The rhetoric of modernity, the logic of coloniality and the grammar of decoloniality. *Cultural Studies, 21*(2–3), 449–514.
Mignolo, W. (2011). *The Darker Side of Modernity: Global Futures, Decolonial options.* Durham, NC, and London: Duke University Press.
Mignolo, W. (2021). *The Politics of Decolonial Investigations.* Durham, NC, and London: Duke University Press.
Montaigne, M. (1580/2018). *Essais de Michel de Montaigne.* New York: Franklin Classic Treade Press.
Nagib, L., & Jerslev, A. (Eds.). (2013). *Impure Cinema: Intermedial and Intercultural Approaches to Film.* London: I.B. Tauris.
Nail, T. (2015). *The Figure of the Migrant.* Stanford, CA: Stanford University Press.
Nail, T. (2018). *Being and Motion.* New York: Oxford University Press.
Nowell-Smith, G. (1997). *The Oxford History of World Cinema* (2nd ed.). Oxford: Oxford University Press.
O'Regan, J. P. (2014). English as a Lingua Franca: An immanent critique. *Applied Linguistics, 35*(5), 533–552.
Piller, I. (2010/2017). *Intercultural Communication: A Critical Introduction* (2nd ed.). Edinburgh: Edinburgh University Press.
Pineda, P., Celis, J., & Rangel, L. (2020). On interculturality and decoloniality: *Sabedores* and government protection of indigenous knowledge in Bacatá schools. *Compare: A Journal of Comparative and International Education, 50*(8), 1175–1192.
R'boul, H. (2021). North/South imbalances in intercultural communication education. *Language and Intercultural Communication, 21*(2), 144–157.
Rosén, J., & Wedin, Å. (2018). Same but different: Negotiating diversity in Swedish pre-school teacher training. *Journal of Multicultural Discourses, 13*(1), 52–68.
Santos, B. (2014). *Epistemologies of the South: Justice against Epistemicide.* Boulder, CO: Paradigm Publishers.

Santos, B. (2018). *The End of the Cognitive Empire: The Coming of Age of Epistemologies of the South*. Durham, NC, and London: Duke University Press.

Shohat, E. (2006). *Taboo Memories, Diasporic Voices*. Durham, NC, and London: Duke University Press.

Shohat, E., & Stam, R. (1994/2014). *Unthinking Eurocentrism: Multiculturalism and the Media* (2nd ed.). London: Routledge.

Stam, R. (2003). Beyond third cinema: The aesthetics of hybridity. In A. R. Guneratne & W. Dissanayake (Eds.), *Rethinking Third Cinema* (pp. 31–48). New York: Routledge.

Stier, J. (2019). *Kulturmöten: En introduktion till interkulturella studier*. Lund: Studentlitteratur.

Stier, J., & Sandström, M. (2021). *Interkulturellt samspel i skolan* (2nd ed.). Lund: Studentlitteratur.

Thomson, K., & Bordwell, D. (1994). *Film History: An Introduction*. New York: McGraw-Hill.

Ting-Toomey, S. (1999). *Communicating across Cultures*. New York: Guilford Press.

13 Mediated communication as an entryway into interculturality

Marko Siitonen and Margarethe Olbertz-Siitonen

Introduction

In the early third century – the time of the 'Three Kingdoms' – historian Yu Huan (魚豢) wrote the following text concerning people in the far-away lands to the west, that is, the Roman Empire:

> This country has more than four hundred smaller cities and towns. It extends several thousand *li* in all directions. The king has his capital (that is, the city of Rome) close to the mouth of a river (the Tiber). The outer walls of the city are made of stone. (…) (The people have) a tradition of amazing conjuring. They can produce fire from their mouths, bind and then free themselves, and juggle twelve balls with extraordinary skill. The ruler of this country is not permanent. When disasters result from unusual phenomena, they unceremoniously replace him, installing a virtuous man as king, and release the old king, who does not dare show resentment. The common people are tall and virtuous like the Chinese, but wear *hu* ('Western') clothes.[1]

This text, called the *Weilue* (魏略), and translated here by John E. Hill, is a typical example of a mediated account of the other. Such accounts have existed most likely as long as the art of writing itself. Together with images, music, artefacts, and so on, descriptions such as the one in the *Weilue* have made it possible for 'foreign' ideas, religions, and ideologies to spread. They have also allowed for people to challenge existing notions of both themselves and of others. In short, they have been, and continue to be, key for what we may call interculturality.

In this chapter, we explore how mediated communication may act as an entryway into learning (about) interculturality. We approach the topic as educators working in the context of higher education, and therefore focus on adult learners. The chapter opens with a general look into the relationship between mediated communication and intercultural communication. We briefly discuss the illustrative and distortive role that media plays in our conceptualisations of culture and related concepts. We then move on to consider the educational and transformative power of mediated communication in the field of intercultural instruction. Towards the end of the chapter, we offer two concrete examples of how educators

DOI: 10.4324/9781003345275-16

might go about utilising mediated communication in the practice of intercultural education.

Our approach to intercultural communication may be labelled *social constructionist* (e.g., Berger & Luckmann, 1967). This means that we are generally less interested in people's 'given' social categories than the ways they make (cultural) group membership apparent and meaningful in communication. In other words, we take culture and interculturality to be interactional and discursive outcomes (see, for example, Piller, 2017; Stokoe & Attenborough, 2015), which is an understanding that opposes a common, inherently essentialist view according to which communication can be automatically treated and studied as *intercultural* when people who are considered to be different from each other are involved. While within the latter perspective, intercultural communication and interculturality are often seen as predetermined, problematic, and exotic (or as a source of misunderstandings and conflict; see Triandis, 2000, 2012), we approach constructions of and orientations to group membership as a normal part of everyday interaction and discourse.

As an interactional, social outcome, interculturality is dynamic and fluid. Thus, culture or group membership may *occasionally* become relevant for people, for example, in the form of 'intercultural moments' (Bolden, 2014), rather than invariably being 'switched on' just because interactants belong to or identify with a certain imagined community. This view appreciates interculturality as contextual and situated, which is consequential for how we study and teach about intercultural communication. It allows us to ponder questions that are of timely societal relevance, such as under which circumstances do people make group membership apparent and meaningful, how do they bring up and go about differences and similarities in writing and talking, and what do they accomplish by doing so (see Piller, 2017).

Pedagogically, our approach entails that we avoid teaching about cultural 'facts', which can only be collections of stereotypical representations of imagined others, or established truths about intercultural communication. Instead, we encourage our students to engage with culture as an unstable, complex, and sometimes overemphasised social construct, and to observe and analyse interculturality as it becomes visible (or not) in their everyday lives, be it online, in print media, or in interaction with people around them. The broad learning outcome of such intercultural education is to be able to critically reflect on everyday uses of the notions of 'culture' and 'intercultural communication', to be able to question and dismantle cultural representations (but also to appreciate them as such), and to be able to revisit one's own assumptions related to identity and group membership. We thereby align with Lee's (2005: 212) call for higher education that fosters "critical thinking through intercultural dialogue" and helps learners think beyond their cultural frameworks. The kind of critical thinking Lee refers to is to be seen rather as a moral obligation instead of a political mission. Still, it resonates with so-called critical pedagogy and its 'commitments' (Fasset & Warren, 2007), which include fostering dialogue and an understanding of the connection points between the everyday and the systemic, as well as highlighting the centrality of language and communication, and the fluid and complex nature of systemic power and privilege.

We also agree with Dervin (2016: 81), who asserts that "there is need to recognize and accept that, as researchers and practitioners, we can only reach a practical simplification of intercultural phenomena". He proposes a (liquid) realistic approach to intercultural communication that navigates between simple and complex ideas. Accepting this stance means that intercultural communication instruction is seen as an ongoing project with a moving target that can never truly be 'reached', and where failure (at times) is also an option. Instead of looking for hegemonic knowledge, both educators and learners are seen as explorers embedded into the process of constructing culture. From this viewpoint, the aim of education becomes something of a shared journey emphasising joint knowledge-creation. This is a challenging proposition, and, in our experience, something many students – even in the context of higher education – seem not ready for. For some, it is not idealistic enough, and for others, it does not offer the kind of tangible and 'safe' answers they yearn for.

Educators working within the broad field of intercultural education have for long utilised methods stemming from experiential or situated learning. This is also the approach we adopt here. While the exercises we describe towards the end of the chapter can and have been included within traditional didactic teaching modules, they allow for the participants to draw on their own experiences and highlight their own agency as learners.

The importance of mediated communication for intercultural communication

Why focus on mediated communication? Building on the example presented in the beginning of the chapter, our stance is that it is primarily through mediated communication that people living in the globalised world learn about and are in contact with 'others', and make sense of the social world in which they live in. From films to news to social media to video games, mediated communication occupies a central position in our everyday lived reality and therefore our understanding of the world around us. This view should not be mistaken to represent a juxtaposition in comparison with face-to-face communication. Indeed, so much of our communication and interpersonal relationships today are 'hybrid' (Haythornthwaite & Wellman, 2002), that such dichotomies are generally best avoided. Our approach here reflects that of Couldry and Hepp (2007: 5), who assert that "a theory of the construction of *social* reality must at the very least pay attention to a key element in the construction of social life today, which is mediated communications". Their argument emphasises the fundamental nature with which our social world is interwoven with media, and how media-related practices even intersect with face-to-face communication.

The starting point outlined earlier follows in the footsteps of Anderson (1983), who proposed that large-scale group identities such as national identities are constructed as an imagined belonging to other (mostly distant) people and places and produced in part with the help of media. Indeed, it is important to keep in mind that "any community beyond face-to-face interaction has to be imagined" (Eriksen in Breuilly, 2016: 628). From Anderson's (1983) *imagined communities* to Billig's (1995) *banal nationalism*, mediated communication is central in how contemporary logics of constructing in-groups and out-groups function. This includes concepts such as 'culture', 'ethnicity', 'race', and many more.

Mediated communication therefore allows us to imagine the world around us and our place within it. Appadurai (1996) has proposed that it is the transnational circulation of people and media that broadens our views on what is possible. Referring to the wide range of source materials to "imagine with" that media offers us (p. 53), he proposes that our mediatised world shapes the way we are able to imagine our social selves.

Mediated communication factors into intercultural communication along a number of axes. Martin and Nakayama (2010: 21–26) speak of the 'technological imperative', which for them includes (1) increased information about peoples and cultures; (2) increased contact with people who are different from us; (3) increased contact with people who are similar to us who can provide communities of support; and (4) changes in thinking about identity, culture, and technology. Such effects are so all-encompassing and have the potential of touching so many aspects of our lives, that, perhaps unintuitively, their importance may become easy to neglect.

Overlooking mediated communication

In the field of intercultural communication and intercultural instruction there has traditionally been a tendency to downplay mediated communication and communication technology, or even actively shut them outside of the general area of interest. This can be seen in content choices of many of the textbooks written on intercultural communication, as well as in the statements of focus of certain key journals in the field. Using a smaller but illustrative example, in the preparation for this book we received a list of questions and potentially interesting themes coined by students. None of the questions in the list dealt with communication technology or mediated communication in any way!

It is possible that at least some of this disregard can be explained with early scholarship on mediated communication and how it has come to be characterised. Indeed, there exists a whole school of thought based on research done in the 1980s and '90s that built a case of how mediated communication could not be as 'rich' as face-to-face communication (Daft & Lengel, 1984), and how social cues were 'filtered out' by technology in communication (Culnan & Markus, 1987). Viewpoints such as these continue to resonate to this day and are something we are used to encountering as educators. In their extreme form, they propose that mediated communication is not as 'real' as face-to-face communication, and that, therefore, intercultural contact that happens through it is not 'real' either.

Another possible reason for the aversion to include mediated communication into intercultural communication research and instruction may stem from the essentialist viewpoint that since a great deal of technology-mediated communication does not (or, in some cases, did not) feature immediately perceivable identity markers such as skin colour or the way people speak, it may be difficult to discern whether the technology-mediated communication a person engages in should be considered intercultural. This perspective becomes all the more understandable when one takes into account the long tradition of focusing on (face-to-face) nonverbal communication in the field of intercultural communication. The seminal writings of Edward T. Hall (1959, 1969) helped lay out this path with analyses of, e.g., proxemics and chronemics. Hall and many of his contemporaries worked from a very pragmatic viewpoint and ended up proposing a prescriptive approach to culture that focused on differences (for a historical overview, see Leeds-Hurwitz, 2009). Similarly, the neighbouring field of intergroup contact and communication has been historically built on clear and dichotomous group divisions such as contact between 'Black' and 'White' soldiers (Dovidio, Gaertner, & Kawakami, 2003). Understanding the influence of this starting point opens a possibility for interesting thought experiments that can be further explored with students. The question becomes: How big a part of interculturality in our minds is resting on the assumption of perceivable (external) differences? The same exercise, of course, can be used to illustrate the narrow ways in which concepts such as diversity are often operationalised.

Finally, even though artefacts certainly feature in the scholarship on nonverbal communication, it is possible that many a researcher and educator do not truly recognise contemporary media and communication technology as 'cultural'. Rather, television, radio, cell phones, or computers are viewed as if they are neutral or apolitical. However, this is not the case. Technology is always created by someone, somewhere, and for some purpose. While it is true that humans ultimately decide how to utilise its *affordances* (Gibson, 1986), that is, the possibilities offered to us by objects in our environment, technology itself can also be seen as embodying certain kinds of values and ideologies. For example, even seemingly neutral tools that we may use on a daily basis such as internet search engines and similar automated algorithms have been demonstrated to reinforce racism through the way they manipulate their users (Noble, 2018).

Again, a thought-experiment may make things clearer. Imagine how we today try to understand the lifeworlds of those who lived a thousand years ago. How we focus on the way the people of the past built their dwellings, fed themselves, and moved from place to place, or the way their tools enabled them to alter their surroundings. Now, imagine the same being done to 'us', but from a thousand years into the future. How many of the things we take for granted in our lives – from railroads to electric networks to bicycles to cell phones – will undoubtedly appear alien to our future observers, as exemplars of a culture long lost. While some affordances of technology may be self-evident to distant observers, others will be lost in time. After all, technology such as communication media still needs people to give it meaning and decide how they want to use it. Such is the analytical view on media and communication technology that we could adopt today, when trying to understand our contemporary social reality.

Mediated communication in intercultural instruction practice

How would the practice of intercultural instruction look like if the aforementioned concepts and approaches were utilised? In the next paragraphs, we will detail two practical learning tasks we have found helpful in introducing mediated communication, here especially online media and virtual teamwork, into our intercultural communication classes. Both learning tasks are described with sufficient detail so that interested educators should be able to adapt and reproduce them in their own teaching.

The first learning task (Table 13.1) asks the students to search for and analyse social media content that speaks about cultural contact with the students' own in-group. This can be any social category they identify with, such as nationality or ethnicity. Whether from YouTube, TikTok, WeChat, Instagram, or any of the other applications that are popular within and across certain regions, language group, or subculture, analysing such material can give us great insight into how social categorisation is communicatively accomplished. Since the target of these commentaries is something the students themselves identify with, their analysis should allow for us to explore the affective dimension of interculturality. The analysis should be open-ended, but it can be scaffolded by a list of ready-made questions as well as any relevant literature that the course in question utilises.

This task has been included in a course dealing with (cultural) narratives and discourses, but could easily fit into a course focusing on contemporary media landscapes as well. One of the benefits of such an exercise is that it allows for the students (and the teacher!) to step out of their habitual 'bubble' of communication media and learn of the media landscapes around the world. The exercise promotes a variety of voices and readings. Sharing these among the class participants offers a useful entry point into broader discussions concerning the way cultures and

Table 13.1 A sample task for analysing social media

Task:
Search for social media content that speaks about cultural contact with a cultural in-group you identify with.
  Analyse the content from the viewpoint of intercultural contact and communication. You may, for example, use the following questions to guide your analysis:

- What kind of discursive positioning is evident in the text?
  - Who is positioning whom?
  - What kind of right and responsibilities are implied?
- How is intercultural contact depicted, what kind of narrative of contact is produced?
- What kind of similarities of differences can you recognise in comparison with other forms of mediated communication you know about?
- How do you, as a viewer, feel about these narratives and positionings?
- As a viewer/listener/reader, are you offended, amused, or nodding in agreement? When and why?

Present your findings in your group/class. Discuss and compare what you found.

cultural contact are made visible. One way to extend the exercise is by asking for additional analysis of the way users comment on and discuss the content. There, questions related to the student's own voice may also become relevant. Do they participate in such discourses at all? Why, or why not? What could one learn from or achieve with such participation? Another way to extend the discussion is to focus on underlying power issues, including economic realities and other divisions that may cause hierarchies or inequalities. Such questions may also be used as a segue to other topics related to agency, social constructionism, and so forth.

The second learning task (Table 13.2) differs from the first in its focus on the students' own social interaction instead of content produced by others. This exercise has been included in a course titled 'International Management'; it is the final task in a series of group assignments and focuses on virtual teamwork. The learning task works best in online learning situations, especially so-called telecollaboration or virtual exchange programmes (e.g. Dooly, 2017) and similar cases where participants are globally dispersed. We have utilised this learning task for example during the COVID-19 pandemic, which forced many institutes of higher education throughout the world to move their teaching online. An important prerequisite for this learning task is that participants are distributed into small virtual teams in the beginning of the course, and that the groups remain the same throughout. In the case of International Management, in the assignments (learning packages) preceding the one described here, participants are asked to study, discuss, and critically reflect on aspects of globalisation, public relations, the popularity of so-called value dimensions in the field of international management, issues related to 'diversity management', and leadership communication. Because of potential geographical distribution of the participants, most of the tasks are designed to function asynchronously. These include mutual writing tasks such as creating a Wiki entry together, writing a short reflection in a shared document, and discussing a topic on a shared forum. However, we recommend encouraging the students to engage in synchronous communication such as video meetings (especially during the final assignment) as this might contribute to the functionality of the tasks (fostering, for example, immediate discussion).

The final learning package of the course, then, deals with global virtual teamwork from the perspective of international management. Since the course participants were actively involved in actual international and globally distributed teamwork during the entire course, they are asked to analyse and critically reflect their own experiences as virtual team members and relate them to readings on the topic. The task description refers to 'assigned readings'. These could be any contemporary empirical research papers focusing on the topic that the teacher sees fit to include.

The assignment combines several benefits. Not only does it inspire the application of previous research findings and concepts studied during the course (and in preparation for this task in particular) to a concrete and personally relevant case, but it is also inherently self-reflective. For example, by asking the course participants to evaluate their virtual teamwork on the one hand (How did we work as an international team? and What could we have done better?), and to

Table 13.2 A sample task for analysing global virtual teamwork

Your task is to analyse your virtual teamwork during this course.

1. Preparation (individual part)

    Think about your group work and team interaction during this course and write down your experiences. What did you observe? What kind of feelings did the group work evoke in you? Your notes can relate to anything, for example language use, identity and group membership, the role of technology, the role of 'virtuality', the timing and coordination of collaboration, conflicts, support and trust, outcomes, practices of collaboration, leadership, etc.

    Read the assigned research articles. Remember to read critically, keeping in mind the points made earlier in your studies as well as in other readings. All group members should read the assigned articles. The idea is to establish a common starting point for everyone. You can also return to them in the analysis of your own virtual group work.

    In addition, each group member should pick one extra research article from the list provided to you by the teacher. Agree with your group beforehand who of you reads which text. Each group member is expected to read only one paper for the analysis. Please make sure that group members don't accidentally read the same paper.

2. Analysis (group task)

    While working on the group task together you can use any communication tool or channel you want. However, this part of the assignment might work best if you met synchronously at least once. Please analyse your own virtual group work:

    - Talk about your observations and agree on the focus of your analysis.
    - Tell each other shortly what 'your' article was about.
    - As a group, discuss how the papers you read in preparation relate to your observations and experiences. Reflect the findings presented in the articles against your group collaboration. (Do you agree with the findings of previous research or is it possible to question and criticise these studies based on your own experiences?)
    - Critically reflect on your collaboration in terms of group work and 'virtuality'. (What worked, what didn't, why? What could you have done better?)
    - Relate your analysis to international management: What do your observations possibly mean for managing international virtual teams? Come up with recommendations for international managers (based on your own experiences and the readings).
    - Remember to take notes of the group meetings!

3. Report (group task)

    You can choose between recording a short group presentation, or handing in a short, shared document:

Group presentation (5 to 10 minutes)	Or	Mutual document (2–3 pages)
You can create a video recording of your group presentation either by editing individually recorded videos together or recording audio that is collected to presentation slides.		You can create a shared online document and work on presenting your analysis and findings in written form. Remember that the document doesn't need to be only textual; you may include pictures, graphs, or similar.

develop literature- and experience-based suggestions for international managers on the other hand, the students are encouraged to think about relevant skills and competences, and how they themselves fared and possibly improved along these lines. This practice acknowledges recent criticism within the area of intercultural communication competence which exposes top-down assessment (often based on technical and essentialising intercultural competence models) as patronising, arbitrary, and even unethical (Borghetti, 2017; Ferri, 2018; see also Dervin, 2016; Holliday, 2012; Olbertz-Siitonen, 2021).

While some of the pre-readings we use in this assignment address questions of culture and intercultural communication (from different paradigmatic perspectives), the task description deliberately avoids reference to the role of social categorisations. This open-endedness aims to provide students authority over their accounts, allowing them to choose to draw on and justify cultural explanations or – equally reasonable – to 'ignore' (imagined) group membership beyond their core team. One underlying idea here is that such an approach offers opportunities to understand culture as a situated construct that may disappear behind varying language proficiencies, technological challenges, time differences, connectivity, and task orientation, or purposefully surface during conflicts and disagreements, etc. Ideally, this learning task contributes to building a critical stance towards overemphasised meanings of culture and to appreciating interculturality as dynamically and socially embedded in everyday mediated communication.

The risks and benefits of mediated communication in intercultural education

Utilising mediated communication in intercultural education comes with both risks and possibilities. Mediated communication is a powerful tool that allows us to explore the world beyond our immediate surroundings and to directly engage with others in different social realities. It has the potential of enriching our view into the variation of human behaviour and social organising. However, the lens of mediated communication is not only illustrative but also distortive. It can show us a world we did not know existed, but it can also paint that world in simplistic colours that strengthen our tendency to social categorisation into in-groups and out-groups. A great deal of media builds on the logic of reification, whether it be about culture, ethnicity, race, religion, or any other similar social category. In doing so, it ends up contributing to the 'false fixing of boundaries' (Baumann, 1996: 10–11) that intercultural education should strive to question.

For example, mediated communication is consistently used in constructing images of 'the enemy' by building strategic narratives that tap into the target audience's values and fears. News and documentaries may become 'weaponised' (Grigor, 2020), and it may be difficult for the learners to distance themselves from the content they see every day even when analysed in an educational context. Social media algorithms contribute to so-called antagonism, where members identifying into one social category end up avoiding connections with perceived out-group members (Calais Guerra et al., 2013). Overall, affordances of mediated communication can easily be utilised to emphasise differences and therefore feed into the creation and maintenance of in-groups and out-groups. This, too, can be difficult to become aware of, especially if one does not include a significant amount of information into the course design concerning how media technologies operate.

On the other hand, mediated communication holds great promise as well. Research has illustrated how technology-mediated intercultural communication can reduce stereotypical thinking (Tavakoli et al., 2010), increase awareness of existing 'cultures' (Diehl & Prins, 2008), and broaden viewpoints and raise consciousness of the linguistic and cultural diversity surrounding them (Levy, 2009). Referring to the affordances of the internet, Mollov and Schwartz (2010: 215) assert that "the internet can transverse geographical and even to some degree political barriers". Whether intercultural education is able to tap into this possibility or rather ends up strengthening existing barriers is a key question for educators.

One of the simplest and perhaps most surprising benefits of utilising mediated communication in intercultural education is that it brings the topic close to the lived reality of the participants. Put simply, practically everyone in the context of higher education has some insight into mediated communication as a lens into interculturality. In our experience, sometimes it happens that a student sees intercultural communication as something that happens to 'someone else', or that they personally do not have enough expertise or experience in it. This is especially prevalent in those cases where interculturality is extensively seen through the lens of (inter)nationality or ethnicity. However, taking mediatisation as a starting point means that intercultural communication is *everywhere* and for *everyone*. No one can live their life in a vacuum, and all of us take part in weaving the intersubjective pattern of the social world.

Emphasising joint agency and 'ownership' of the topical matter goes hand in hand with a social constructionist starting point. As we have seen, from such a viewpoint human agency matters, and we have a say in the construction of social reality. This view is also compatible with technology and mediated communication (e.g. Bijker et al., 1987). Furthermore, an emphasis on joint agency leads easily to a key learning goal that can be included in a variety of learning activities: an awareness that the social world, including concepts such as culture, ethnicity, race, and so forth, is *made by us* together, and therefore can also be *remade by us* (Berger & Luckmann, 1967: 106). For example, in order to help students understand what reification of culture means, one should find ways in which they can participate in the process of reification in practice; catch themselves and each other 'doing it'.

A final pedagogical goal that we want to highlight here and that links to a focus on mediated communication is the concept of enhancing participants' media literacy. Being something of an emancipatory concept, the idea behind enhancing media literacy is that if we increase our "ability to access, analyze, evaluate and create messages across a variety of contexts" (Livingstone, 2003: 1), we can become more active participants in shaping our own lives and the societies we live in.

Conclusion

As educators in the context of higher education, we often come across deeply embedded ideas in our students that relate to culture(s) being a territory on the one hand and something one carries along and cannot escape on the other. Many of our students have learned and internalised (e.g. during their prior school years) that national or ethnic group memberships are the epitome of 'difference' or 'diversity', and that knowing about predefined differences will be beneficial for their interactions with a thus imagined other. In fact, asking students about their expectations at the beginning of our courses on intercultural communication, almost exclusively yields responses in terms of 'learning more about other (national) cultures'. This implies that for many, culture and interculturality represent something unfamiliar and difficult, even mysterious, and 'not their immediate concern'. It takes considerable time and effort to unpack these notions with the students and jointly find less restrictive ways to approach interculturality that highlight agency as well as multilayered, situated identities. If students were allowed to develop more nuanced insights into interculturality in their earlier education, they would be better equipped to expand their understanding in the university-level courses that are linked to questions of intercultural communication. Instead of having to return to the basics and deconstruct seemingly factual knowledge about the global social world, we could move on already to more pressing and current issues of living in an interconnected social reality, such as experiencing and critically reflecting on mediated forms of interculturality.

Hand in hand with an apparent exotification of culture and interculturality, we note scholarly as well as everyday (students') tendencies to overlook crucial interconnections with digital affordances and media. While not a problem per se, we propose that shutting mediated communication outside of the focus of intercultural communication and instruction is potentially detrimental. Mediated communication plays such a large role in the life of practically all higher education students and all those who operate within academia today, that including it opens a plethora of possibilities for the interested educator.

Our hope is that through the argumentation and examples presented in this chapter, we have been able to demonstrate how focusing on mediated communication may be beneficial for the intercultural communication curriculum. Since all higher education is necessarily mediatised, and since practically everyone embedded within this context is somehow entangled in globalised flows of mediated communication, such a focus offers a way for us to 'demystify' intercultural communication. For both the student and the teacher, it is rewarding to be able to explore tangible sites and discourses where culture is made real and relevant. This makes it also easier to develop an active stance towards intercultural communication, a stance that highlights agency, change, and responsibility. Incorporating mediated communication into the intercultural communication curriculum gives us an important tool with which we can understand ourselves and the way we position ourselves in the world, as well as how we view and come into contact with others. Simultaneously, it allows for us to develop various types of media literacies

(Livingstone, 2003), which are frequently highlighted among the so-called 21st-century skills and competencies in the form of digital literacy (Chalkiadaki, 2018).

As mentioned in the previous section, one of the possible pitfalls of utilising mediated communication in the context of intercultural communication education relates to the way media follows the logics of reification. That is, mediated communication is rife with content that emphasises and (re)creates seemingly fixed boundaries between in-groups and out-groups, and at times even the way the technology itself is built may feed into that process. There is a danger here that relates to Lee's (2005: 210) warning about being satisfied to introduce "a multiplicity of voices for the sake of inclusivity" into the intercultural curriculum. According to Lee (2005: 207), the outcome that intercultural education should aim for is that of enhancing communication, whether it be between groups or individuals, and that this aim cannot be reached by simply adding 'multiculturality' or 'diversity' in an effort to render "multicultural education into some kind of cultural quota system". Similarly, simply adding 'diverse' examples of mediated communication into the course contents is not enough to enhance intercultural learning and dialogue. It requires noticeable effort to escape simplistic operationalisations of culture and related concepts. Luckily for the interested educator, there is a considerable body of research into technology-mediated communication available which may be used in developing an advanced understanding of the possibilities and limitations of the context.

Note

1 Yu Han, "The Peoples of the West" in *Weilue*, trans. John E. Hill (2004), https://depts.washington.edu/silkroad/texts/weilue/weilue.html.

References

Anderson, B. (1983). *Imagined Communities: Reflections on the Origin and Spread of Nationalism*. London: Verso.

Appadurai, A. (1996). *Modernity at Large: Cultural Dimensions of Globalization*. Minneapolis, MN: University of Minnesota Press.

Baumann, G. (1996). *Contesting Culture: Discourses of Identity in Multi-Ethnic London*. Cambridge: Cambridge University Press.

Berger, P. L., & Luckmann, T. (1967). *The Social Construction of Reality: A Treatise in the Sociology of Knowledge*. London: Penguin Books.

Bijker, W. E., Hughes, T. P., & Pinch, T. (Eds.). (1987). *The Social Construction of Technological Systems: New Directions in the Sociology and History of Technology*. Cambridge, MA: MIT Press.

Billig, M. (1995). *Banal Nationalism*. London: Sage.

Bolden, G. (2014). Negotiating understanding in 'intercultural moments' in immigrant family interactions. *Communication Monographs, 81*(2), 208–238.

Borghetti, C. (2017). Is there really a need for assessing intercultural competence? *Journal of Intercultural Communication, 44*. http://immigrantinstitutet.se/immi.se/intercultural/nr44/borghetti.html.

Breuilly, J. (2016). Benedict Anderson's Imagined Communities: A Symposium. *Nations and Nationalism, 22*(4), 625–659.

Calais Guerra, P., Meira, W., Cardie, C., & Kleinberg, C. (2013). A measure of polarization on social media networks based on community boundaries. *ICWSM Proceedings.* 7th International AAAI Conference on Weblogs and Social Media (ICWSM 2013), Boston, USA.

Chalkiadaki, A. (2018). A systematic literature review of 21st century skills and competencies in primary education. *International Journal of Instruction, 11*(3), 1–16. https://doi.org/10.12973/iji.2018.1131a.

Couldry, N., & Hepp, A. (2007). *The Mediated Construction of Reality.* Cambridge: Polity Press.

Culnan, M., & Markus, M. (1987). Information technologies. In F. Jablin, L. Putnam, K. Roberts, & L. Porter (Eds.), *Handbook of Organizational Communication: An Interdisciplinary Perspective* (pp. 420–443). Newbury Park, CA: Sage.

Daft, R., & Lengel, R. (1984). Information richness: A new approach to managerial behavior and organizational design. In L. Cummings & B. Staw (Eds.), *Research in Organizational Behavior* (Vol. 6, pp. 191–233). Greenwich, CT: JAI Press.

Dervin, F. (2016). *Interculturality in Education: A Theoretical and Methodological Toolbox.* London: Palgrave Macmillan.

Diehl, W. C., & Prins, E. (2008). Unintended outcomes in second life: Intercultural literacy and cultural identity in a virtual world. *Language & Intercultural Communication, 8*(2), 101–118.

Dooly, M. (2017). Telecollaboration. In C. A. Chapelle & S. Sauro (Eds.), *The Handbook of Technology and Second Language Teaching and Learning* (pp. 169–183). Hoboken, NJ: Wiley & Sons.

Dovidio, J. F, Gaertner, S. L., & Kawakami, K. (2003). Intergroup contact: The past, present, and the future. *Group Processes & Intergroup Relations, 6*(1), 5–21. http://doi.org/10.1177/1368430203006001009.

Fassett, D. L., & Warren, J. T. (2007). *Critical Communication Pedagogy.* London: Sage.

Ferri, G. (2018). *Intercultural Communication: Critical Approaches and Future Challenges.* London: Palgrave Macmillan.

Gibson, J. (1986/2015) *The Ecological Approach to Visual Perception: Classic Edition.* New York: Psychology Press.

Grigor, I. (2020). *Weaponized News: Russian Television, Strategic Narratives and Conflict Reporting.* Doctoral dissertation, University of Helsinki.

Hall, E. T. (1959). *The Silent Language.* New York: Doubleday & Company, Inc.

Hall, E. T. (1969). *The Hidden Dimension.* New York: Anchor Books.

Haythornthwaite, C., & Wellman, B. (2002). The Internet in everyday life: An introduction. In B. Wellman & C. Haythornthwaite (Eds.), *The Internet in Everyday Life* (pp. 3–44). Oxford: Blackwell.

Holliday, A. (2012). Culture, communication, context and power. In J. Jackson (Ed.), *The Routledge Handbook of Language and Intercultural Communication* (pp. 37–51). London: Taylor & Francis.

Lee, T. M. L. (2005). Intercultural teaching in higher education. *Intercultural Education, 16*(3), 201–215. https://doi.org/10.1080/14675980500211808.

Leeds-Hurwitz, W. (2009). Notes in the history of intercultural communication: The foreign service institute and the mandate for intercultural training. *Quarterly Journal of Speech, 76*(3), 262–281.

Levy, M. (2009). Technologies in use for second language learning. *The Modern Language Journal, 93*, 769–782.

Livingstone, S. (2003). *The Changing Nature and Uses of Media Literacy.* Media@LSE electronic working papers (4). Media@Lse, London School of Economics and Political Science, London, UK.

Martin, J. N., & Nakayama, T. K. (2010). *Intercultural Communication in Contexts* (5th ed.). Boston, MA: McGraw-Hill.

Mollov, M. B., & Schwartz, D. G. (2010). Towards an integrated strategy for intercultural dialogue: Computer-mediated communication and face to face. *Journal of Intercultural Communication Research, 39*(3), 207–224.

Noble, S. U. (2018). *Algorithms of Oppression: How Search Engines Reinforce Racism.* New York: New York University Press.

Olbertz-Siitonen, M. (2021). Practical applications of naturalistic inquiry in intercultural education. *Journal of Praxis in Higher Education, 3*(2), 52–78. https://doi.org/10.47989/kpdc127.

Piller, I. (2017). *Intercultural Communication: A Critical Introduction.* Edinburgh: Edinburgh University Press.

Stokoe, E., & Attenborough, F. (2015). Ethnomethodological methods for identity and culture: Conversation analysis and membership categorisation. In F. Dervin & K. Risager (Eds.), *Researching Identity and Interculturality* (pp. 89–108). New York: Routledge.

Tavakoli, M., Hatami, J., & Thorngate, W. (2010). Changing stereotypes in Iran and Canada using computer mediated communication. *Journal of Intercultural Communication, 23.* https://www.immi.se/intercultural/nr23/tavakoli.htm.

Triandis, H. C. (2000). Culture and conflict. *International Journal of Psychology, 35*(2), 145–152.

Triandis, H. C. (2012). Culture and conflict. In L. A. Samovar, R. E. Porter, & E. R. McDaniel (Eds.), *Intercultural Communication: A Reader* (pp. 34–45). Boston, MA: Wadsworth.

14 Teaching interculturality
The ecology of self-reflection as a priority

Nathalie Auger

Introduction: Renewing interculturality by creolising it

In this book dedicated to the renewed teaching of interculturality, we are faced with an interesting challenge. As such, to say that we wish to renew interculturality, to teach it 'differently', means in concrete terms and etymologically that we integrate a vision, an approach of the 'other', as well as the other him-/herself in the theories and practices that we propose. It is as if we, as researchers, were able to propose an intercultural approach that contains its own principles. This makes it possible to formulate a coherent theorisation.

Proposing a renewal of intercultural approaches by encouraging the adoption of other practices from China and other contexts is therefore very fruitful. Thus, in my opinion, and it is the ambition of this book, we are witnessing a creolisation of interculturality that favours the conceptualisation of this field. Indeed, E. Glissant (1996: 17) in *Introduction to a Poetics of Diversity* maintains that

> *the world is becoming creolised*, that is to say that the cultures of the world, brought together in a lightning-fast and absolutely conscious manner today, are changing by exchanging with one another through irremissible clashes, merciless wars, but also through advances in consciousness and hope that make it possible to say, without being utopian or rather by accepting to be utopian, that today's humanities have difficulties abandoning something they have been sticking to for a long time, namely that the identity of a being is only valid and recognisable if it is exclusive of the identity of all other possible beings.[1]

It is by accepting contacts, sometimes conflicting ones, that we can envisage advances in consciousness. This will be the subject of my chapter, which is rooted in my experience as a researcher in France, and in the South of the country in particular. Thus, if everyone can problematise his or her experience in the space and time lived, the intercultural approach becomes, in my opinion, an ecology of reflection on oneself which is conducive to an understanding of the other. Thus, we are far from the canonical vision of interculturality that has been (and continues to be) widely shared, and consists of a respectful dialogue between people of so-called different cultures. While the ambition is laudable and has been widely disseminated by international institutions such as the Council of Europe, the theories of interculturality that underpin these approaches hardly allow for rational conditions of achievement. In fact, according to these intercultural approaches, it is a matter of respecting the other in his or her difference above all, while finding a common language. No indication is given of the difficulties that might arise during the encounters, i.e. in reality, during intercultural interactions and the means to overcome them. Conflicts and differences of opinion are ignored, even though they have been an inherent part of interactions according to, e.g., French discourse analysts since the 1990s (Vion, 1992, 1998; Kerbrat Orecchioni, 1990, 1992, 1994).

These analyses have shown that in a given space-time, interactions are played out which always oscillate between the irenic and the conflictual, in a continuous manner. Understanding that interactions are the very essence of intercultural encounters is essential for those who do not want to naively enter intercultural education and training.

Interculturality rooted in space and time: The example of the University of Montpellier

I would like to offer a first example: my working context in France. My university in Montpellier in the south of France is a two-hour drive from Spain and is situated 'opposite' the Maghreb countries (Morocco, Algeria, Tunisia), on the other side of the Mediterranean Sea. This spatial context is very important and its location in the heart of the Mediterranean basin is not innocuous. Interestingly the oldest faculty of medicine in Europe is to be found in the centre of Montpellier. And if one takes a closer look at the building of the faculty, one realises that it is adjacent to the cathedral of Montpellier. In the Middle Ages, Christian doctors of Montpellier and France were not allowed to open human bodies to study anatomy. However, they found a way to develop their knowledge of the human body. When corpses were not identified by their families, during funerals in the cathedral, Arab doctors from Morocco, Algeria, Tunisia, and other Mediterranean countries visiting Montpellier were asked to perform autopsies and show the Christian doctors their findings on human bodies. Nothing prohibited this practice for Arab doctors.

It is therefore thanks to intercultural exchanges that medicine made progress in Europe and that the University of Montpellier became the oldest and most advanced medical school. This experience represents a symbol that helps us understand and integrate the fact that the notions of space and time are crucial in intercultural issues. If Montpellier had not had this specific geographical location; if, over time, Arab doctors had not shared their experience with their Christian counterparts, knowledge would not have been able to progress. It is through creolisation, through crossbreeding, that humans advance in their knowledge of the world.

Language biography: Revealing intercultural experiences

My vision of interculturality has always been, as a prerequisite, to return to one's own biography, anchored in a singular time-space. This biography allows us to understand, starting from ourselves, how we perceive interculturality because it is from *who we are* that we perceive the other.

Thus, with my colleagues Gail Prasad and Emmanuelle Le Pichon-Vorstman, we wrote a book based on the biographies of researchers working on issues of multilingualism, education, and, of course, interculturality. In this book, our aim was to show that biography, and in particular the language biography of scientists, leads to a personal vision of interculturality, including languages (Prasad, Auger, & Le Pichon-Vorstman, 2022). The language biography is a specific exercise, well-known to researchers since Bush's work (2006) on personal accounts of speakers' languages in South Africa. These biographies reveal the intercultural relations that exist between us and others, through our languages (attraction, rejection, desire, etc). This narrative, subjective, and introspective work allows us to better objectify the way we conceptualise multilingualism and interculturality. It also shows both our specificities and our unity, our coherence, shaped by our contexts over time. Since all human beings have relationships with languages through personal experiences, this process is common to all.

In order to be consistent with my point, I would like to go back to my own language biography. I grew up in the East of Paris in a very multilingual and multicultural neighbourhood – therefore the idea that multilingualism and multiculturalism are the norm was obvious to me from the beginning. This is probably why I find it hard to imagine that other people would not see diversity as I do. I feel that it is by better understanding my own process of intercultural construction that I could also better understand the diversities of viewpoints and accept other perspectives.

Interculturality through the eyes of other researchers

Approaching interculturality requires one to enter an intercultural process with other researchers, to define one's own vision of the field.

I was of course greatly influenced by European researchers, especially French scholars such as Abdallah-Pretceille and Porcher who introduced the notion of interculturality in France. As pioneers, they succeeded in drawing attention to the concept, particularly in order to deal with the diversity of increasingly multilingual and multicultural classes in France. Fred Dervin (2011b) then worked a lot on this concept too, in particular by coupling it with discourse analysis to show very finely the movement of representations in interactional exchanges.

In a similar vein I also contributed to enriching research and education in the field. But I differ from certain European authors on various points, such as M. Byram (1992) or J. C. Beacco (2000) who proposed a definition of intercultural competence (for, e.g., learners) which is still widely used today. Though one cannot underestimate the ambition to identify, describe, and then teach these skills; danger comes when one tries to assess these skills since they necessarily change, depending on intercultural experiences and representations co-constructed by people when they interact. It is very complex to try to pin down such *moving elements* as *static skills*. Therefore, some tests of intercultural competence proposed in the USA seem to me quite unreliable. First, they are managed by private companies which are reluctant to explain their approach and which (let us never forget!) charge for the test. Second, it is quite possible to answer the questions set in these tests in the way the examiners expect, without necessarily sharing their values on intercultural issues, concerning, e.g., humanism. Far more dangerous in other even more radical theoretical proposals, such as in the business world and the work of Hofstede (2001), the definition of intercultural competence aims not only at assessing learners but also at developing strategies to get the other to adhere, more or less, to one's vision. In any case, by making others believe that their representations are shared (i.e. the way they see and experience the world), companies aim at financial gain *first and foremost*. This is fundamental distancing from the humanist goals of interculturality since the human being is objectified in order to make her/him act as *expected*. While this may be a somewhat valid vision in corporate spheres, it cannot be the one shared by 21st century educators.

My work also differs from scholars such as Candelier (2007) who classifies interculturality as one of the four plural approaches in his influential Framework of Reference for Pluralistic Approaches to Languages and Culture (FREPA/CARAP). In the framework Candelier categorises these approaches as follows: *language awareness, cross-comprehension between languages, interculturality,* and *teaching content through diverse languages*. In my view, interculturality is a conceptual framework which underpins all the other approaches. For instance, one cannot practice language awareness without interculturality. Languages, like any other phenomenon, are the result of representations, of processes of putting things into perspective with a view to finding differences and/or similarities, and the same applies to intercomprehension between languages (e.g. French and Italian). Finally, teaching a language through a discipline implies thinking about the specific cultural relationships linked to this discipline, anchored in a precise context. As such, in geopolitical terms, how to conceive of the notion of 'globalisation' when it does not refer to the same reality. These examples show that interculturality is not, in my opinion, an approach alongside the other three plural approaches, but it is the foundation, the indispensable meta-perspective for a good understanding of *intercultural issues* such as languages.

Diverse methodologies for intercultural purposes

The factors that have allowed my conception to evolve, in the sense of setting in motion my theories and practices of interculturality, are undoubtedly my work 'with' (and not 'on' or 'for') students and then families whose languages are more or less explicitly, consciously, discriminated against, such as gypsies, Roma, and migrants, both in France and in Canada. Over time, I realised that one cannot propose an intercultural approach without working 'with' others. Working 'on' discriminated populations does not implement the principle of reciprocity that is contained in the very notion of interculturality. On the contrary, researchers often act in a form of meta-, overhanging posture, which can slide towards the dangerous slope of condescension, if one is not careful. On the other hand, one can have a good conscience about doing something considered as good 'for' others. Even if the idea is to welcome the languages and cultural experiences of the speakers, with a benevolent spirit, it is advisable not to speak 'for' others, not to find ideas or solutions in their place, so as not to infantilise them. Here again, overbearing positions should be avoided if one is truly committed to an intercultural approach. Working 'with' the pupils and their parents has enabled me to reconsider many of my ideas, such as taking more into account the voices of young people and their families, and their perceptions of, e.g., schools and languages. I realised that I had many stereotypes as well and these experiences allowed me to deconstruct them just as I could perceive the deconstruction of negative representations about university researchers, teachers, and schools among students and their parents in the course of our joint research work.

My analytical methodologies are therefore essentially qualitative. Through a detailed analysis of discourses, it is possible to grasp the representations and stereotypes at work, in their dynamic movement in a given intercultural situation (White, 2018). However, in the course of my work, I have not excluded more quantitative methodologies that allow me to give, at a given time, an image, a photograph of representations and stereotypes. This is what I proposed in my doctoral thesis on stereotypes in French foreign language textbooks in use in Europe at the beginning of the 21st century (Auger, 2007/2015). Obviously, the stereotypes that I have identified in my research are static, but it seems to me that this work may be of interest in order to give a picture as true to life as possible. For studies on the evolution of speakers' perceptions, it will be relevant to take this 'photograph' at different times. Finally, in order to carry out analyses of the very movement of stereotypes or representations, of tipping points, of transformations, qualitative approaches such as discourse and interaction analyses are indispensable.

I do not exclude experimental approaches either. For example, in a study with the Gypsy population of Perpignan (France), who are in great distress at school, a recurring representation, both from the Gypsy community and from the teachers, is that the fact that the young people speak Gypsy hinders their success at school. However, Gypsy is not a language listed as such, linguistically speaking. We researchers therefore had to propose an experimental device to compare the language practices of the Gypsy community with those of the Catalan-speaking inhabitants of the region (particularly the elderly) whose practices seemed to be similar to those of young Gypsies. A device for reading a comic book without text made it possible to compare different elements such as lexicon, syntax, and prosody. Thanks to this experimentation, we were able to conclude that the linguistic differences between the two communities of speakers were not very significant, that there was also intercomprehension between Gypsy and non-Gypsy speakers and that 'Gypsy' was the regional language shared by all, but that, for reasons of identity (to distinguish oneself from the other) another name was used to refer to and represent the language.

This example reinforced my belief that intercultural studies need to be open to different methodologies if they are to shed light on complex issues. In order to do so, it is important to differentiate the object from the field and from the methodology. Our research project was indeed intercultural, however, depending on the field and the issue raised, the methodology may vary. If qualitative approaches are common in intercultural studies, let us pay attention to the fields that need to be problematised by this approach, and let us choose the most relevant methodologies according to our objectives. In short, *let us remain open*.

Towards the interculturalisation of interculturality

The formula of 'interculturalising interculturality', proposed first by Dervin and Yuan (2021) and Dervin and Jacobsson (2021, 2022), is a recursive loop that allows us to question interculturality in its very conceptualisation and its methodologies. Sociologist and philosopher Edgar Morin (1990), in his *Theory of Complexity*, problematises the notion of a recursive loop and proposes that it should become central to thinking in the human and social sciences. To speak of 'interculturality of interculturality', of 'knowledge of knowledge', or of 'nature of nature' allows us to pose a recursive loop that pushes the questioning of the notion to its paroxysm. Thus, this principle of organisational recursion that is the recursive loop generates products and effects that are themselves producers and consumers of what produces them. A process is recursive when the result of the process itself has an influence on its beginning. Thus, working on the 'interculturality of interculturality' allows us to better understand its foundation.

In my opinion, reflection on this recursive loop allows us to transcend the duality so characteristic of the intercultural – *attraction–rejection, attraction–repulsion* – in order to assume the dissolution, or at least a certain erasure, of binarity. For Edgar Morin (1990), the human being cannot be purely rational, scientific, having succeeded an archaic, barbaric being. The human being is both emotional and rational. These two aspects allow, in my opinion, to problematise the complexity of interculturality. This is why, in my seminars and training courses, I am interested in linking these two aspects together: the rational and the emotional. How can we understand the emotional and the rational? The functioning of emotions and reason, to which we will return later, can be understood through a meta-reflexive posture that offers a saving suspension of time to think about interculturality.

Examples of projects illustrating my vision of interculturality

Various research projects have led me to develop this reflection. For instance, in the MALEDIVE (Majority Language and Diversity)[2] project funded by the Council of Europe for the European Centre for Modern Languages, the aim was to get teachers to reflect on their attitudes, actions, and beliefs concerning multilingualism and interculturality in their classes and, more broadly, in society, through various documents and activities (Auger, 2018). Through the identification of their emotions, representations, and reasoning that got them to think as they do at a given time, the objective is to make them, through a meta-reflexive look, more sensitive and at the same time reasonable (in the etymological sense of 'arranging') in order to apprehend diversity in their professional context. There are therefore no right or wrong answers in teacher education and training, but a personal path that is proposed to each individual, on the understanding that the limits of reflection and emotions are always those of physical or verbal violence.

These trainings show that teachers who work in a context of linguistic and cultural diversity, through an initial reflection on their own language and cultural biography, subsequently recognise these experiences more favourably for their pupils. In another project, Conbat+[3] (Content-based teaching + Plurilingualism/Pluriculturalism), which involved various disciplines, we also integrated this pathway from languages and cultures as resources to work with pupils. In this training programme, the aim was to teach subjects such as mathematics, science, history, geography, and art, while using the students' languages and cultures. In this way, the teaching starts from the learner, puts the learner at the centre, and it is these cultural and linguistic experiences that will help compose and construct teaching. Interculturality is a powerful way of linking formal (institutional learning), informal (family, friends), and non-formal (associations, clubs) experiences, and of reflecting on the complexity of our identities and practices (Auger & Kervran, 2011). During the European project SIRIUS[4] Education and Migration, we worked from this assumption, recognising the variety of experiences of young migrants in Europe while encouraging them to live and share new social and language practices in formal, informal, and non-formal spaces. By taking the image of the sunflower to represent the young person, we wanted to indicate that the person is always at the centre of the process, and that the different petals symbolise the spaces where it is possible to experience cultural and language situations, on a human scale, around them, referred to as a 'learning territory' (i.e. the materialisation of spaces that allow learning, without temporal discontinuity). Not only are links created for the young person, but new contacts are also created between spaces: teachers meet associations and places of culture, with families to help build pathways for young people and vice versa (Sauvage & Auger, forthcoming).

These projects also aim to show that scientific work can have an impact on macro-contexts, prescribing it to encourage our institutions to change their representations. Interculturality certainly aims at promoting a balance that includes cultural minorities. This question is very important to me because, in France, there are many languages and diverse cultural experiences in schools but these languages are hardly taken into account in the school system, while ministries deplore the lack of internationalisation of schools. I have therefore proposed a model, *the language diamond*, to ensure that multilingualism and multiculturalism become resources for teaching and learning. The diamond symbolises our cultural and languages experiences, which are precious resources. It is our memory, our experiences, which will enable us to look ahead to the future. The diamond has facets that can be cut, polished, and made to shine, which correspond precisely to the use of these resources. This scheme is maximalist and holistic, it includes everyone's various dimensions of languages and cultures. A very important facet of the diamond is to identify and value the languages and cultures of the students. All too often, many teachers are unaware of the cultural and language experiences their students experience, and therefore do not summon them. Another aspect of the diamond corresponds to the awareness that these language and cultural experiences are resources for teaching and learning. The commitment to use multilingual and multicultural materials for thinking and learning is also central: books, textbooks, posters, videos, etc. Mutual tutoring between students is also recommended as part of the diamond. Tutoring is not only about helping minority students since the latter have access to languages and cultural experiences that can also help and contribute to other students' learning. It is important to make relationships in class more symmetrical in this respect. Another facet emphasises going out of the classroom to visit the many multilingual and multicultural places around us that we often ignore: places of culture, shops, and streets where diverse languages and cultures are resources for learning. Co-education with parents also matters here. In France, the inclusion of parents in schools is not very common, whereas the diversity of parental backgrounds represents an interesting opportunity for reflection on learning. Finally, a last facet encourages teachers to work together with school managers, staff such as supervisors, and nursery assistants.

The aim of the diamond and the aforementioned multifaceted approach is a paradigm shift from a heteroglot or translanguaging vision to a maximalist and holistic approach to languages and cultures, a panlanguage approach where these language and cultural experiences are taken into account as an immeasurable whole. All students can benefit from this approach, whatever their resources, in order to develop social cohesion and multiple values in our contemporary societies.

Thus, these projects create modelling reflections which, in turn, offer spaces that question and link different scientific disciplines together, allowing for a better understanding of the essence of interculturality.

'The interculturality of interculturality': The necessity of interdisciplinarity

To understand interculturality, it is necessary to question it. One possible approach is to ask what 'the interculturality of interculturality' is. To illustrate this questioning, I would like to go back to a personal experience that had a strong impact on me when I was young. In the 1980s, when I was a teenager, there was a major anti-racist movement in France called 'Touche pas à mon pote' (that we could translate into 'do not touch my friend'). Sometimes, however, I felt uncomfortable because I was aware that, even though I wanted to defend anti-racist ideas, I could be prejudiced against certain groups of people. I felt ashamed because I didn't know how stereotypes and representations were constructed. Thanks to social psychology, I understood much later how 'imaginary images of others' are formed. It is therefore essential, when teaching interculturality, to draw from different disciplines, to link them together, in order to answer a question such as why stereotypes can be generated about such and such a category of people. The fields of *sociology, neuroscience*, and *psychology* (especially *social psychology*), which were previously quite unknown to me, being a trained linguist, are essential to 'interculturalise interculturality' (Dervin & Jacobsson, 2021). Even if the field of interculturality has always called upon a plurality of bibliographical references to build itself, I have, for my part, really felt the need, based on these personal experiences, to make the disciplines of 'reason' work with those of 'emotion'. This questioning thus requires the 'linking' (Morin, 1990) of disciplines.

For me, it is a way to give a closer account of our human functioning, which is so complex and made of both impulses and reflections. During my training sessions with pre-service teachers, I explain that the first step is to dare to recognise one's emotions and prejudices, even if one is uncomfortable with one's feelings. This step is essential to proceed with the work of deconstructing stereotypes. If one does not recognise one's emotions, one cannot, in my opinion, enter the intercultural process.

All these considerations lead me to explain my ways of teaching interculturality in what follows.

Teaching interculturality in action

To be able to feel emotions, you have to live experiences. I therefore always propose to feel/reflect on an authentic document, e.g. a comic strip, press clippings, videos, photos. For example, in the comic strip *What? Me? A Racist?* published by the European Commission (1998), different people successively meet on the street and experience negative or positive emotions. A Black man is insulted by a man who tells him to 'go back to your country'. The insulted person does not respond and then, when he crosses the street, takes offence at the fact that so many people are waiting in front of a job centre. He calls them 'idle', 'lazy'. Men queueing outside an office see a young woman walk by and whistle at her, calling her a 'doll', suggesting to take her for a drink. The young woman walks away, scandalised, and meets two young men holding hands a little farther on. She is outraged. The male couple walks away, undaunted, and come across a woman wearing a headscarf and her son. They stare at her and feel indignant about her hijab, which they say is a sign of 'a lack of integration'. The mother and son meet the first man from the beginning of the story, who was vilifying a Black person. The son thinks the man is too fat and should go on a diet! Through this comic strip that I often give students to analyse, we experience emotions together, we recognise them and the associated prejudices, and then we reflect on how to study them.

This experience of 'chain racism' allows one to recognise oneself, either in the one who expresses or suffers from the aforementioned stereotypes. Of course, I don't ask the students to share personal emotions or prejudices with the rest of the class. What interests me here is to show the processes at work, not from the outside, but from the inside, from our own experience, from our own private lives. My goal is also to show that no one is exempt from the action of stereotyping or being stereotyped. Psychology and anthropology explain to us that these categorisations allow us to control an emotion, to reassure ourselves thanks to categorisation, and, paradoxically, they allow us to live in society. Our representations, which are sorted out in a cognitive way, as neuroscience explains, are affected by other ways of life. In this case, the emergence of emotions such as anger, sadness, and fear but also joy, is irrepressible. They lead to what Favre (2019) calls a shortening of the thought process, which generates a stereotype that puts the other at a distance.

Living through visual and discursive experiences allows us to understand that the utterer, the one who produces the stereotypes, is not actually talking about the other: he is talking about himself, his habits, what he likes, what bothers him, what he dislikes. In my opinion, it is therefore essential to develop an ecology of reflection on oneself. I argue that the intercultural experience does not say anything about the other but that it tells about me, about the other *through me*.

This process does not happen smoothly. It can lead to verbal or physical violence, which is why my first analyses of intercultural communication focused on this subject. As such violence is the Rubicon not to be crossed, and it is not up to us to judge it but rather to describe it in order to understand how to act on this process. With Romain (Auger & Romain, 2015) I identified four steps of verbal violence. The first step is what we called 'potential violence', which is linked to the fact that sometimes we are more or less in a good mood, depending on our physiological or emotional states. These states have an impact on future conflicts. Another factor is the space-time context. Simply because spaces are confined (a lift, a public place) or time is short (delay, too many people queuing), conflicts will be all the more present and may take the form of intercultural conflicts. If actions are taken before this first stage occurs, such as improving living conditions for people and taking into account their wellbeing, this potential violence is likely to be avoided. If this is not the case, the second stage identified will be what we refer to 'embryonic violence'. Following a problem from stage 1 (context or personal), one person challenges another and issues a prejudice, a cliché concerning his or her way of acting, language and speech, cultural experience, etc. To avoid this stage, only intercultural education can defuse these conflicts already at work in the form of stereotypes. If this is not the case, the third stage, the 'crystallised violence', takes place. Once someone has expressed a prejudice or stereotype, the categorised person will usually respond and the conflict will only escalate. This response may also lead to a final and fourth step, which is 'physical violence'.

To illustrate these stages, let me mention an anecdote that I experienced when I started teaching French as a foreign language in Montpellier. It occurred when President Jacques Chirac had decided to resume nuclear testing off the coast of Australia ('potential violence' stage: context put at risk). I had an Australian student and this student was obviously very angry about the situation and he didn't want to work in class. He had come to Montpellier, sent by his company to study the language. He thought that French politics was disastrous and he laughed a lot in class, disturbed the others and kept saying 'Hiro-Chirac' ('embryonic violence' stage: interpellation, stereotype) – a portmanteau word composed of *Hiroshima* and *Jacques Chirac*. Of course, feeling attacked and threatened, it would have been tempting for me to respond to the attacks ('crystallised violence'). Fortunately, I had learnt my intercultural communication lessons (but with little practice). One morning, I brought the press of all political orientations that can be found in France, from the far right to the far left, and we studied the articles with the students on the issue of resuming nuclear tests. We saw that there were very divergent opinions in the press and in the public opinion, with people who were in favour and people who were against. What was very interesting was to understand the various reasons that had led people to take a stand, e.g. arguments of security, the army, ecology, health. This experience of intercultural conflict, which I only knew about from theoretical books on interculturality, was really founding for me. It helped me defuse the conflict and understand that a nation can cover various representations of the world, which annihilates the temptations of stereotyping.

Teaching interculturality as an ecology of self-reflection

It is a sweet dream to imagine that teaching interculturality will solve societal problems such as racism, homophobia, or any type of categorisation of a given group. Who wouldn't like to see interculturality bring diplomatic peace, fluidity in relations that would allow us to go beyond drastic judgements? However, if we follow some of the principles developed in this chapter, it seems that the task is a challenging one since it is a question of moving from a *solid vision* to a *liquid vision* of interculturality (Dervin, 2011a) and that only the personal journey, through our emotional experiences and reflections, can allow us to deconstruct our own and shared stereotypes. Far from implementing specific strategies or skills, it is more a matter of working on oneself. This implies that we must feel safe enough to let go of our certainties about ourselves and about the other and accept to live this journey, which can be very destabilising. When I teach interculturality, what I would like my students to learn in the end is how to learn, in particular to learn how to identify their feelings, their emotions, what they (re)teach us. It is very difficult to accept and to admit that one is angry, sad, or afraid. It often takes a lot of courage to welcome these feelings in an honest and sincere relationship with oneself. Our five senses can allow us to feel and trigger our emotions: what we taste, what we hear, what we can touch, what we see, what we smell. Our senses connect us to our beliefs and sometimes generate stereotypes. It is then a question of developing, once the feelings have been identified, a meta-reflection to understand the reason for the existence of these stereotypes. But we should not underestimate the difficulties that this reflection brings into play. Indeed, emotions are linked to the short circuit of thought, the reptilian brain which is there to protect us. A negative sensation should allow us to quickly decide whether to flee, to confront, etc. This survival mechanism is more important for humans than a 'long', 'meta' reflection of our emotions. Only time and distance allow this long circuit of thought to operate. In this second moment, which is the moment of reflection, it is therefore a question of observing and finding out: finding out about the historical context, discussing with others, daring not to draw hasty conclusions, leaving potential judgements on hold.

Working on interculturality means daring to experience discomfort, because daring to let go of one's certainties, daring to look at oneself without obviously being in a psychotherapeutic or psychoanalytical activity, requires courage. Being in contact with one's emotions can be very destabilising. It is a personal relationship, from *self to self*. Thinking personally, perhaps differently, may also take us out of the group. Deconstructing stereotypes, by disturbing certain categories that we may have constructed, might thus lead to a feeling of loneliness and sometimes this feeling can be uncomfortable as well. It is therefore important when teaching interculturality to provide a safe context for discussions in order to move forward intellectually.

Following Bachelard (1938/1967), for whom epistemological obstacles represent ultimately the key to solving a given problem, it is important to reassure students of our human functioning, even if it is sometimes disturbing. These elements of knowledge may lead them to think with new data. Of course, some students are self-conflicted because being in contact with their emotions, their stereotypes may sometimes be very unpleasant. A 'safe' framework allows us to say that conflict is already the rearrangement of categories and prejudices. No one knows what path this de-/reconstruction will take, but a conflict is already the signal that it has begun. I always congratulate the students when they rebel, when they are against the framework and the scientific elements that I pose. I explain to them that this is a sign that they are affected and that, if they react emotionally, it is because the 'short-circuit' of their thinking cannot for the time being allow them to reflect more deeply on the reasons for their response. Long-term engagement will allow, little by little, to work on a long reflection which will allow one to consider new scientific and contextual elements.

Life and thought are constantly shifting and this is the movement that I am trying to initiate in my students. Conflict is energy and the energy of movement is already the sign of a reorganisation of self-reflection.

Notes

1 My translation from French into English.
2 https://maledive.ecml.at/.
3 https://conbat.ecml.at/Theproject/tabid/246/language/en-GB/Default.aspx.
4 https://siriusfrance.jimdofree.com/.

References

Auger, N. (2007/2015). *Construction de l'interculturel dans les manuels de langue*. Paris: L'Harmattan/EME.
Auger, N. (2018). Le MOOC MALEDIVE: un site d'auto-formation pour les enseignants de langue et de culture qui accueillent des élèves migrants dans leur classe. *ContACTES, 2459–2986*, 61–69.
Auger, N., & Kervran, M. (2011). Construction identitaire et compétence plurilingue: des principes à la mise en œuvre de séquences interdisciplinaires (projet européen Conbat+). *Tréma, 33–34*, 35–44.
Auger, N., & Romain, C. (2015). *Violence verbale et école*. Paris: L'harmattan, Enfance & Langages.
Bachelard, G. (1938/1967). *La Formation de l'esprit scientifique*. Paris: Librairie philosophique J. Vrin.

Beacco, J.-C. (2000). *Les dimensions culturelles des enseignements de langue*. Paris: Hachette, coll. Références.

Busch, B. (2006). *Language Biographies for Multilingual Learning*. Cape Town: PRAESA.

Byram, M. (1992). *Culture et éducation en langue étrangère*. Paris: Hatier/Didier, coll. LAL.

Candelier, M. (Ed.). (2007). *LE CARAP, un instrument au service de l'éducation plurilingue*. Strasbourg: CELV, Conseil de l'Europe.

Dervin, F. (2011a). A plea for change in research on intercultural discourses: A 'liquid' approach to the study of the acculturation of Chinese students. *Journal of Multicultural Discourses*, 6(1), 37–52.

Dervin, F. (2011b). Quand la didactique des langues et des « cultures » emprunte à l'anthropologie…. *Journal Des Anthropologues*, *126–127*, 255–272.

Dervin, F., & Jacobsson, A. (2021). *Interculturaliser l'interculturel*. Paris: L'Harmattan.

Dervin, F., & Jacobsson, A. (2022). *Intercultural Communication Education: Broken Realities and Rebellious Dreams*. Singapore: Springer.

Dervin, F., & Yuan, M. (2021). *Revitalizing Interculturality*. London: Routledge.

European Commission, DG X – Information, Communication, Culture and Audiovisual Media, Secretariat-General. (1998). *What? Me? A Racist?* Brussels: Publications Office.

Favre, D. (2019). *Transformer la violence des élèves : Cerveau, motivations et apprentissage*. Paris: Dunod.

Glissant, E. (1996). *Introduction à une poétique du divers*. Paris: Gallimard.

Hofstede, G. (2001). *Culture's Consequences, Comparing Values, Behaviors, Institutions, and Organisations Across nations*. London: Sage Publications.

Kerbrat-Orecchioni, C. (1990/1992/1994). *Les interactions verbales* (Vol. 3). Paris: A. Colin.

Morin, E. (1990). *Introduction à la pensée complexe*. Paris: Le Seuil.

Prasad, G., Auger, N., & Le Pichon-Vorstman, E. (2022). *Multilingualism and Education: Researchers' Pathways and perspectives*. Cambridge: Cambridge University Press.

Sauvage, J., & Auger, N. (forthcoming). Familles migrantes en situation précaire, fracture numérique et éducation informelle, formelle et non formelle. L'exemple du projet européen SIRIUS à Montpellier. In P. O. Weiss, & A. Maurizio (Eds.), *L'éducation aux marges en temps de pandémie. Précarités, inégalités et fractures numériques*. Pointe-à-Pitre: Presses universitaires des Antilles.

Vion, R. (1992). *La communication verbale, analyse des interactions*. Paris: Hachette, Université Communication.

Vion, R. (dir.) (1998). *Les sujets et leurs discours, énonciation et interaction*. Aix-en-Provence: Presses universitaires de Provence.

White, J. (2018). *Apprendre à rencontrer l'autre, les effets de la réflexion guidée sur le discours des étudiants universitaires en mobilité*. Thèse de doctorat. Université Paul-Valéry Montpellier 3.

15 A Finnish approach to promoting intercultural encountering in primary schools

Oona Piipponen

Introduction

Interculturality is polysemous, like an artwork that appears different each time it is contrasted against a different wall colour. There are as many forms of interculturality as there are intercultural situations. It is a good thing that the concept can be applied to diverse contexts. However, polysemy is also a challenge to researchers and educators: How can we know we are talking about a shared idea? If everyone understands interculturality differently, how can teachers teach about it, and how can learners learn it?

I will use an old Indian folktale about the blind men and the elephant as an analogy for interculturality. In the story, six blind men have heard about the elephant, but have never encountered the animal themselves. Each man approaches the elephant from a different direction. The first blind man feels the elephant's trunk and deduces that the elephant must be like a snake. The second takes a hold of the elephant's ear and says that the elephant must be like a fan. The third touches its legs and professes that the elephant must be like a tree. The fourth blind man approaches the elephant's tusks and gathers that it is like a spear. The fifth faces the elephant from the side and states that it must be like a wall. Finally, the sixth blind man grabs a hold of the elephant's tail and says that the elephant is like a rope.

What happens next depends on which version of the story you retell. Do the blind men engage in dialogue and collaboration to put the pieces together? Do they each insist they alone know the full truth? Interculturality is like the elephant; how it is defined depends on which part of the elephant you happen to be holding. This is my first reflection on the idea of 'interculturalising interculturality', proposed by Dervin and Jacobsson (2022) and put into practice by the editors of this volume: What would happen if the blind men engaged in dialogue? How do different theorisations or practical expressions of interculturality speak to each other?

In this chapter, I discuss how I have explored the elephant of interculturality. I came to the concept as a primary teacher with personal experience of moving between different school systems internationally, yet no clear pedagogical methods to teach it in my classroom. I embarked on a doctoral research project

DOI: 10.4324/9781003345275-18

to better understand what children's interculturality might look like. Kaikkonen (2004) has proposed three kinds of intercultural pedagogies: pedagogies of knowledge, encountering, and conflict resolution. To this I add a pedagogy of critical interculturality, which deals with dismantling colonial power structures (Gorski, 2008). I decided to focus on children's intercultural encounters, because I wanted to understand how children engage in encountering each other. This perspective was crucial, as it illuminated how intercultural education tends to be very adult-centric.

Not all intercultural encounters necessarily lead to intercultural learning, and not all kinds of pedagogies support reciprocal encountering (Jackson, 2018; Kaikkonen, 2004; Piipponen, 2022). Over three academic years, I developed a children's story exchange between classrooms in different countries. What surprised me during the study was just how much both the learning space and learning community influenced the potential for encountering. It was not enough to organise an exchange between primary classrooms in different countries; the teachers had to deliberately engage with the children to create a classroom culture that supports trust, respect, and a sense of community (Piipponen et al., 2021). The classroom culture was co-created by the teachers and children through a dynamic process of open-ended inquiry, so the intercultural story exchange evolved organically. To be successful, the teachers needed to go against conventional teacher-led pedagogies and distribute power also to the children. In what follows, I will outline my approach to promoting children's intercultural encountering, which involves encouraging children's participation, experiential learning, and a dynamic approach to interculturality. The approach was inspired by what I will call a Finnish educational philosophy, which values the holistic growth of the child, supported by the highly professional and autonomous teacher.

Finnish educational philosophy

If interculturality is the elephant in my research, Finnish educational philosophy is the forest that it lives in. In this section, I will cover four themes from Finnish educational philosophy that have influenced my research: (1) schools should provide equitable opportunities to learn for all; (2) children are active agents and childhood is a special period in their lives; (3) autonomous teachers can be trusted to make pedagogical decisions locally; and (4) the purpose of primary education is to support the holistic growth of the child. I give examples of how these themes were visible in practice during the development of an intercultural story exchange project for 10- to 11-year-olds.

In Finland, schools need to provide equitable opportunities to learn for all. In my research project, a major driver for pedagogical choices was how feasible the intervention would be in different school contexts. Intercultural learning interventions such as travelling abroad have tended to be offered to socioeconomically privileged students. One of the reasons I chose the Storycrafting method is that it is simple to use and does not require any expensive software or training. During Storycrafting, a scribe writes down the storyteller's improvised oral story exactly as it is told. A Storycrafting exchange can be adapted to different kinds of school contexts; in my project, we exchanged the stories via email and shared cloud drives, but it could easily be organised as a letter exchange as well. Furthermore, the Storycrafting method creates a space for encounters between people, and because telling stories is an innate part of being human, it is an accessible method for most people. Children are familiar with improvising a story through their experiences of imaginative play, and although adults often worry about whether children will have any ideas for what to tell, when given enough thinking time, most children come up with a story quite easily. The method is thus suitable to most children.

The Finnish educational philosophy sees children as active participants in their learning (Lonka, 2018). It is therefore important to consider children's prior experiences and interests, which may influence their motivation to engage in learning. The Storycrafting method lets children choose freely what they would like to tell about. This is unusual in a school setting, where typically the teacher chooses what children should write about (Karlsson, 2013). During my research intervention, the children were in the steering seat as they could tell stories that they enjoyed, and their purpose was to entertain their exchange partners as well. Because Storycrafting is an oral method where a scribe writes down what the teller says, it does not limit children to write only the words that they know how to spell. It is also important that the final story is not evaluated by others, because the authorship belongs to the storyteller. The method is about celebrating the child's voice.

The Finnish educational philosophy trusts autonomous teachers to make pedagogical decisions locally. In Finland, teachers gain a masters-level degree at university to become qualified professionals. The core curriculum is a broad general curriculum and teachers have a lot of professional autonomy to implement the curriculum as they see fit. With their specialised training that includes educational psychology, child development, and understanding and implementing educational research, teachers can make informed judgements about how to carry out learning activities in the classroom (Lonka, 2018). Therefore, the teachers participating in the intercultural exchange implemented the project in a way that fits with the classroom culture in their local contexts. For example, the teachers varied the size of the groups depending on what they perceived the children needed. Sometimes the teacher modelled the Storycrafting activity with the whole class to build a sense of class community, and at other times children worked together in smaller groups so that individuals had more agency to tell the kind of story they wanted.

In Finnish, the field of educational sciences in university is known as *kasvatustiede*, literally 'the study of raising children'. Finnish primary school teachers thus have a holistic view of the purpose of education as something that is more than just academic learning. Raising children involves being responsive to the child's stage of development and core psychological needs. Children need to feel that they belong to a social group (relatedness), that they can have influence their lives (autonomy), and that they can be successful when they act in the world (competence) (Ryan & Deci, 2017). Therefore, in developing the intercultural exchange between children, it became important not only to promote encounters between the exchange partners, but also to develop a sense of belonging and community within each class. Feeling safe and valued in one's own group was seen as foundational to developing intercultural encounters with the unfamiliar exchange partners.

Challenges to teaching children interculturality

When I started my doctoral research in 2015, I found that there was not yet very much prior research that investigated children's intercultural learning, and recent reviews of research demonstrate that the same trend continues still (Rapanta & Trovão, 2021; Walton et al., 2013; Zhang & Zhou, 2019). Where research exists, the papers often report similar challenges.

In many schools, interculturality is integrated through superficial celebrations of diversity, for example in the Nordic countries (Mikander et al., 2018). Some research has suggested that in international schools or national schools where the student body is composed of different nationalities, religions, or language groups, students develop positive attitudes towards diversity due to everyday intercultural contact (Schwarzenthal et al., 2019). However, not all contact is necessarily positive, and schools should not leave intercultural learning to chance. Furthermore, often in educational discourses, the implied recipients of intercultural education are students with immigrant backgrounds (Hummelstedt et al., 2021; Zilliacus et al., 2017), even though all classrooms exhibit diversity in students' micro-cultures and are by nature intercultural (Bash, 2014).

At other times, intercultural education may fall into the trap of tokenism. According to Wong (2018), teachers regularly use guided reflection to teach students to think critically about their intercultural experiences. However, as students become habituated to the method, they might learn to respond in ways that are expected by the teacher. Are their reflections, therefore, anything more than a performance (Lanas, 2017)? Will students be able to apply their learning in real-life situations? Furthermore, intercultural learning may be reduced to tokenistic nods when teachers prioritise other learning outcomes in an overcrowded curriculum (Cochran-Smith, 2021; Davies, 2022).

Another challenge to teaching interculturality to children (and adults for that matter) is that many well-meaning teachers may unintentionally reinforce cultural stereotypes when they plan 'cultural' activities, which are usually focused on national culture (Alvaré, 2017; Roiha & Sommier, 2021). This can lead to reinforcing societal power structures as well as to the discrimination of certain groups (Hummelstedt, 2022). This problem is perpetuated by teacher education institutions, where discourses often still support a fixed view of culture, and tend to 'other' students from immigrant or minority groups (Gorski, 2009; Hummelstedt-Djedou et al., 2018).

Many researchers have tried to make a list of all the knowledge, skills, attitudes, behaviours, and values that make up intercultural competence (Deardorff, 2006, 2020; Barrett, 2018). However, the danger is that talking only about a person's innate ability may ignore the role that context has on an intercultural situation. There is some evidence that discourses are diversifying in the field. In a recent study, Rapanta and Trovão (2021) have shown that instead of using the term 'intercultural competence', some researchers are beginning to use more dynamic conceptualisations such as intercultural learning or dialogue.

Finally, all dominant theories on interculturality (e.g. Bennett, 1998; Byram, 2008; Deardorff, 2006) seem to be based on research with adults. Studies show that children's or adolescents' learning tends to remain at a superficial level when they participate in intercultural interventions that are based on adult-centric theories (Ruest, 2020; Lau, 2015). It is important to also have evidence on how children learn to encounter each other in intercultural situations. These challenges pave the way for developing a different way to teach interculturality to children.

Interculturalising interculturality through children's perspectives

Could the concept of children's interculturality bring something new to the dominant discourses of interculturality, where the normative intercultural learner is assumed to be an adult, or at least adult-like? Here is my second attempt to unpack the idea of interculturalising interculturality (see Dervin & Jacobsson, 2022).

According to contemporary discourses, often the purpose of education is to prepare children and young people for a complex adult world, where they will need qualifications and competencies for employment, and proper socialisation to contribute to society as a citizen of a nation (Biesta, 2014). Within this discourse, intercultural education is often seen as a solution to societal problems in the adult world, such as building competencies for an international labour market (Jackson, 2018), integrating immigrants to a national setting (Faas et al., 2014; Portera, 2020), or promoting social justice in society (Pais & Costa, 2020; Sobre, 2017). Children are thus construed as 'adults-in-becoming', and educational activities aim to teach children knowledge and skills that move children from their current state of childhood towards adulthood (Qvortrup, 2009). This deficit view positions children as incomplete and ignorant rather than complete and knowledgeable.

In many intercultural learning theories, the ideal intercultural citizen is implied to be an adult. Therefore, the normative intercultural learner is also assumed to be an adult or adult-like, and teaching methods are derived from adult education. Guided critical reflection is often a central element in adults' intercultural learning (Jackson, 2018). An example of this is the *Autobiography of Intercultural Encounters* commissioned by the Council of Europe (2009). The roughly 20-page document encourages the learner to produce written reflections of an encountering experience by answering guiding questions. A similar 'child-friendly' version has been produced for younger learners, which can be used orally rather than in written form. Research shows that the *Autobiography* supports adults' intercultural learning, but there is some evidence that the questions are too complicated for adolescent learners (Ruest, 2020). The version intended for younger learners has been the object of little research (e.g. Rivieccio, 2021). However, I argue that teaching interculturality to children using guided reflection is not necessarily meaningful to children, as children may be used to answering questions to please the teacher rather than reflect on their own perspectives (Howe & Abedin, 2013; Wong, 2018). Due to their position of authority, teachers may be unwittingly leading children to mirror their own views of interculturality.

Children are in some ways the same as adults and also different (Punch, 2002). Children participate in a shared culture with adults, but they can also have cultural knowledge and repertoires they share exclusively with other children (Johanson, 2010). The field of childhood studies, which investigates children's culture (James & James, 2012), supported me in thinking about children's interculturality. In the 1980s and 1990s, there was a turn in the research, which is commonly referred to as the new sociology of childhood. Around the same time, the United Nations Convention on the Rights of the Child (1989) was born. Children are seen by both as active agents in their own lives, with experiential knowledge and the right to have an influence on issues that concern them (Karlsson, 2020).

Children's cultural experiences are predominantly moulded by their everyday lives. They revolve around their local communities, such as family, friends, and school. Children are used to narrating about their experiences by telling small stories, which relate the events of everyday life (Puroila et al., 2012). They also engage regularly in negotiating with peers during play (Corsaro, 2003; Hakkarainen, 2013). Children already have lots of informal experiences of intercultural and intracultural encountering when moving between their communities and learning from others. Children rarely engage in formal written or spoken reflection outside an educational setting. I propose that making use of children's existing cultural repertoires help them to engage in and learn from intercultural encounters with other children.

An example from my doctoral research illustrates the dominance of adult interculturality conceptually and in practice. When implementing a children's intercultural story exchange for the first time, I believed I was good at listening to children. After reading aloud a story from the exchange partners to my students, I decided to organise an open-ended class discussion to give the children an opportunity to share their thinking. However, I had not taken into consideration that the children interpreted the purpose of the discussion differently. Having a reflective discussion was a method that I as an adult was very comfortable with, but it was not a natural way for children to encounter each other. During the discussions, the children objectified their exchange partners and seemed to try to give answers that would please the teacher. When I replaced the guided reflection with a drawing activity, the children were better able to direct their messages to their exchange partners instead of the teacher (Piipponen & Karlsson, 2019).

Developing an intercultural story exchange with children

During my doctoral research, I developed a story exchange project where children told stories using the Storycrafting method. The Storycrafting method is a Finnish innovation that promotes encounters between adults and children, where all participants are valued equally (Karlsson, 2013). During Storycrafting, the scribe says to the teller, *Tell me a story. I will write it down exactly the way you tell it. When the story is finished, I will read it out to you, and if you want, you can make any changes or corrections* (adapted from Karlsson, 2013). The stories were exchanged between partner classes in Scotland and Finland during the first cycle of research, then between classes in Belgium and Finland for the next two cycles. After hearing a partner class's story during the first cycle, the children were given opportunities to orally comment on their exchange partners' story. This was changed in the second and third cycles, where the children drew an illustration of the story and told their own stories, which were sent back to the exchange partners. The stories were told in the school language (English or Finnish) and translated by the teachers. Both original and translated versions were read aloud to the recipients.

In the study, children found ways to encounter their exchange partners using their existing cultural repertoires (Piipponen, 2022). Cultural repertoires are ways of being, thinking, feeling, and acting that are based on our personal or collective experiences. Four repertoires were especially prominent: everyday, peer, narrative, and play. Everyday repertoires are activities that children are familiar with in their daily lives, like sleeping, eating, or playing. Peer repertoires consist of insider knowledge that has developed in children's peer groups, such as shared interests and hobbies, or inside jokes. Narrative repertoires are children's experiences of storytelling conventions. In my research, children were competent in creating tension in their stories, for example. Play repertoires are ways that children invite each other into play. The Storycrafting method afforded children with unusual freedom to take the story in different directions and improvise, which is very similar to the process of imaginative play.

I had to struggle for a long time to understand how the children were encountering their exchange partners, given that they never saw each other face to face. Together with my colleagues, I discovered that children created narrative tension and interest using, for example, exaggeration, plot twists, humour, and taboos in order to prompt an affective response from their audience (Piipponen & Karlsson, 2019). They often wanted to make their audience laugh! Here is an extract from a story which captured the exchange partners' imaginations. By illustrating the partners' stories, the recipients of the stories could show which parts of the story had been most interesting to them.

> Once upon a time there was a fat cat and it was a silver tabby with blue eyes called Beanz and it went on a spaceship. Then when he came back to Earth he landed in KFC.[1] Cats aren't allowed in KFC because they are an animal so he went to a pet shop instead. Beanz decided, because he was so handsome, he wanted to get a man makeover. Then he made best friends with another cat named Ziggy. They decided to go on a walk and when they went on a walk, they met a guy who thought he could fly. He tried to fly by jumping off a cliff. He landed in the sea and he got swallowed up by a big, fat, humongous, obese, swag, ugly, scary, big-teethed mammoth called Jeff Henry Jake Jaffa

Cake Jamie Hetty Betty Plonker Stevo. Beanz and Ziggy decided to jump in after them and it didn't end so well.

(Told by 10- to 11-year-old students, school in Scotland)

The drawings were sent back to the storytellers so that they could see how their story had been received. In this case, the exchange partners had noticed the detail of the fat cat and the difficult-to-translate word 'swag', which they had interpreted through their social media repertoires by adding a hashtag not mentioned in the original story. The children recognised the tongue-in-cheek tone of the story, and reciprocated by telling another fun, light-hearted tale. Intercultural encountering was present in the acts of telling, drawing, reading, listening, viewing, and imagining the stories and the storytellers, as the participants co-constructed a shared narrative culture (Piipponen & Karlsson, 2021).

Even though the exchange was 'international' – taking place between groups located in different countries – the content of the children's stories was not centred on national culture. When given the choice, the children told stories that were fun or exciting, that reflected their special interests, or that reaffirmed their relationships with others (Piipponen & Karlsson, 2019). In short, they engaged in exchanging a dynamic form of (children's) culture that was created in the specific local contexts of the exchange project.

A dynamic approach to interculturality

A dynamic approach to intercultural learning means learning *through* intercultural encountering rather than *about* cultures. Like many colleagues in this book, I understand culture as a dynamic process rather than a static entity: we maintain existing culture or create new culture over time by interacting with each other, and belong simultaneously to various cultural groups (Piipponen, 2022). An example of a static intercultural approach would be teaching facts about national traditions or customs. By contrast, in a classroom that follows the dynamic approach, the students could be collaborating with a partner class to create a shared work of art. This kind of holistic learning is a form of experiential inquiry, where children engage cognitively, socially, emotionally, and physically in the learning process. Rather than focusing on achievements of individuals, a dynamic approach supports the learning of the entire community. A static approach is usually teacher-led, but the dynamic approach distributes power also to the children. The challenge of this approach is that, currently, many school systems in the world are implementing neoliberal reforms, which focus on effectiveness, measurement, individual performance, and promoting narrow competencies (Biesta, 2014) – which, in short, produce a static approach to intercultural learning (Lanas, 2017; Rapanta & Trovão, 2021). Of course, elements of both approaches can co-exist in a classroom, but as a teacher I found that I had to work much harder to enable the dynamic approach.

How can teachers shift their pedagogies towards a dynamic approach to interculturality? There is no one-size-fits-all method that would lead to change in your classroom. Arriving at a dynamic approach requires going through a process of inquiry in your specific local context with your students (Piipponen, 2022). When developing intercultural learning with my students and colleagues, I started with the idea of exchanging children's culture. To this end, the Storycrafting method was useful because it allowed children to tell freely, drawing from their cultural repertoires.

The teacher's role at the beginning was to model how to listen actively and write down children's stories without making evaluative judgements during the process. Once the children became proficient using the method, they could work with a partner or in a small group to scribe each other's stories. The teacher's role shifted to one of reflective observation and enabling the children to participate in developing the learning space. For example, children often asked if they could take turns scribing and telling a story in their small group. This showed the teacher that the children valued communality, so she provided further opportunities for the children to send the stories not only to their exchange partners, but also read them aloud to their classmates. By being responsive to the children's initiatives and ideas, the teachers were able to support their agency. The story exchange evolved over time in response to the students' and teachers' cycles of action and reflection (Piipponen, 2022).

Let's return to the elephant again. How could a dynamic approach contribute to interculturalising interculturality? Think about an elephant always on the move. The elephant is born, grows up and goes through different life stages, and so changes whilst still being an elephant. It travels from one place to another, adapting to its surroundings. How would the blind men perceive the elephant if they met with it in a forest, in a field, or in a wildlife rehabilitation centre?

As researchers move towards more dynamic conceptualisations, this means interculturality will be expressed more often through a local rather than a universal lens. Therefore, when reflecting on intercultural learning in practice and in theory, one could think about these questions:

1. Who teaches/researches interculturality?
2. Who are the learners?
3. In which language(s)?
4. How is 'culture' defined? How is 'cultural difference' understood?
5. Where does intercultural education/research take place? Where is it not taking place?
6. Which ideologies guide the teacher's pedagogies?
7. What kind of teaching methods are used?

Situating intercultural encounters within their local context means that researchers and teachers have to pay more attention to more than just the communicative interaction. I propose that viewing encountering as experiential learning can help teachers to take better account of the learning context.

A Finnish approach to promoting intercultural encountering 209

Reuniting emotion and reason through experiential learning

A dynamic approach to intercultural learning entails that children can draw from their own cultural repertoires and experiences, as well as engage in new experiential forms of learning. Promoting experiential learning can be a challenge as education systems are not neutral; how we educate reflects what we value. Since the Enlightenment period, Western education has been influenced by a philosophy of rationalism, which separates subject from world, body from mind, thinking from feeling, and reason from emotion (Duncan & Sankey, 2019). Take a moment to imagine a classroom interaction where a teacher is leading the students through a whole-class discussion. What are the implicit rules that the participants are following? What kinds of children's initiatives are acceptable to the teacher, and what other kinds are checked? A typical Western school classroom privileges rationality and suppresses children's emotions, even though contemporary knowledge of learning views the body and mind as interconnected systems (Duncan & Sankey, 2019). In the same vein, Lanas (2017) criticises an intercultural education that is emotion-free and focused narrowly on utility, given that emotions are central in negotiating intercultural situations.

In his philosophy of experience, Dewey (1938/2015) unites the subject and the world, body and mind, and thought and feeling in a situation through the concept of experience. In effect, it is not possible for the mind to detach itself during an intercultural situation. Rather, an experience is formed when a person interacts with the world and other people in it whilst simultaneously drawing from the memories, habits, emotions, social norms, and language that derive from prior experiences. Focusing only on cognition ignores the holistic nature of experience. Learning through experience should allow students to engage with the full spectrum of experiential knowledge that is broader than just cognition. Prior research shows that not all intercultural encounters lead to deeper intercultural learning (e.g. Lau, 2015; MacKenzie et al., 2016; Peiser, 2015). I propose that intercultural experiences lead to learning when they are meaningful to the student. Meaningful intercultural experiences have an aesthetic quality, which means the experience engages the emotions and imagination, and connects to prior knowledge (Piipponen & Karlsson, 2021).

How can a teacher, then, influence the quality of students' intercultural encountering experiences? It is not possible to gain an insider view of students' experiences, but by working together with the students, it is possible to develop the learning space so that it is more conducive to encountering. In my research, I realised that teacher-led discussions *about* encountering were inhibiting children from actually encountering their exchange partners (Piipponen & Karlsson, 2019). After that experience, I went back to examine the research data and, together with my colleagues, we analysed which dimensions of the learning space supported or hindered intercultural encountering (Piipponen et al., 2021). When the dimensions were well aligned, the two groups of children could engage in reciprocal encountering, where they collaborated as equal participants. Table 15.1 describes how the dimensions of power, knowledge, relatedness, purpose, structure, continuity,

Table 15.1 Seven dimensions of the learning space influence whether a space of reciprocal encountering can be created in a children's story exchange

Dimensions of the learning space	Questions	Space of reciprocal encountering
Power	Who has influence through speaking or acting?	Power should be democratically rather than authoritatively distributed so that children also have autonomy to influence the learning space.
Knowledge	How is knowledge defined? What are the boundaries of knowledge?	The space should value dynamic, experiential, situated knowledge, so that children can use their cultural repertoires, which are often dismissed in institutional settings in favour of conventional academic knowledge.
Relatedness	How do participants connect with each other?	Supporting a warm, respectful form of relatedness in the learning space is important for making the children feel they are part of their community, so that they feel comfortable to encounter the unfamiliar exchange partners.
Purpose	What is the purpose of learning?	The purpose of the learning space should aim for holistic growth of the learners, because decontextualised skills and knowledge are not enough to support reciprocal encountering in complex sociohistorical contexts.
Structure	How is the learning space structured?	The learning space should be structured so that it supports reciprocal encountering between the participants. For example, a class discussion about the partner school students does not support reciprocity, whereas the students directed their responses to the exchange partners by drawing an illustration of their partners' story and sending it back to them.
Continuity	How much do past learning spaces influence the current space?	The dimension of continuity acknowledges the influence that past experiences have on a learning space; over time, a new tradition or classroom culture is developed.
Meaningfulness	To what extent is the learning made meaningful and relevant for the learners?	Meaningfulness is fulfilled when the learning authentically connects to learners' lives. In a space of reciprocal encountering, children's contributions are appreciated and their initiatives are encouraged.

Source: Adapted from Piipponen (2022).

and meaningfulness contributed to forming a space of reciprocal encountering. The related questions can guide teachers or researchers to reflect on the nature of the learning space and help them to become aware of possible barriers.

Conclusion

The elephant uses its legs to move, its tail for swatting flies, and its ears to hear and cool down. Interculturality is multifaceted, and it is fruitful for researchers and teachers to approach it from different standpoints. In this chapter, I have argued that dominant intercultural theories and practices are adult-centric, and children's intercultural learning will be enhanced by investigating interculturality from children's perspectives. I presented a dynamic approach to developing children's intercultural encountering in primary schools, which involves developing the learning space together with children through inquiry. Intercultural encountering can be viewed as experiential learning, which supports children's holistic growth. This kind of learning cannot be reduced to narrow, measurable learning outcomes, but rather a teacher should observe and reflect on the quality of the learning space and its potential for supporting encounters between equal subjects. As a final reflection on the notion of interculturalising interculturality (Dervin & Jacobsson, 2022), I would like to propose that learning from children's interculturality may 'interculturalise' the scope of adult interculturality as well.

The story exchange intervention was influenced by a Finnish educational philosophy, which promotes equal opportunities for all children to learn, views children as active and knowledgeable participants in the learning process, and trusts professional and autonomous teachers to develop the learning space so that it is appropriate for the children in their local context. Being aware of one's educational philosophy supports teachers in making informed pedagogical choices that promote intercultural learning. Teaching interculturality is an ongoing process of inquiry where the teacher learns together with the children.

Note

1 A fast food restaurant.

References

Alvaré, B. (2017). "Do they think we live in huts?" – Cultural essentialism and the challenges of facilitating professional development in cross-cultural settings. *Ethnography and Education*, *12*(1), 33–48. https://doi.org/10.1080/17457823.2015.1109466.

Barrett, M. (2018). How schools can promote the intercultural competence of young people. *European Psychologist*, *23*(1), 93–104. https://doi.org/10.1027/1016-9040/a000308.

Bash, L. (2014). The globalisation of fear and the construction of the intercultural imagination. *Intercultural Education*, *25*(2), 77–84. https://doi.org/10.1080/14675986.2014.885223.

Bennett, M. J. (1998). Intercultural communication: A current perspective. In M. J. Bennett (Ed.), *Basic Concepts of Intercultural Communication: Selected Readings* (pp. 1–34). Boston, MA: Intercultural Press.

Biesta, G. (2014). Measuring what we value or valuing what we measure? Globalization, accountability and the question of educational purpose. *Pensamiento Educativo*, *51*(1), 46–57. https://doi.org/10.7764/PEL.51.1.2014.5.

Byram, M. (2008). *From Foreign Language Education to Education for Intercultural Citizenship: Essays and Reflections*. Clevedon: Multilingual Matters.

Cochran-Smith, M. (2021). Rethinking teacher education: The trouble with accountability. *Oxford Review of Education*, *4*(1), 8–24. https://doi.org/10.1080/03054985.2020.1842181.

Corsaro, W. A. (2003). *We're Friends, Right? Inside Kids' Culture*. New York: Joseph Henry Press.
Council of Europe. (2009). *Autobiography of Intercultural Encounters*. https://www.coe.int/en/web/autobiography-intercultural-encounters.
Davies, T. (2022). Towards a praxis of difference: Reimagining intercultural understanding in Australian schools as a challenge of practice. *Pedagogy, Culture & Society*. https://doi.org/10.1080/14681366.2022.2027002.
Deardorff, D. (2020). Defining, developing and assessing intercultural competence. In G. Rings & S. Rasinger (Eds.), *The Cambridge Handbook of Intercultural Communication* (pp. 493–503). Cambridge: Cambridge University Press. https://doi.org/10.1017/9781108555067.036.
Deardorff, D. K. (2006). Identification and assessment of intercultural competence as a student outcome of internationalization. *Journal of Studies in International Education*, *10*(3), 241–266. https://doi.org/10.1177/1028315306287002.
Dervin, F., & Jacobsson, A. (2022). *Intercultural Communication Education: Broken Realities and Rebellious Dreams*. London: Springer.
Dewey, J. (2015). *Experience and Education*. Indianapolis, IN: Kappa Delta Pi. (Original work published 1938).
Duncan, C., & Sankey, D. (2019). Two conflicting visions of education and their consilience. *Educational Philosophy and Theory*, *51*(14), 1454–1464. https://doi.org/10.1080/00131857.2018.1557044.
Faas, D., Hajisoteriou, C., & Angelides, P. (2014). Intercultural education in Europe: Policies, practices and trends. *British Educational Research Journal*, *40*(2), 300–318. https://doi.org/10.1002/berj.3080.
Gorski, P. C. (2008). Good intentions are not enough: A decolonizing intercultural education. *Intercultural Education*, *19*(6), 515–525. https://doi.org/10.1080/14675980802568319.
Gorski, P. C. (2009). What we're teaching teachers: An analysis of multicultural teacher education coursework syllabi. *Teaching and Teacher Education*, *25*(2), 309–318. https://doi.org/10.1016/j.tate.2008.07.008.
Hakkarainen, P., Brėdikytė, M., Jakkula, K., & Munter, H. (2013). Adult play guidance and children's play development in a narrative play-world. *European Early Childhood Education Research Journal*, *21*(2), 213–225. https://doi.org/10.1080/1350293X.2013.789189.
Howe, C., & Abedin, M. (2013). Classroom dialogue: A systematic review across four decades of research. *Cambridge Journal of Education*, *43*(3), 325–356. https://doi.org/10.1080/0305764X.2013.786024.
Hummelstedt, I. (2022). *Acknowledging Diversity but Reproducing the Other: A Critical Analysis of Finnish Multicultural Education*. Doctoral Dissertation, University of Helsinki. https://helda.helsinki.fi/handle/10138/342840.
Hummelstedt, I. P., Holm, G. I., Sahlström, F. J., & Zilliacus, H. A.-C. (2021). Diversity as the new normal and persistent constructions of the immigrant other – Discourses on multicultural education among teacher educators. *Teaching and Teacher Education*, *108*, 103510. https://doi.org/10.1016/j.tate.2021.103510.
Hummelstedt-Djedou, I., Zilliacus, H., & Holm, G. (2018). Diverging discourses on multicultural education in Finnish teacher education programme policies: Implications for teaching. *Multicultural Education Review*, *10*(3), 184–202. https://doi.org/10.1080/2005615X.2018.1511341.
Jackson, J. (2018). *Interculturality in International Education*. London: Routledge.

James, A., & James, A. (2012). *Key Concepts in Childhood Studies* (2nd ed.). London: Sage.
Johanson, K. (2010). Culture for or by the child? 'Children's culture' and cultural policy. *Poetics, 38*(4), 386–401. https://doi.org/10.1016/j.poetic.2010.05.002.
Kaikkonen, P. (2004). *Vierauden keskellä: Vierauden, monikulttuurisuuden ja kulttuurienvälisen kasvatuksen aineksia*. Jyväskylä: Jyväskylän yliopistopaino.
Karlsson, L. (2013). Storycrafting method – To share, participate, tell and listen in practice and research. *European Journal of Social & Behavioural Sciences, 6*(3 Special Issue), 1109–1117. https://doi.org/10.15405/ejsbs.88.
Karlsson, L. (2020). Studies of child perspectives in methodology and practice with 'osallisuus' as a Finnish approach to children's reciprocal cultural participation. In E. E. Ødegaard & J. S. Borgen (Eds.), *Childhood Cultures in Transformation: 30 Years of the UN Convention of the Rights of the Child in Action* (pp. 246–273). Amsterdam: Brill/Sense Publisher.
Lanas, M. (2017). An argument for love in intercultural education for teacher education. *Intercultural Education, 28*(6), 557–570. https://doi.org/10.1080/14675986.2017.1389541.
Lau, S. M. C. (2015). Intercultural education through a bilingual children's rights project: Reflections on its possibilities and challenges with young learners. *Intercultural Education, 26*(6), 469–482. https://doi.org/10.1080/14675986.2015.1109774.
Lonka, K. (2018). *Phenomenal Learning from Finland*. Helsinki: Edita.
MacKenzie, A., Enslin, P., & Hedge. N. (2016). Education for Global Citizenship in Scotland: Reciprocal partnership or politics of benevolence? *International Journal of Educational Research, 77*, 128–135. https://doi.org/10.1016/j.ijer.2016.03.007.
Mikander, P., Zilliacus, H., & Holm, G. (2018). Intercultural education in transition: Nordic perspectives. *Education Inquiry, 9*(1), 40–56. https://doi.org/10.1080/20004508.2018.1433432.
Pais, A., & Costa, M. (2020). An ideology critique of global citizenship education. *Critical Studies in Education, 61*(1), 1–16. https://doi.org/10.1080/17508487.2017.1318772.
Peiser, G. (2015). Overcoming barriers: Engaging younger students in an online intercultural exchange. *Intercultural Education, 26*(5), 361–376. https://doi.org/10.1080/14675986.2015.1091238.
Piipponen, O. (2022). *Children Encountering Each Other Through Stories: Developing a Dynamic Approach to Interculturality in Primary Schools*. Doctoral Dissertation, University of Eastern Finland. https://erepo.uef.fi/handle/123456789/26784.
Piipponen, O., & Karlsson, L. (2019). Children encountering each other through storytelling: Promoting intercultural learning in schools. *The Journal of Educational Research, 112*(5), 590–603. https://doi.org/10.1080/00220671.2019.1614514.
Piipponen, O., & Karlsson, L. (2021). "Our stories were pretty weird too" – Children as creators of a shared narrative culture in an intercultural story and drawing exchange. *International Journal of Educational Research, 106*, 101720. https://doi.org/10.1016/j.ijer.2020.101720.
Piipponen, O., Karlsson, L., & Kantelinen, R. (2021). From ambivalent spaces to spaces of reciprocal encountering: Developing classroom culture in an intercultural story exchange. *Journal of Multilingual and Multicultural Development*. https://doi.org/10.1080/01434632.2021.1920027.
Portera, A. (2020). Has multiculturalism failed? Let's start the era of interculturalism for facing diversity issues. *Intercultural Education, 31*(4), 390–406. https://doi.org/10.1080/14675986.2020.1765285.

Punch, S. (2002). Research with children: The same or different from research with adults? *Childhood*, *9*(3), 321–341. https://doi.org/10.1177/0907568202009003005.

Puroila, A., Estola, E., & Syrjälä, L. (2012). Does Santa exist? Children's everyday narratives as dynamic meeting places in a day care centre context. *Early Child Development and Care*, *182*(2), 191–206. https://doi.org/10.1080/03004430.2010.549942.

Qvortrup, J. (2009). Are children human beings or human becomings? A critical assessment of outcome thinking. *Rivista Internazionale Di Scienze Sociali*, *117*(3–4), 631–653.

Rapanta, C., & Trovão, S. (2021). Intercultural education for the twenty-first century: A comparative review of research. In F. Maine & M. Vrikki (Eds.), *Dialogue for Intercultural Understanding* (pp. 9–26). London: Springer.

Rivieccio, P. (2021). Questioning questions in autobiographies of intercultural encounters. *International Journal of Bias, Identity and Diversities in Education*, *6*(1), 47–59. https://doi.org/10.4018/IJBIDE.2021010104.

Roiha, A., & Sommier, M. (2021). Exploring teachers' perceptions and practices of intercultural education in an international school. *Intercultural Education*, *32*(4), 446–463. https://doi.org/10.1080/14675986.2021.1893986.

Ruest, C. (2020). The autobiography of intercultural encounters: Mixed results amongst Canadian adolescents. *Language and Intercultural Communication*, *20*(1), 7–21. https://doi.org/10.1080/14708477.2019.1681438.

Ryan, R. M., & Deci, E. L. (2017). *Self-Determination Theory: Basic Psychological Needs in Motivation, Development and Wellness*. New York: Guilford Publications.

Schwarzenthal, M., Schachner, M. K., Juang, L. P., & van de Vijver, F. J. R. (2019). Reaping the benefits of cultural diversity: Classroom cultural diversity climate and students' intercultural competence. *European Journal of Social Psychology*, 1–24. https://doi.org/10.1002/ejsp.2617.

Sobre, M. (2017). Developing the critical intercultural class-space: Theoretical implications and pragmatic applications of critical intercultural communication pedagogy. *Intercultural Education*, *28*(1), 39–59. https://doi.org/10.1080/14675986.2017.1288984.

Walton, J., Priest, N., & Paradies, Y. (2013). Identifying and developing effective approaches to foster intercultural understanding in schools. *Intercultural Education*, *24*(3), 181–194. https://doi.org/10.1080/14675986.2013.793036.

Wong, D. (2018). Intercultural learning may be impossible in education abroad: A lesson from King Lear. *Frontiers: The Interdisciplinary Journal of Study Abroad*, *30*(3), 38–50. https://doi.org/10.36366/frontiers.v30i3.428.

Zhang, X., & Zhou, M. (2019). Interventions to promote learners' intercultural competence: A meta-analysis. *International Journal of Intercultural Relations*, *71*, 31–47. https://doi.org/10.1016/j.ijintrel.2019.04.006.

Zilliacus, H., Holm, G., & Sahlström, F. (2017). Taking steps towards institutionalising multicultural education – The national curriculum of Finland. *Multicultural Education Review*, *9*(4), 231–248. https://doi.org/10.1080/2005615X.2017.1383810.

16 Remarks and conclusion

Towards an endless and centreless glissando of interculturality

Fred Dervin

We must get back to interculturality again and again

The tendency to better remember unfinished tasks than completed ones has a name: the Zeigarnik effect (Denmark, 2010). Interculturality has that effect on us as scholars and educators but also students of the notion. Interculturality is the 'limitless' encounters of people, ideas, artefacts. *We must get back to it again and again.* This is the main message of this book – which was not meant to provide us with ultimate answers and guidance about teaching interculturality.

The chapter authors, mostly located in the 'Western' corner of the world, were asked to reflect upon modes of conceptualising, criticising, inquiring, problematising, and writing about teaching interculturality (see original questions to authors in Chapter 1). What they have done for and with us is to interrogate the 'imaginary being' of interculturality (to refer back to a metaphor from Chapter 1) by adding to its *puzzles*. While some appear to be more convinced of the 'strength' of what they do with interculturality in education, the vast majority of authors are curious about the 'limitless' of the notion. For Schoenberg (2003: 114):

> We must become conscious that there are puzzles around us. And we must find the courage to look these puzzles in the eye without timidly asking about the "solution." It is important that our creation of such puzzles mirror the puzzles with which we are surrounded, so that our soul may endeavor—not to solve them—but to decipher them.

Let me reformulate this for our purpose: The chapter authors did not intend to (help us) *solve* the puzzles of interculturality but to *decipher* them for and with you the reader – in other words, to help appreciate, catch, comprehend, perceive, understand them 'temporarily'. (Note: *Cipher* in *decipher* comes from Arabic for 'zero, empty, nothing'.) As a whole, the book represents *a snapshot of a snapshot of a snapshot* … of the wide range of perspectives on teaching interculturality, even within the 'West' – making *otherwise* within this somewhat monolithic label a partial reality too.

There is no solution to interculturality but endless combinations of (temporary) answers to decipher. Teaching interculturality *otherwise* means to treat interculturality as it is: a multifaceted, changing and unfinished notion that deserves to be discussed and problematised *again and again* with others.

Two of the Chinese students who took part in the project behind this volume refer to interesting metaphors that reaffirm the 'limitless' complexities of interculturality:

> "From my perspective, interculturality may be like potatoes to some extent. Potatoes have different names in different parts of China. Some call them 马铃薯, 洋芋, and others 土豆."

> "Today I came across an interesting thought in Robyn Moloney's lecture, which she borrows from Fred Dervin: 'Interculturality is a chest of drawers.'[1] Hearing this sentence, I opened my drawer to see what was in it. I am not a meticulous person. My drawers are messy. The colors inside are also very rich, and the dates when various things are put in are different. Some things I haven't even taken out of the drawer in a year. I think that's right. Different things collide in my drawers. If I just shove them in in a mess, sometimes, it's going to be a disaster."

Towards endless and centreless glissandos of interculturality

Several aspects of teaching interculturality 'otherwise' were considered in the book as the chapter authors engaged with the idea of interculturalising interculturality (Dervin, 2021; Dervin & Jacobsson, 2022). As a reminder, interculturalising interculturality is not an end in itself but a lifelong process of opening up the way we deal with, e.g., teaching interculturality. The neologism *interculturalising* might give the illusion that there is a possible end or that it might lead to 'a state of readiness'. Unfortunately, all languages have their limits and the English language does not allow me to propose a hint at 'never-endingness' with the word interculturalising – unless I repeat *interculturalising* ad infinitum as in *interculturalising interculturalising interculturalising interculturalising interculturalising ... interculturality.*

(To be clear: One can never be ready with interculturality or *interculturalising* it.)

Let me just discuss one example from my colleague and friend Andreas Jacobsson who proposes the stimulating idea of *polycentrism* in Chapter 12 – considering many different centres of knowledge production about interculturality, taking into account the fluidity of language, for enriching its teaching. I see a potential problem with this label which has to do with how to relate and link these different centres. In other words, how to infuse some *inter-* between different centres. I also see a potential danger of turning interculturality as an object of research and education into a *monopolylogue*, i.e. an "entertainment in which one actor performs as many characters" (*Merriam Webster*) – one voice having the power to *choose to speak for* others. I am thinking here of a piece of music by Camille Saint-Saëns (1835–1921), *Orient et Occident op. 25* (1869), which he composed for the opening of the 345-metre wide and 193-km long Suez Canal in Egypt. The piece is said to combine 'Eastern' and 'Western' musical elements, and starts with 'European' tones and rhythm, continues with 'softer' and freer (imagined) music from the 'East' (e.g. pentatonic melodies) and ends with a return to the 'West' with a fugue (which is considered as the most complex and appreciated form of 'Western' music). In *polycentralising* interculturality we might run the risk of experiencing a similar awkward transition between, e.g., the 'West' and the 'East' (with either re-presented as simpler and stereotyped, depending on where one is located), creating samples and patchworks of simplified imaginary beings (Alexander Frame makes a similar point in Chapter 2; see R'boul, Chapter 17, Afterword). We must also remember that *there are multiple centres within a given centre* (e.g. Saint-Saëns uses musical elements from fantasised homogeneous centres) and many chapters from this book hint at polycentrism within the 'West' too. Finally, without dialogue, connections, and intense and honest negotiations between scholars and educators from different parts of the world – but also from the same region and country – this might not work. Opportunities for cooperation between *centres* appear to be limited today in our neoliberal/capitalistic global academic worlds (one tends to work with 'official' partners, reproducing global economic, political, and institutional hierarchies). Thinking from a polycentric perspective could work for teaching interculturality if one reflects on questions such as: Who is (not) talking in discussions of interculturality in teaching? Who is (not) talking about other centres and centres within centres? Who is (not) allowed to talk and for whom? Who is (not) talking to whom? Who is (not) answering? Who is (not) listened to? Who is (not) listening? Who is (ab)using the other knowledge-wise?

I would like to propose a musical metaphor for describing what interculturalising interculturality (ad infinitum) could mean for teaching, moving away from centres: *an endless and centreless glissando*. Used in music, the word 'glissando' comes from 'Italianised' French *glissez*, which means 'to slide'. A glissando is a musical slide across a span of notes performed on an instrument, continuously ascending or descending. One of the most famous glissandos is found in George Gershwin's *Rhapsody in Blue* (1898) which opens with a trilling clarinet going up more than two octaves. I suggest that 'sliding about' (not just between notes in a 'logical' up or down order but *about, around, on all sides*) in endless and centreless glissandos represents an interesting approach to interculturalising interculturality. Instead of jumping from a single centre to 'visit' another, sliding endlessly through scholars, ideas, concepts, ideologies, languages ... (regardless of where they are located), refraining from reproducing naively and robot-like 'preferred', 'sponsored', or 'dominating' stances from those dictating what the field of interculturality is about, corresponds to a challenging and stimulating approach. Interculturality as both a social and scientific phenomenon is itself complex, limitless, polysemous, uncontrollable, and changeable but also incomplete. Trying to 'catch' this imaginary being is treacherous since one cannot but lock interculturality into a cage, feeding it with preferred (limited) ideologies, economic–political positions, 'pet' concepts, etc. An endless and centreless glissando approach, with an obligation to look at the unstable geo–economic–political positions of *east, north, south, west* could allow us to let 'chance' operate in discovering other ways of engaging with interculturality, in different languages and translations, in different kinds of sources (fields of research rather than just 'an' intercultural field; philosophy, the arts, music, fiction, etc.), and in simple *things* around us (e.g. an encounter on the subway, an object). Sliding about through these with both curiosity and humility, I can re-revise (again and again)[2] my take on interculturality, not with an aim to 'finalise' it (that would not make sense) but to continue reflecting and engaging with the notion *lifelong*. Teaching/learning ('tearning', see Chapter 1) interculturality could mean to train people to help themselves become aware of, reconsider, liberate themselves and others from the dominating ideologies that pretend to be more 'scientific' than others, orders to think and act, beautified discourses, one-sided critiques, biases, lies, manipulations, that they have been fed with – *lifelong*. One must remember that replacing, e.g., one ideological take on interculturality by another 'order' still needs to be worked upon.

We must turn interculturality around in all directions, performing endless and centreless glissandos in the labyrinth of thoughts that the notion represents.

Interculturality-r-us. *We construct interculturality as an object of research and education with others* non-stop.

Important takeaways for *otherwising* interculturality

> Is there a thought that would be worthy of not being thought again?
> (Canetti, 1989: 23)

In the Introduction to this volume, I proposed a guide for reading the chapters (see Table 1.1). Re-reading all the chapters that compose this book, using the reading guide, one notes snapshots of potential centrisms in what the authors (and myself) shared with us. The proposed glissando should help us detach ourselves a bit from such centrisms – temporarily until we attach ourselves to another centrism, from which we must push ourselves away again, *sliding about*. In what follows I list some of the takeaways from the book that I consider to be important for teaching interculturality *otherwise* – feel free to add other ones!

- Constantly perform an *archaeology of the ideas and terms used* within our field(s) and beyond, as well as in as many different languages as possible to avoid reinventing the wheel (which is often 'broken') and giving the impression that we have found something new to say, leading in fact to "humiliated repetition" (Barthes, 1975: 41–42). The more we know, the readier and more comfortable we might be to 'slide about'. Let's build up curiosity in our students instead of merely feeding them with our (limited) knowledge!
- In teaching interculturality, *help self and others help themselves 'decipher'* interculturality rather than help them try to 'solve' it (which is impossible). Falsely miraculous recipes such as models of intercultural competence (see

Layne and Chakrapani, Chapter 10; and Piipponen, Chapter 15) could be avoided since they cannot reflect the 'limitless' of interculturality.
- *Be critical of our own criticality* to avoid 'attacking' others while our own positions and thoughts cannot but be criticisable too (see, e.g., Chen and Dervin, Chapter 9). Using a comment made by Claudel, Barthes (2002: 86) asserts that critique is "knowledge [*connaissance* in French] of the other and co-birth [*co-naissance, a play-upon-word based on French for knowledge and birth*] of self to the world" (my translation). My criticality of the other requires criticality of self in order to avoid turning my criticality into caricatures and simplifications. Jasmin Peskoller puts it nicely in Chapter 3 when she writes about "practise what you preach" in critical interculturality. She adds: "critically rethinking, reshaping, redefining, reassessing, and reviewing through multiperspectivity constitutes an intercultural process that should present a standard course of action in any academic discipline or educational context".
- Pay attention to the *way we speak of interculturality* in education, listening to ourselves and considering the consequences that our discourses might have on others – and others' discourses on us. For example, how often do we use strong modals such as *must* or *should* versus softer ones like *could* and *might* to introduce and discuss what we expect from the notion? Do we tend to refer to our approach using the definite article *the* – as in *the intercultural approach is the most appropriate* ... ? We can also reflect on why it is that we use certain terms (e.g. empathy, respect, democracy) and not others. *Who is forcing us (in)directly to construct interculturality around them?*
- There is a need for us to identify, reflect on, and act upon *our own centrisms and others'*. Centrisms defeat interculturality; centrisms lead to sameness and destroy opportunities for glissandos. These could include (in alphabetical order):
    - *Adult-centrism* (ignoring the voice of children, believing that they are 'intercultural dummies'; see Piipponen, Chapter 15, but also Jacobsson et al., 2023)
    - *Anthropo-centrism* (disregarding the influence of non-humans in intercultural encounters)
    - *Authority-centrism* (making sole references to globally preferred and popular scholars)
    - *Concept-centrism* (using fashionable words without always questioning them)
    - *Corner-of-the-world-centrism* (dividing the world ex-/implicitly into the West, Europe, Finland, China, Global South, etc.)
    - *Criticality-centrism* (believing that one's critiques of interculturality – and (in)directly of others – are the only (in)valid ones)
    - *Field-centrism* (remaining anchored in one single field of research when interculturality is interdisciplinary par excellence)
    - *Ideology-centrism* (basing one's work on a specific ideology – which is not always declared as such – e.g. *democracy-talk, diversity in unity,*

interculturality as a way of disseminating/'spreading' knowledge about self, Reconciliation)
- *Institution-centrism* (presenting one's institution as a leading centre of knowledge on interculturality, ignoring the fact that many such centres are also working hard to enrich our knowledge of interculturality in other parts of the world)
- *Lingua-centrism* (using specific ways of speaking and 'flavouring' interculturality in English and other languages, assuming others share these 'flavours', and showing a complete lack of interest in 'real' multilingualism in research and education)
- *Nation-centrism* (constructing (research in) one's country as a good/bad example of interculturality 'management')
- *Times-centrism* (making assumptions about today's world compared to the past in terms of interculturality – as in 'the world has never been as diverse as today')

I have used a certain number of metaphors in the Introduction (Chapter 1) and this concluding chapter to refer to interculturality. I would like to leave you with two of these metaphors which I think summarise well what my co-editors and I as well as the chapter authors had to say about the notion. *Interculturality is a multiform imaginary being which has a Zeigarnik effect on us.* Its unfinished and complex shapes in research and education force us to come back to it again and again. If we decide not to take these elements into account when we teach interculturality – or simply refuse to teach it – it does not really matter. Interculturality will still 'operate' in its own intricate and unstable ways; *interculturality does not really need us.* And as one of our students said about ignoring the complexities of interculturality: "There is an old saying in China: 地球缺了你不会不转的, which means 'the earth will still rotate without us.'" While reflecting back on the book and reading Hamza R'boul's Afterword, the reader might want to consider these last assertions for themselves.

Notes

1 See Dervin, 2022a.
2 Repetitions intended.

References

Barthes, R. (1975). *The Pleasure of the Text*. New York: Farrar, Straus, Giroux.
Barthes, R. (2002). *Essais critiques*. Paris: Seuil.
Canetti, E. (1989). *The Secret Heart of the Clock*. New York: Farrar, Straus, Giroux.
Denmark, F. L. (2010). Zeigarnik effect. *The Corsini Encyclopedia of Psychology* (online). London: Wiley. https://onlinelibrary.wiley.com/doi/abs/10.1002/9780470479216.corpsy0924.
Dervin, F. (2021). *Critical and Reflexive Languaging in the Construction of Interculturality as an Object of Research and Practice* (19 April 2021). Digital series of talks on plurilingualism and interculturality, University of Copenhagen.

Dervin, F. (2022a). Series editor foreword. In R. Moloney, M. Lobytsyna, & J. De Nobile (Eds.), *Interculturality in Schools: Practice and Research* (pp. x–xv). London: Routledge.
Dervin, F., & Jacobsson, A. (2022). *Intercultural Communication Education: Broken Realities and Rebellious Dreams*. London: Springer.
Jacobsson, A., Layne, H., & Dervin, F. (2023). *Children and Interculturality in Education*. London: Routledge.
Schoenberg, A. (2003). *A Schoenberg Reader: Documents of a Life*. New Haven, CT, and London: Yale University Press.

17 Afterword

Theorising and teaching interculturality otherwise: *What 'otherwise'?*

Hamza R'boul

Theorising and teaching interculturality 'otherwise' entail having a deep understanding of the 'mainstream' and the 'dominant'. The 'otherwise' goes beyond the 'mainstream' and provides novel insights into how theorising and teaching interculturality could be exercised. However, in the case that mainstream knowledge producers take charge of theorising and teaching interculturality 'otherwise', then there is a possibility that they will be reproducing the same dominant knowledges in other forms and modalities under the guise of 'otherwise'. Therefore, it is essential to probe into the question of whether the 'otherwise' can be produced by the same epistemologies and voices that have developed the 'mainstream'. Is it really 'otherwise' when the 'mainstream' is enunciating again? These are epistemological challenges to the very premise of the 'otherwise'. I argue that its alternativising essence is not fulfilled as long as the same perspectives are being remoulded with the 'mainstream' speaking the 'otherwise'.

Other pertinent questions could include: *Is the 'otherwise' non-Western? Is the 'otherwise' Southern? Can the Global North transcend its Western logics to construct a genuine possibility of generating alternative knowledges?* Again, the Global South does not necessarily theorise and teach interculturality *otherwise* because it can be re-expressing Western epistemologies through Southern voices. These are key questions in setting the preliminary frame of reference to ascertain that we are actually theorising and teaching interculturality 'otherwise'. The 'otherwise' is an opportunity to disrupt the 'dominant' and 'mainstream', but it remains unclear to what extent the 'otherwise' is represented through alternative lenses with alternative knowledges. The 'otherwise' should not be used to recast the 'dominant' to sound and look 'peripheral' and 'non-popular' enough to be seen as 'otherwise'.

Whenever the 'otherwise' is theorised and discussed, we may be running the risk that dominant knowledges are reshaping and reproducing themselves through alternative manifestations that allow them to continue occupying the same superior status in interculturality through assuming essential roles in the process. Dominant knowledge producers may take the liberty of capitalising on the burgeoning 'decolonial turn' and the 'otherwise' in interculturality to not theorise and teach otherwise but to reproduce themselves otherwise while keeping their epistemological tenets intact. We are then faced with an epistemic chameleon when dominant knowledges assume their legitimacy in theorising the 'alternative' and the 'otherwise'. What is problematic is that the Global South has to read the Global North even in its decolonial discourses and narratives, but the Global North can get away without reading, citing, and discussing the Global South even in its attempts to theorise the 'otherwise'. Theorising and teaching interculturality 'otherwise' requires first developing a deep understating of the 'what', 'how' and 'what for' of the dominant epistemologies before proceeding to work on the 'otherwise'. Ignoring this condition may pave the way for re-enacting the dominant in the *otherwise's clothing*.

It may be a bold statement to argue that 'otherwise' has already been there since it is the knowledges of the Global South, but there is certainly a great deal of legitimacy propelling this claim. Do we indeed need to theorise the 'otherwise'? Or we should only grant more visibility to the Global South since it is the 'otherwise'. The Global South has nothing but its place in theorising the 'otherwise', and if this is seized by the Global North and its dominant knowledges, then what is left for the subaltern? This is not an argument to halt the Global North from participating; it is rather a call to zoom into what we do not know or what we haven't paid enough attention to and then endeavour to explore its significance in theorising the 'otherwise'. We cannot simply surmise that there is no 'otherwise', and we can already go ahead and theorise the 'otherwise' as if it were novel and ground-breaking work. Again, the 'otherwise' has always been there, but it needs to be recognised and visibilised. The quest for theorising and teaching interculturality otherwise aggravates the Global South's epistemic dependency since the very attempts to disrupt the ascendency of the Western cognitive empire are enunciated through Western lenses.

The 'otherwise' is an opportunity for those who have not been privileged enough to have their voices heard. The 'otherwise' may have always been there but we did not care to check, read, and cite. We may engage in theorising and teaching interculturality 'otherwise' without consulting the alternative perspectives that have been there for a while; we may ignore their contributions and go ahead to make use of their struggles to teach them what they should do and how they should understand the 'otherwise'. These dynamics exemplify epistemic exploitation, which refers to "when privileged persons compel marginalised knowers to educate them [and others] about the nature of their oppression" (Berenstain, 2016: 569). It delivers the assumption that 'I understand your struggles and your need for alternative approaches to teaching interculturality, and I am qualified and privileged enough to offer them to you without you participating'. For instance, it is important to examine and unsettle the complex politics of knowledge through the 'otherwise' in Africa by centring the often-ignored ontologies, ecologies, and perspectives of African intellectuals on the decolonisation of knowledge and politics (Ndlovu-Gatsheni, 2021a). Interculturality for Africa is quite different from what interculturality may mean to the US. Interculturality for Africa may be about how their relations with the other are conditioned by power struggles while, for the US, it may mean managing cultural diversity. That is why 'otherwise' remains a contested notion and we may use it to mean different things that are not necessarily characterised by similar premises.

Even in postcolonial and decolonial studies, which are essentially premised upon the idea of the 'otherwise', Marxist and secular forms of resistance have been foregrounded in postcolonial discourse; the majority of prominent postcolonial works produced in the 1980s and 1990s prioritised the secular and Marxist dimension of anticolonial liberation struggles since 'resistance' within postcolonialism has been understood in secular terms. Postcolonial historians and critics sidelined religious anticolonial movements in favour of secular and Marxist liberation movements (El Amrani, 2021). Such an insight warrants that what is advanced as 'decolonial', 'alternative', and 'otherwise' may again be the 'mainstream' and the 'dominant'. Theorising the 'otherwise' can be perceived as an opportunity to participate in the current 'trends' in interculturality research by drawing on decolonial theories without acting on the skewed geopolitics of knowledge and epistemic injustice. The scholarships that challenge the dominant knowledges get sidelined and *otherwised* due to the need to maintain the mainstream intact and due to the 'unverified' yet innovation and originality of these scholarships (Dervin & Jacobsson, 2022).

'Teaching interculturality otherwise' already makes the assumption that the 'otherwise' is possible and it has never been there before. Even if it is possible, then *what* 'otherwise' is possible? Is it the type of reasonings that allow for ostensible alternative perspectives of what interculturality is about while maintaining the dominant mainstream knowledges? We cannot teach otherwise unless we theorise otherwise, but it remains questionable what 'otherwise' can be 'made' possible in both theory and practice. The confluence of power, knowledge, and politics problematises the possibility of promoting alternative knowledges and an 'otherwise'. The very premise of detaching teaching interculturality from the epistemological underpinnings of intercultural research is another issue in the sense that teaching interculturality may not entail the same epistemological depth and nuance of intercultural communication. Affirming the possibility of the 'otherwise' necessarily stipulates that we all acknowledge the self-ascribed universality existent in the dominant interculturality literature. The possibility the Global North may be taking over the 'traditional' and 'characteristic' intercultural labour of the Global South which is thinking about some fields and concepts 'otherwise' is again complicating the 'supposed' primacy of Southern epistemologies in sustaining alternative imaginaries of interculturality. Actually, we may need to theorise and do the 'otherwise' *otherwise* in order to generate a more genuine process of 'otherwising' and 'alternativising'. The 'otherwise' should not be a variant of Western ways of theorising and teaching interculturality.

The Global North and South may construe teaching interculturality otherwise differently depending on their needs, objectives, and logics. 'Otherwise' can be interpreted depending on our answers to whether teaching interculturality is about ensuring the smooth functioning of intercultural encounters, or about balancing intercultural relations through disrupting epistemic, linguistic, and cultural hierarchies. My 'otherwise' is not someone else's otherwise because we view the dominant and the otherwise differently depending on our geopolitical location and conditions. Teaching interculturality otherwise should carry substantial implications for reimagining the core objectives of what interculturality, as a theory of social reality, is trying to achieve. The focus is usually on managing cultural diversity under the premise that reorganisation is effective in ensuring balanced intercultural encounters. Intercultural communication needs to assume more impact by prioritising the deconstruction and unsettling of historical and contemporary power structures (R'boul, 2022). The 'otherwise' would be repeating the same litanies if it was not about recognising the different ways through which diverse individuals across the human globe perceive, make sense, and provide meaning to their existence (Ndlovu-Gatsheni, 2021b). The exigency to discuss theorising and teaching interculturality otherwise is evidence of the skewed geopolitics of knowledge in the field and, thus, both modalities need to centre linguistic, cultural, and epistemic inequalities. Teaching interculturality needs to encompass the reconsideration of these hierarchies and differentialisms; otherwise, the 'otherwise' is only a metaphor.

Theorising the 'otherwise' is appealing and interesting, but we may not be able to clearly differentiate between the dominant and the 'otherwise' as they may be overlapping and enunciated through similar voices and epistemologies. After recognising this dilemma, it is also essential to establish how the 'otherwise' is not only in and from the Global South. There are some Global South(s) in the Global North since they do not follow the dominant trends (R'boul, 2021). There has already been a lot of work on identity, competence, othering, and self, that is why it may be the right time to signal an epistemological shift towards more pressing issues. As a final note, 'otherwise' in Arabic can be translated to 'بطريقة أخرى' (in another way), بصورة مختلفة (in another picture), and خلاف ذلك (unlike that). These definitions may help set the agenda for how the work on 'otherwise' can be done in order to genuinely theorise and teach 'otherwise'.

References

Berenstain, N. (2016). Epistemic exploitation. *Ergo: An Open Access Journal of Philosophy*, 3, 569–590.

Dervin, F., & Jacobsson, A. (2022). *Intercultural Communication Education: Broken Realities and Rebellious Dreams*. London: Springer.

El Amrani, A. (2021). Desecularising the postcolonial resistance: The role of Islamic spirituality in the framing of Moroccan anticolonial thought. *The Journal of North African Studies*. https://doi.org/10.1080/13629387.2021.1975272.

Ndlovu-Gatsheni, S. J. (2021a). The cognitive empire, politics of knowledge and African intellectual productions: Reflections on struggles for epistemic freedom and resurgence of decolonisation in the twenty-first century. *Third World Quarterly*, 42(5), 882–901. https://doi.org/10.1080/01436597.2020.1775487.

Ndlovu-Gatsheni, S. J. (2021b). Epistemic injustice. In F. J. Carrilo & G. Koch (Eds.), *Knowledge for the Anthropocene* (pp. 167–177). Cheltenham: Edward Elgar Publishing.

R'boul, H. (2021). North/South imbalances in intercultural communication education. *Language and Intercultural Communication*, 21(2), 144–157. https://doi.org/10.1080/14708477.2020.1866593.

R'boul, H. (2022). Epistemological plurality in intercultural communication knowledge. *Journal of Multicultural Discourses*. https://doi.org/10.1080/17447143.2022.2069784.

Index

adult-centric 201, 204–205, 214, 219
agency 62, 73, 145–146, 150, 175, 179, 182–183, 202, 208
anti-racism 43, 92, 96, 104
autobiography 8, 47, 121, 143, 188–189, 193, 204
autoethnography 26, 72, 74, 77, 79, 82–84

bias 4, 10, 16, 24, 80, 118, 126, 150, 161, 218
Black Lives Matter 43, 147

categorisation 19, 27, 80, 112, 129, 137, 144, 164, 178, 181, 196–197
children 8–9, 38, 61–63, 73, 78–79, 92–93, 101–106, 114, 131–133, 165, 167–168, 201–214, 219
citizenship 1, 40, 50, 62–63
climate change 43, 65, 91, 136–137
communication studies 16, 77, 161
community 11, 21–22, 47, 58, 64, 78, 83, 88–90, 94, 101–102, 106–107, 121, 131, 145–146, 148, 174, 176, 191, 201–203, 205, 207, 210
competence 5, 7, 15, 35, 39–41, 46, 48, 63, 66–67, 73, 80, 104, 107, 126, 130, 137, 144–145, 149, 151, 157–158, 163, 181, 189, 190, 202–204, 218, 225
conflicts 18, 56, 59, 64, 128, 131–132, 134, 137, 181, 188, 196
COVID-19 11, 62, 114, 128–129, 131, 135, 179
criticality 1, 5, 8, 116–119, 122–123, 126, 130, 219
critical turn 159, 161
culture 2, 15–22, 24–40, 42–43, 45–50, 55–60, 63, 65–66, 72, 78–82, 84, 86, 90–96, 101–107, 111–114, 116–118, 121, 123–124, 126, 128, 130, 132–133, 138, 143–147, 149–151, 159–160, 163–166, 169, 173–178, 181–183, 187–188, 190, 193–194, 201–203, 205, 207–208, 210
curriculum 38, 49, 61, 63, 78, 91, 93, 104–107, 111, 113–114, 130, 134, 144, 147–150, 161–162, 167, 183–184, 202

decentring 20, 23–24, 163
decipher 215, 218
decolonial 1, 9, 71–72, 85, 123, 130, 143–144, 146–147, 151, 161–163, 166, 222–225
democracy 1, 5, 32, 38, 40, 55–58, 62, 64–65, 67, 118, 126, 144, 148, 210, 219
dichotomy 3, 47, 73, 121, 150, 175, 177
discomfort 123, 197
diversity 11, 15, 21–22, 24, 26, 28, 34, 36–43, 46–50, 56–57, 59–60, 63–67, 71–72, 83–84, 89, 105–108, 129, 134, 137, 144, 148–150, 158, 163, 168, 177, 179, 182, 184, 187, 189, 192–194, 203, 219, 223, 225
dominant 1, 5, 16, 22, 28, 57–59, 64, 104, 111, 113, 116, 130, 133, 143, 145–147, 149, 157, 161–162, 166, 204, 211, 217–218, 222–225
drawers 6, 108, 216
drawing 205, 207, 210
dynamic approach 201, 207–209, 211
dynamics 16, 20, 26–27, 47, 64, 223

education for emergencies 8, 128–129, 131–139
emotions 9–10, 35, 67, 192–193, 195–198, 209
encounters 17, 35–37, 42–43, 47–48, 60, 65–67, 72, 74–78, 82–83, 126, 160, 164, 188, 201–205, 208–209, 211, 215, 219, 224–225

Index

English 3, 5, 8, 10, 15–16, 21–22, 30, 34, 44, 49, 73, 102, 105–106, 120–121, 124–125, 128, 145, 147, 150, 160, 163, 168, 216, 220
equity 26, 28, 56, 61, 64, 83, 101, 104, 131, 165, 201
etymology 2, 117
Eurocentrism 67, 154, 159, 162–163, 165

gender 6, 66, 83, 114, 130, 133, 151
glissando 216–219
global education 73
globalisation 34, 55, 65, 67, 158, 166, 179
global south 4, 21, 162, 219, 222–225
Gundara, Jagdish 65, 88–89, 92, 94–95

hegemony 21, 112, 145–147, 149–150, 175
higher education 4, 9, 15, 88–89, 92, 116, 128, 134, 157, 159, 168–169, 173–175, 179, 182–183

identity 8, 16–20, 22, 25–30, 34–36, 38–40, 43, 45–46, 48–50, 58, 60–61, 67, 79–80, 83, 85–86, 105–107, 111, 113–114, 121, 130, 138, 145–151, 161, 167, 174–177, 180, 187, 191, 193, 225
ideologemes 116
ideology 1–2, 5, 9, 59, 66, 79–81, 83, 117–126, 128, 133, 143–145, 147, 149–150, 159, 161–163, 173, 177, 208, 217–219
imaginary 1–5, 7, 9, 11, 113, 115, 194, 215, 217
inclusion 15, 22, 26, 28, 36, 38, 56–57, 59, 61–62, 64, 84, 101, 105, 108, 148, 194
indigenous 34–35, 43, 72, 78, 101–104, 106–107, 130, 161
Institute of Education 8, 88, 96–98
intercultural communication education 4, 21, 122, 159, 161–162, 184
interculturalidad 161, 169
interculturalising interculturality 4, 6–7, 9, 10, 20–22, 36, 113, 118, 162–164, 166–167, 192, 204, 208, 211, 217
interculturality-as-altering 116–119, 123, 125–126
interdisciplinarity 15, 38, 40, 66, 90–92, 94–97, 129–130, 132, 134, 136, 138, 157, 194, 219
interepistemic 146, 161
intergroup 16, 20, 26–27, 177

internationalisation 73, 128, 157, 193
interpersonal 16–17, 20, 24, 26, 71, 76, 146, 175
intersectionality 43, 112, 116, 118, 130, 133, 143–144, 149, 151

knowledges 106, 133, 162, 222–224

language education 5, 23, 38, 40–41, 46–47, 49, 73, 102–103, 105–106, 144, 150, 168
lenses 3, 128–131, 134, 137–138, 222–223

management 15–17, 19–20, 22–24, 26–27, 30, 63–66, 148, 166, 179–180, 220
mediated communication 9, 173–178, 181–183
metaphor 75, 126, 147, 166, 215–217, 220, 225
migrants 8, 60–63, 79–81, 102, 138, 144, 148, 152, 157, 190, 203–204
Minzu 4–5, 11, 146
mirror 8, 34, 103, 121, 126–127, 205, 215
monolingual 48, 102, 107, 150
movement 43, 59, 80, 88, 160, 189, 191, 198
multicultural 1, 5, 34, 39–40, 48, 57–60, 65, 67, 73, 88–90, 92–97, 111, 144, 147–148, 150–152, 157–158, 167, 184, 189, 193–194
multilingual 2, 34, 38, 40, 48, 62–63, 102, 106–107, 149–150, 167, 189, 193–194, 220

neoliberalism 55, 65, 67, 207, 217
non-essentialism 7, 21, 25, 29, 35–36, 46, 69, 80, 84, 101, 116, 118, 123, 126, 163, 191, 222

observality 8, 116–127
otherness 40, 59, 60, 74–75, 77, 80–85
otherwise 1, 3, 7, 10–11, 80, 82, 119, 129, 215–216, 218, 222–225

philosophy 1, 59, 67, 72, 74, 76–77, 89–90, 104, 111–113, 119, 144, 158, 164–166, 169, 192, 201–202, 209, 211, 218
politics 1–2, 4, 9, 18, 19, 22, 29–30, 43, 46, 48, 55–56, 60, 62, 65, 66, 71, 75, 81, 83, 89, 91, 101, 104, 118, 122, 126, 129, 131–133, 135–138, 143–144, 147–148, 150–151, 158–164, 166, 168, 174, 177, 182, 190, 196, 217, 223–225

Index 229

polycentric 9, 160, 163, 216, 217
postcolonial 17, 27, 41, 112–113, 130, 147, 149, 159, 224
postmodern 17, 20, 24–26, 36, 46
primary education 38, 149, 200–202, 211

racism 38–39, 42–43, 47, 56, 61, 79, 92–94, 96–97, 101–102, 104–105, 108, 114–115, 128–129, 134, 138, 177, 194, 195, 197
reconciliation 101, 104–105, 107–108, 220
reflexivity 77, 79, 118, 122–123, 126, 143, 149–150
relativism 29, 59, 60, 158
rethink 3–4, 36, 66, 108, 117, 162–163, 169, 219

senses 119–126, 197
similarities 11, 26, 36, 38, 42, 44, 49, 58, 60, 66, 80–81, 115, 174, 178, 190
simplexity 27
small cultures 22, 26, 130, 144, 146, 151
social media 18–19, 114, 124, 129, 175, 178, 181, 185, 207
stereotypes 9, 15, 18, 20, 27–29, 42–49, 73, 80, 82, 103–104, 146, 158, 160, 166, 174, 182, 191, 194–198, 202, 217

Storycrafting method 73, 201–202, 205–206, 208
story exchange 9, 201, 205, 208, 210–211
struggle 59, 79–80, 88, 91–92, 144–145, 158, 168, 206, 223–225

tasks (learning) 41, 78, 178–181
teacher aide 8, 72, 74, 77, 79–84
textbooks 47, 104, 114, 150, 158–159, 163, 176, 191, 194
tolerance 6, 39, 43, 61, 104, 148, 167
transcultural 1, 36, 43, 57–58, 65, 118, 146
translanguaging 1, 194

unity 50, 90, 112, 166, 189, 219
universalism 58, 63, 162
unthink 3–4, 117, 163, 165

violence 58, 101, 151, 193, 196

Western 6, 11, 21, 29, 58, 63, 66, 103, 111–112, 116, 143, 146, 151, 159, 161–163, 166, 173, 209, 215, 217, 222–224
world cinema 163–165, 169

Zeigarnik effect 215, 220

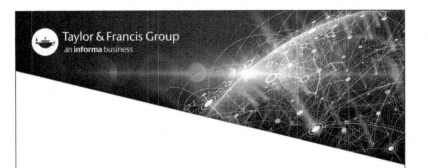